CHANGES IN PRACTICE AND LAW

Thomas Molony (1865–1949), last lord chief justice of Ireland.
By William Orpen. Courtesy of the Honorable Society of King's Inns.

Changes in Practice and Law

*A selection of essays by members of the legal
profession to mark twenty-five years of
the Irish Legal History Society*

DAIRE HOGAN
AND
COLUM KENNY

EDITORS

FOUR COURTS PRESS
in association with
THE IRISH LEGAL HISTORY SOCIETY

Typeset in 11pt on 13pt EhrhardtMtPro *by*
Carrigboy Typesetting Services *for*
FOUR COURTS PRESS LTD
7 Malpas Street, Dublin 8, Ireland
www.fourcourtspress.ie
and in North America for
FOUR COURTS PRESS
c/o ISBS, 920 N.E. 58th Avenue, Suite 300, Portland, OR 97213.

© the individual contributors and Four Courts Press 2013

A catalogue record for this title is available
from the British Library.

ISBN 978 1-84682-415-9

All rights reserved.
Without limiting the rights under copyright
reserved alone, no part of this publication may be
reproduced, stored in or introduced into a retrieval system,
or transmitted, in any form or by any means (electronic, mechanical,
photocopying, recording or otherwise), without the prior
written permission of both the copyright owner and
publisher of this book.

Printed in England
by Antony Rowe Ltd, Chippenham, Wilts.

Foreword

As patrons of the Irish Legal History Society, we are delighted to mark the twenty-fifth anniversary of its foundation. The society was formally inaugurated on 12 February 1988 under the patronage of the Hon. Mr Justice Finlay, chief justice of Ireland, and the Rt Hon. Lord Lowry, lord chief justice of Northern Ireland. As successors to these distinguished judges, we are pleased and honoured to contribute this foreword.

The Society's silver anniversary is commemorated by this timely and remarkable book of essays on changes in practice and law in Ireland and Northern Ireland. This volume reflects the Irish Legal History Society's mission to encourage the study and advance the knowledge of the history of Irish law by scholarly works. Within you will find a treasure trove of information and stories. We commend the distinguished contributors to the volume of essays for their erudition, which marks this milestone anniversary in admirable fashion.

Legal history is concerned with not only the institutions and doctrines of the law, but also the many personalities that the law attracts. The law is after all a human endeavour of great nobility, concerned as it is with justice and respect for the rule of law. It could also be described as a drama with an array of remarkable characters who walk on and off the stage with the passage of time. The timelessness is captured well by this book.

The contributors' essays chart the transformation that has occurred in the legal professions in Ireland, north and south. To choose just one example, Colum Kenny's chapter on the advance of women in the legal profession between 1901 and 2012 provides an aspect of the change we have witnessed in our lifetimes. Professor Kenny refers to the *Weekly Irish Times* of 21 October 1939, which contained an article titled 'women in strange employment', based on the returns of the 1936 census. It referred to female carpenters, cabinet-makers, motor mechanics, barristers, solicitors and pawnbrokers. How times have changed! Women are entering the legal professions in increasing numbers, in many instances outnumbering their male colleagues.

For one author of this foreword the essay by the Hon. Mr Justice Hugh Geoghegan holds a very special interest, as she devilled with him and was a member of the midland circuit. The essay evokes the vibrancy and collegiality of the circuit.

The society does tremendous work to make Irish legal history accessible. Its members are drawn from Ireland and abroad, including members of the judiciary, practising lawyers, academic lawyers and historians. This volume further advances the discipline and should spark interest in the wider community and among undergraduate law students throughout the island's many third level colleges during their studies.

Finally, we express our gratitude to the editors, Mr Daire Hogan, solicitor, and Professor Colum Kenny, for their efforts in preparing this volume. We wish the Irish Legal History Society continued success for the future.

The Rt Hon.	The Hon.
Sir Declan Morgan	Mrs Justice Susan Denham
Lord Chief Justice of Northern Ireland	Chief Justice of Ireland
Royal Courts of Justice,	Four Courts,
Belfast	Dublin

Contents

FOREWORD		v
IRISH LEGAL HISTORY SOCIETY PUBLICATIONS		ix
EDITORS' PREFACE		xi
LIST OF CONTRIBUTORS AND EDITORS		xiii
DETAILS OF ILLUSTRATIONS		xv
1	*Eheu fugaces*: fifty years in the Northern Ireland courts Robert Carswell	3
2	The changing role of equity in the Irish courts in the twentieth century Ronan Keane	23
3	The changing face of the circuits during the past twenty-five years Hugh Geoghegan	37
4	Judges of the midland circuit, 1924–94 *An editorial addendum*	41
5	Fifty years in a rural law practice Robert Pierse	50
6	Was there a criminal bar and what happened to any such tradition? Patrick Gageby	69
7	The Honorable Society of King's Inns: developments in legal education, 1988–2013 Mary Finlay Geoghegan	89
8	The regulation and education of the solicitors' profession in Northern Ireland, 1976–2012 Alan Hewitt	103

9	'You just have to get on with it': the advance of women in the legal profession, 1901–2012 *Colum Kenny*	127
THE SOCIETY'S FOUNDATION		153
CELEBRATING THE SOCIETY		155
IRISH LEGAL HISTORY SOCIETY SUCCESSION LISTS		157
INDEX		161

Irish Legal History Society publications

1 Daire Hogan and W.N. Osborough (eds), *Brehons, serjeants and attorneys: studies in the history of the Irish legal profession* (1990)
2 Colum Kenny, *King's Inns and the kingdom of Ireland: the Irish 'inn of court', 1541–1800* (1992)
3 Jon G. Crawford, *Anglicizing the government of Ireland: the Irish privy council and the expansion of Tudor rule, 1556–1578* (1993)
4 W.N. Osborough (ed.), *Explorations in law and history: Irish Legal History Society discourses, 1988–1994* (1995)
5 W.N. Osborough, *Law and the emergence of modern Dublin: a litigation topography for a capital city* (1996)
6 Colum Kenny, *Tristram Kennedy and the revival of Irish legal training, 1835–1885* (1996)
7 Brian Griffin, *The Bulkies: police and crime in Belfast, 1800–1865* (1997)
8 Éanna Hickey, *Irish law and lawyers in modern folk tradition* (1999)
9 A.R. Hart, *A history of the king's serjeants at law in Ireland: honour rather than advantage?* (2000)
10 D.S. Greer and N.M. Dawson (eds), *Mysteries and solutions in Irish legal history: Irish Legal History Society discourses and other papers, 1996–1999* (2000)
11 Colum Kenny, *King's Inns and the battle of the books, 1972: cultural controversy at a Dublin library* (2002)
12 Desmond Greer and James W. Nicolson, *The factory acts in Ireland, 1802–1914* (2003)
13 Mary Kotsonouris, *The winding-up of the Dáil courts, 1922–1925: an obvious duty* (2004)
14 Paul Brand, Kevin Costello and W.N. Osborough (eds), *Adventures of the law: proceedings of the 16th British Legal History Conference, Dublin 2003* (2005)
15 Jon G. Crawford, *A star chamber court in Ireland: the court of castle chamber, 1571–1641* (2005)
16 A.P. Quinn, *Wigs and guns: Irish barristers and the Great War* (2006)
17 N.M. Dawson (ed.), *Reflections on law and history: Irish Legal History Society discourses and other papers, 2000–2005* (2006)
18 James Kelly, *Poynings' Law and the making of law in Ireland, 1660–1800* (2007)
19 W.E. Vaughan, *Murder trials in Ireland, 1836–1914* (2009)
20 Kevin Costello, *The court of admiralty of Ireland, 1575–1893* (2011)
21 W.N. Osborough, *An island's law: a bibliographical guide to Ireland's legal past* (2013)

22 Felix M. Larkin and N.M. Dawson (eds), *Lawyers, the law and history: Irish Legal History Society discourses and other papers, 2005–2011* (2013)
23 Daire Hogan and Colum Kenny (eds), *Changes in practice and law: a selection of essays by members of the legal profession to mark twenty-five years of the Irish Legal History Society* (2013)

ALSO AVAILABLE

The Irish Legal History Society (1989)

Volumes 1–7 are published by Irish Academic Press.

Editors' preface

Changes in practice and law is a selection of essays by members of the legal profession, including judges, counsel and solicitors, who explore a number of transformations in their profession both north and south of the border, over different time frames. They chart developments in aspects of practice and law that are of significance not only to lawyers but also to the societies that they serve.

Reflecting on the fleeting nature of time, Lord Carswell, formerly lord chief justice of Northern Ireland and a lord of appeal in ordinary, recalls and reflects upon fifty years in the courts of Northern Ireland, at the bar and on the bench. Hugh Geoghegan considers the changing nature of circuits during recent decades. From these contributions parallels can be drawn between the pressures of changing times, and the response of the bar, north and south. The editors have prepared a series of brief biographical sketches of the judges of the midland circuit, of which Mr Geoghegan was a member, and these sketches in themselves are a demonstration of the legal and social changes which took place in circuit practice in the course of the twentieth century.

The former chief justice of Ireland, Ronan Keane, discusses the role of equity in the Irish courts as it evolved over the past century, and the different course that certain equitable doctrines have taken in this country and in England.

The significant developments in the regulation and education of the solicitors' profession in Northern Ireland between 1976 and 2012 are described and put in context by Alan Hewitt, while Robert Pierse writes of fifty years in a rural law practice in Kerry. Mary Finlay Geoghegan describes the transformation of professional education for the bar at King's Inns in recent decades.

Patrick Gageby contributes a chapter on the evolution of a criminal bar in Ireland, and on the contrast between the continuity of certain themes in criminal legal practice over the years – indeed, over the centuries – and the redundancy of others.

Colum Kenny also contributes a chapter on the dramatic advances which women have made in the legal profession since the start of the twentieth century.

These essays mark the twenty-fifth anniversary of the foundation of the Irish Legal History Society in 1988, and are a demonstration of the breadth and the scope of the society's objective, to encourage the study and advance the knowledge of the history of Irish law.

The editors wish to express their thanks to all the contributors to this volume, to the Lord Chief Justice of Northern Ireland and the Chief Justice of Ireland for their gracious foreword, to Julitta Clancy for the preparation of the index and to Four Courts Press for assistance at all stages of the production process.

DAIRE HOGAN & COLUM KENNY

Contributors and editors

ROBERT CARSWELL was raised to the peerage as Baron Carswell in 2004, and was a lord of appeal in ordinary 2004–9.

MARY FINLAY GEOGHEGAN is a judge of the Irish high court.

PATRICK GAGEBY is a senior counsel in Dublin.

HUGH GEOGHEGAN retired as a judge of the Irish supreme court in 2010.

ALAN HEWITT was formerly senior partner in L'Estrange & Brett, solicitors, Belfast, and president of the Law Society of Northern Ireland in 2002.

DAIRE HOGAN is a solicitor and a former president of the Irish Legal History Society.

RONAN KEANE retired as chief justice of Ireland in 2004.

COLUM KENNY is professor of communications, Dublin City University.

W.N. OSBOROUGH is professor emeritus, University College Dublin, and a former president of the Irish Legal History Society.

ROBERT PIERSE of Pierse and Fitzgibbon, solicitors, Listowel, Co. Kerry has more than fifty years' experience in general practice.

Details of illustrations

Front cover

Royal Courts of Justice, Belfast. By Vincent McDonnell (2009).
Courtesy of the artist and the Law Society of Northern Ireland.

Back cover

Averil Deverell BL. Artist unknown.
Courtesy of the Bar Council of Ireland.

Deverell was one of the first two women called to the bar in Ireland or Britain, in Dublin on 1 November 1921. This portrait hangs in the Law Library, Dublin. Photographer: Saro Scuto.

Frontispiece

Thomas Molony, last lord chief justice of Ireland, wearing the ceremonial 'collar of SS'. By William Orpen.
Courtesy of the Honorable Society of King's Inns.

Leaf 1

Judges of Ireland, Four Courts, Dublin, 6 April 1921.
Courtesy of the Bar Council of Ireland.

This photograph, a memorial to the last persons to constitute the judiciary of Ireland as a single jurisdiction, was taken by Lafayette at the Four Courts, Dublin, on 6 April 1921.

Seated (*left to right*): Lord Justice James O'Connor, Lord Chief Justice Thomas Molony, Lord Chancellor James Campbell, Lord Justice Stephen Ronan, Mr Justice W.H. Dodd.

Standing (*left to right*): Mr Justice Arthur Samuels, Mr Justice William Moore, Mr Justice John Ross, Mr Justice John Blake Powell.

The judges had gathered for the usual ceremonial opening of the Easter law sittings, when the chancellor Sir James Campbell (later Lord Glenavy) held his last levee in the benchers' chamber. This 'was largely attended by the judges and members of the bar'. No such ceremony had been held during the troubled year of 1920. The photograph appeared next day on the front page of the *Freeman's Journal* along with some other images of the occasion.

xvi   *Details of illustrations*

The *Irish Times* reported that the following judges were 'unavoidably absent': master of the rolls Charles Andrew O'Connor, Mr Justice John Gordon, Mr Justice J.E. Pim, and Mr Justice William Evelyn Wylie. It added that, 'The function brought to mind the fact that the past year had deprived the Bench of four distinguished personalities – the Lord Chief Baron [Christopher Palles, last chief baron who retired in 1916 but died in 1920] and Mr Justice [William] Kenny through death, and Mr. Justice [James Owens] Wylie and Mr. Justice [John George] Gibson through retirement.'

Alone among the judges seen in this photograph, William Moore later sat on the bench of Northern Ireland. There he became lord chief justice in 1925.[1]

Lord Chancellor Campbell was attended on 6 April 1921 by the mace-bearer, the purse-bearer and the train-bearer. A short but remarkable British Pathé newsreel of the occasion exists (56 seconds). 'United Irish Courts meet for the last time', it informs its viewers, and concludes with the mace-bearer holding the chancellor's eighteenth-century ceremonial mace. As may be seen below, the mace was to survive the destruction of the Four Courts.[2]

Frances Kyle and Averil Deverell, on the day of their call in 1921.
Reproduced from the Daily Sketch, *3 Nov. 1921. Original not found.*

Later that same month, Kyle was also called to the bar in Belfast.

Leaf 2

The Four Courts and Public Record Office explode and burn, 30 June 1922.
Courtesy of the National Library of Ireland (Hogan, HOG57).

Remains of the statue of Michael O'Loghlen in the Round Hall of the Four Courts, July 1922.
Courtesy of the National Library of Ireland (IND H245).

O'Loghlen's was the oldest of six statues of eminent Irish lawyers, two seated and four standing, which were destroyed by the explosions and

---

1 V.T.H. Delany, *Christopher Palles: his life and times* (Dublin, 1960), pp 177–87; *Dictionary of Irish biography* for Moore, by Bridget Hourican.
2 *Irish Independent*, 6 April 1921; *Freeman's Journal*, 7 April 1921; *Irish Times*, 7 April 1921 and 15 and 19 July 1922 (including photograph); Pathé <http://www.britishpathe.com/video/lord-chancellors-easter-levee/query/wildcard> (accessed 12 April 2013).

fire at the Four Courts. Sculpted by Patrick McDowell of Belfast and erected between 1843 and 1851, it stood by the chancery court in 1922. The inscription is visible. It reads, 'THE BAR OF IRELAND TO THE MEMORY OF THE RIGHT HONORABLE SIR MICHAEL O'LOGHLEN BART. MASTER OF THE ROLLS. BORN [-] OCTOBER 1789. [DIED 28] SEPTEMBER 1842.' On 4 July 1922 a man was seen making off with its 'very fine life-size marble head' that had lain on the ground.[3]

Leaf 3

Remains of the statue of Henry Joy in the Round Hall of the Four Courts, July 1922.
Courtesy of the National Library of Ireland (IND H248 and Hogan HOG8).

Joy (1766–1838) was appointed chief baron in 1831. Sculpted by his grand-nephew, Bruce Joy, and erected in 1865, the statue stood by the court of exchequer in 1922. Curran wrote of finding all the statues in the Round Hall 'broken and calcined' on 3 July 1922: 'I stuck my thumb into Joy – he had the consistency of cream cheese.'[4]

Leaf 4

The Four Courts gutted.
Courtesy of the National Library of Ireland (NLI IND H240).

The lord chancellor's mace and mace-bearer.
Reproduced from the Irish Times, *15 July 1922, but the image predates the civil war. Original not found.*

A mace was long symbolic of the Irish lord chancellor's authority, and John Dunton about 1699 describes how it lay with the purse on a green velvet cushion in the court of chancery when John Methuen was chancellor.[5] The mace in use in 1922 had been made in Dublin during

---

3 *Freeman's Journal*, 12 and 14 July 1922; *Irish Independent*, 14 July 1922.
4 C.P. Curran, 'Figures in the hall', reprinted in C. Costello (ed.), *The Four Courts: 200 years* (Dublin, 1996), pp 169–76. This volume also includes R. Keane, 'A mass of crumbling ruins: the destruction of the Four Courts in June 1922.' Photographs of O'Hagan's headless statue were also published but the originals appear not to have survived (*Freeman's Journal* and *Irish Independent*, 14 July 1922, with the former reporting that 'the head has been found and is little the worse for its adventure').
5 F. Elrington Ball, *The judges in Ireland, 1221–1921* (London, 1926), ii, 15, citing Bodleian MS, Rawl. D.71.

the 1760s. Part of the mace is seen lying on a red cloth in Gilbert Stuart's portrait of Lord Chancellor John FitzGibbon in 1789.

It was said in 1922 that, 'Every day that the Lord Chancellor sat in the Court of Appeal, the massive silver mace was placed before him; but in order to prevent any possibility of its being stolen, it was fitted with an immovable apparatus attached to the side of his desk. When he rose, it was taken by the crier, and locked into its safe in the Four Courts.' In the Pathé film of Lord Chancellor Campbell's levee in 1921 (above), the mace is displayed by the mace-bearer, Mathew Orr.

Although the Four Courts were destroyed in 1922, the mace was not. Lord Chancellor John Ross wrote that the mace was 'kept in a steel box in the wall of my chamber. It was afterwards taken out, and found to be almost uninjured.' Free State troops brought it to the Four Courts Hotel nearby, for safekeeping. However, on 11 July 1922 a man was charged in a local Dáil court with its theft. 'He said an officer of what was now called the National troops told him he could have it as a souvenir.' P.H. O'Reilly, a solicitor prosecuting 'on behalf of the Republican police', said that the mace had been taken to pieces and each piece wrapped in paper and hidden under the boards of the floor. The chairman of the north city parish court told the accused, 'It is a very serious matter, and you are very lucky that you were not shot, as you would be under the circumstances, in other places.' The police were said to have information that the mace was going to be sent to England.

Having recovered the mace, the new Free State government decided to retain it. Ross believed that it was the property of the Crown and that he should resume possession of it. When the courts next sat in temporary accommodation at King's Inns, he asked that it be handed over to his mace-bearer, but he did not get his way: 'the Free State authorities refused on various grounds that are past understanding.' Having been screwed back together and repaired, it was by the end of 1925 deposited in the National Museum of Ireland, and today is at that museum's decorative arts and history section in the former Collins Barracks, Dublin. It is there described as follows:

> 1925.21 Mace, silver gilt. Formerly belonging to the lord chancellor of Ireland. Large crown on top (fleur-de-lis cresting and orb and cross missing). Head with four compartments alternately repoussé with a shield bearing the letters 'GR', supported by winged cupids. Britannia seated, a shield bearing the French Arms, supported by winged cupids; and Britannia seated. Four supports below head formed of terminal figures. Baluster stem

repoussé with spiral flutings, acanthus leaves and scroll and interlaced work. Flat top of head repoussé with the Royal Arms and supporters and 'GR III' above. Formed on nine separate parts. Bears the Dublin hallmarks for *c*.1760–70 and maker's mark 'WT' for William Townsend. See Irish *House of Commons Journal*, xiv, p. 365 (22 Dec. 1766) – 'Paid to Isaac D'Olier Silversmith for silver mace for House of Lords £286.9.4¾.' Deposited by the Executive Council of Ireland.[6]

The figure of 'Truth' moved from the Four Courts to King's Inns about 1880.
Photographs by C. Kenny, 2001.

Sometime before 1840, this figure of 'Truth' was erected in the centre of the Round Hall at the Four Courts. It is not known who sculpted 'The Gas Woman', as she became known to some, but by April 1880 the piece 'was deemed so unsuitable an ornament – (loud laughter) – that it was removed to the lawn of the King's Inns' at the top of Henrietta Street.[7] Thus escaping from later destruction during the civil war, she came to be nicknamed 'Henrietta'. She was recently knocked down and broken by a lorry, and is no longer on view.

Leaf 5

John Ross (1853–1935), last lord chancellor of Ireland, June 1921– December 1922. A charcoal sketch by Frank Leah, 1922.
Courtesy of the National Library of Ireland (PD Ross – JO (i) IV).

Ross superseded Lord Chancellor Campbell in circumstances that neither he in his autobiography nor Ball in his study of the judges of Ireland addresses. One report indicates that, 'The reason generally assigned for the enforced retirement of Sir James Campbell appears to be that the Executive in Dublin Castle were of opinion that they were not receiving from him the support they thought they had a right to expect.' Nevertheless, Campbell went on to become chairman of the

---

6 *Freeman's Journal*, 12 July 1922; *Irish Independent*, 30 Oct. 1924, 19 and 21 Jan. 1926 and 27 May 1927; *Nenagh Guardian*, 15 July 1922; *Irish Times*, 15 July 1922 and 18 Oct. 1924; John Ross, *The years of my pilgrimage* (London, 1924), pp 296–7. Thanks to Ms Alex Ward of the National Museum of Ireland for details from file 30 A&I 1925.
7 *Irish Times*, 29 Nov. 1894, for an address on Dublin by L.R. Strangways, vice-president of the Photographic Society of Ireland, before a large audience in the Molesworth Hall; Curran, 'Figures in the hall', pp 172–3.

Irish senate, gave advice on drafting the written constitution of the new state and was a formative influence in respect to the Courts of Justice Act 1924.[8]

Leaf 6

Denis Henry (1864–1925), first lord chief justice of Northern Ireland 1921–5.
Courtesy of the National Portrait Gallery, London.

Henry had served as solicitor general (1918) and attorney general (1919) of Ireland. In November 1921 he presided over the first call to the bar in Belfast, that of Frances Kyle and John Clarke MacDermott. A biography of Henry was published in 2000.[9]

Leaf 7

Thomas Molony (1865–1949), last lord chief justice of Ireland 1918–24. By William Orpen.
Courtesy of the Honorable Society of King's Inns.

William Moore (1864–1944), lord chief justice of Northern Ireland 1925–37.
Irish Law Times and Solicitors' Journal, 15 Dec. 1928.

Note that each wears a ceremonial collar of 'SS'.

Moore had served as a judge of the king's bench division of the high court 1917–21, then from 1921 as a lord justice of appeal in Northern Ireland before becoming lord chief justice of Northern Ireland from 1925 to 1937.

Mary Dorothea Heron BA (Queen's University Belfast).
Courtesy of the Bar Council of Ireland.

In 1923 she became the first woman to be admitted a solicitor in Ireland.

---

8   *Nenagh Guardian*, 2 July 1921; *Irish Times*, 18 Oct. 1924; *Dictionary of Irish biography* for Campbell, by Patrick Maume.
9   A.D. McDonnell, *The life of Sir Denis Henry: Catholic Unionist* (Belfast, 2000).

Averil Deverell BL.
The first woman to practise as a barrister in the Irish Free State. Artist unknown.
Courtesy of the Bar Council of Ireland.

This portrait hangs in the Law Library, Dublin. *Photographer: Saro Scuto.*

Leaf 8

Lord Glenavy (formerly Lord Chancellor James Campbell) with Hugh Kennedy, future chief justice, in the garden of Kennedy's house in Clonskeagh, Dublin, 1922–3.
Courtesy of the National Library of Ireland (KEN8).

On 27 January 1923 the executive council of the Irish Free State appointed a 'Judiciary Committee' to advise it on setting up courts and related offices in accordance with the new constitution. Lord Glenavy chaired the committee, and its members included Hugh Kennedy KC, then attorney general. The committee reported within five months.[10]

Mella Carroll (1934–2006).
The first woman appointed as a high court judge in Ireland. Here in her robes as chancellor of Dublin City University, with its then president Prof. Ferdinand von Prondzynski in September 2001.
Courtesy of the Irish Times. *Photographer: Joe St Leger.*

The editors wish to thank Mr John G. Gordon of Napier & Sons, solicitors, Belfast, for his helpful suggestions and assistance in relation to the choice of an image for the front cover. We are also grateful to the archivists and others who have furnished us with copies of the images that are listed above.

---

10 *Freeman's Journal*, 13 June 1923.

Eheu fugaces ... labuntur anni

(Alas, ... the fleeting years glide by)

– Horace, *Odes*, book ii.14

Eheu fugaces: fifty years in the Northern Ireland courts

ROBERT CARSWELL

When I first walked through the door of the Bar Library in 1957 with the other newly called members of the bar of Northern Ireland, it was entering a different world from that which our successors encounter today. For a start, there were only four of us, but that was regarded as a 'big call', whereas the annual September call in Belfast now numbers some twenty-five or so new barristers. We were all men, while calls today are more or less evenly divided between men and women. There was one woman member of the Bar Library, but she was engaged in law reporting and did not take part in advocacy. There was a sprinkling of women solicitors, but no women at any judicial level. That also has changed enormously over the years, and women now play a substantial part in the legal world.

The bar in those days numbered about sixty members, who fitted comfortably into the old Bar Library, a handsome room built as an integral part of the Royal Courts of Justice, opened in 1933. Practically every member had his own desk, in which one could keep stationery etc., and where briefs, cases for opinion and other papers sent out by solicitors were delivered as they arrived. There was a bank of pigeon-holes just outside the door, into which one could leave papers for solicitors for collection. Belfast firms who regularly left papers for counsel would collect returned papers at frequent intervals, and papers to and from country solicitors generally were sent by post. They tended to pile up on counsel's desks, some being more tidy and orderly than others, so the library gave the clear appearance of being a working place, with a busy hum during term.

The facilities were extraordinarily primitive by the standards of today. There were two telephones for the whole Bar Library, both coin-operated and situated in little call boxes outside the door, which were the sole vehicle for both outgoing and incoming calls. Most contact with solicitors was, however, made in writing or by personal interview, and in those earlier days the telephones were not so commonly used and the facilities sufficed for the style and pace of work.

There was an elderly doorkeeper, Sergeant Breheny, who would call counsel's name from the doorway if a solicitor called and asked to see him or if there was a telephone call for him. At the end of the library was the tea room, presided over by a motherly lady, Mrs Steele, who provided tea and coffee and cooked light and plain lunches for the members. This was a great forum for gossip and for discussion of cases, many of which were settled following an encounter (not always accidental) in the tea room. When a jury verdict in a case at hearing was imminent the sergeant would come in and call out 'Jury, please', whereupon many of the barristers would troop out and go into court to hear the result. The number of actions listed in those days was so small that the members as a whole had a lively interest in current litigation. The tea room was a very good social centre for the bar and has its present-day counterpart in the refectory in the glossy new Bar Library building.

Working patterns changed to some extent during my time in practice. When I started it was possible to read papers and write opinions or draft pleadings comfortably enough in the Bar Library, and most people did the bulk of their work there. As time went on and numbers increased it became less quiet and peaceful and correspondingly more difficult to concentrate on one's work. The pattern then shifted to an extent to using the library as a forum, while doing most paper work at home. In those early days the members of the bar, which was always old-fashioned in its methods, had only recently graduated to having their written work typed (only one or two were able to type themselves, and word processors were a long way in the future). It was customary to engage the services of a typist working from home, of which there was a fair supply, and to leave work with her or dictate documents to her to take down in shorthand. Three senior members had reel-to-reel tape recorders, which were the size of a small suitcase, and they used to dictate into these at home and bring them in to the secretary whom they shared. As dictating machines became smaller and more sophisticated, most of us began to arm ourselves with them and leave tapes with our secretaries for transcription.

A new member's pupillage with an established member of the bar was a very personal relationship. It was the traditional learning process at the bar, before we had the benefit of training courses in advocacy, but in those quiet days when work was relatively light one had time to absorb one's master's professional know-how and one gradually learned the valuable unwritten principles of conducting a practice and surviving in a competitive world. As a pupil gained experience he would start to draft pleadings and opinions for his master, who would ideally take time to go over the drafts and any corrections he made to them before the documents went out. In time one might get small cases handed on by a busy master, with the agreement of the solicitors, and a good master would give the pupil some instruction and assistance in how to handle them in court.

The small size of the bar meant that there was something of a club-like atmosphere in the Bar Library. There was an agreeable camaraderie: the tradition of the common law bar as a whole that members were rivals in court but friends outside it genuinely prevailed. One commonly heard counsel who had just lost a hard-fought action congratulate his opponent and invite him for a cup of tea. New members were made to feel a welcome part of the profession. There always seemed to be time for a more senior member, if asked for his help on some topic, to follow the old tradition of putting aside his papers and giving advice and guidance. The overheads of practice were remarkably low by today's standards and the Bar Library subscriptions were deliberately kept at a minimum level for those commencing practice: this carried with it the social advantage that it was genuinely possible for a young person without financial resources to obtain a start in the profession.

The assize system was still in fairly flourishing condition when I was called. Two high court judges would go out twice a year on circuit round the county towns of Northern Ireland for a tour occupying some two weeks. In previous days virtually all the barristers on that circuit would travel around with the circuit, staying and dining together in hotels in the different towns. By the late 1950s the number going on circuit was rather smaller, as only those holding briefs for the various venues would normally attend. Even so, in some of the towns there was a sufficient amount of work to make for a busy couple of days and the circuiteers would have an entertaining evening, as they were obliged by custom to dine with the bar (and fined bottles of wine or port if they failed to turn up). The older members used to tell tales of past members such as Ned Murphy and Tony Babington (both subsequently members of the court of appeal) sitting down together with armfuls of briefs and trying to rationalise the lists and agree what issues were not contested.

There was a more or less elaborate ritual before and after dinner each evening, when it was customary to call upon members of the company to entertain the rest, generally in song. Probationers on their first circuit were always obliged to sing, but if the result was unacceptable they would receive a certificate exempting them for the future.

One judge would act as crown judge in each town and preside over the criminal trials, while the other as the civil judge would hear the civil bill appeals from the county court. They would then exchange duties in the next town. Each judge was entitled to take a registrar with him, usually a young member of the bar, as a sort of equerry-cum-court clerk. Registrars were paid the sum of £200 in old Irish money, which came to £183.12.4 sterling, a considerable windfall for a young practitioner in those days. They travelled with the judges, stayed in the same lodgings and ate their meals with them. They were responsible for seeing to practical details, such as ensuring that the travel arrangements ran smoothly, then sat in court as clerk to call the cases and draft the orders in the civil appeals. The judges' lodgings were a mixed bag. In Co. Down they stayed in the Slieve Donard hotel in Newcastle. In Armagh they stayed in a house on the Mall, where the cuisine was notable. In Enniskillen they were quartered in the old Killyhevlin hotel and in Co. Tyrone the lodging was in Corick, a rather typically run-down Irish country house near Clogher. The best of all was in Londonderry, where they stayed in some style in the Irish Society's house beside the court-house.

The high sheriff was always in attendance at the court, and he and other local worthies were entertained to dinner, along with the crown prosecutors and a few members of the bar. The RUC county inspector came the night before the opening of each assize to brief the crown judge on crime statistics. The next morning the crown judge would inspect a military guard of honour, frequently with a regimental mascot such as a malevolent-looking ram, who would be restrained by a couple of sturdy corporals with a leash on each horn. The commission would be read and the crown judge would address the grand jury – a body of twenty-three local worthies, usually rather grand persons – on the state of law and order in the county. The grand jury then retired to hear a synopsis of the crown case in each prosecution, then if satisfied that there was a case to answer would find that there was a 'true bill' and hand down, or 'present', the bills of indictment on which the subsequent trials were then based. The grand jury, having completed its arduous morning's work, then retired for lunch, at which the judges and crown prosecutors were guests.

Other local personages would come to the lodgings to pay a courtesy call. In Enniskillen Dean MacManaway invariably presented himself and, as the judges well knew, could easily be persuaded to accept a 'ball of malt', *aliter* Irish whiskey. The judges stayed in Enniskillen over the middle week-end, and were commonly entertained to a cruise on Lough

Erne on the police launch and a visit to the RUC training depot. When I was registrar in 1959, in Armagh the escort in the judges' car was an old gentleman who volunteered that he had attended Chief Baron Palles many years ago (very many, as Palles retired in 1916). Lord MacDermott was fascinated and asked how the present day judges compared, to which the other replied, 'Ah, my lord, he was much crosser.' This was probably true, as Lord MacDermott visibly enjoyed the assizes, with a never-ending variety of litigants and witnesses and the freedom from paper work, and was at his most mellow on these visits.

In 1957 the supreme court of judicature consisted of five members, the lord chief justice, two lords justices of appeal and two high court judges, a complement unchanged since the foundation of the court in 1921. One high court judge was designated the chancery judge and the other queen's bench. In practice the lords justices and puisne judges were readily interchangeable: they all took their turn on circuit and on criminal trials at Belfast city commission, the puisne judges regularly sat in the court of appeal and the lords justices would sit when required on civil trials and county court appeals. Civil actions for damages for personal injuries, which constituted most of the civil work, were heard by juries. The numbers coming into the list were very light by comparison with later decades, and commonly only one or two were listed for each court day. Negligence actions were settling into a recognisable shape: it was, after all, less than ten years since the abolition of the defence of common employment and contributory negligence ceased to be a complete bar to a claim. The court of appeal sat sporadically as required, generally not more than a day or two in the week. Chancery and bankruptcy work was steady, while family work constituted only a fraction of what it later became when the grounds for divorce and the jurisdiction in cases relating to children were changed.

There were four courts opening off the Great Hall, in order from the front door nisi prius, court of appeal, chancery and queen's bench. There was also the common court in the north-east corner of the building (now one of the judges' chambers), where the bankruptcy registrar and the chief clerk held their sittings, with occasional use for overflows from the main courts. The judges occupied comfortable and spacious chambers in the 'back corridor' running along the east side of the building, which also housed the administrative and secretarial staff and tipstaves. The judges' assembly room, which has now become the lord chief justice's chambers, was in the centre of the corridor. There was no judges' common room and each judge generally lunched in solitary state in his chambers on fare brought in by his tipstaff from the Bar Library servery.

The administration of the legal system was largely carried out under the auspices of the lord chief justice, assisted by a permanent secretary and a private secretary, both legally qualified, and a small secretarial staff. The offices of the several divisions of the supreme court, located on the upper floors of the building, received a steady stream of callers from solicitors' offices and the general public, relating to the business of the courts. The registrars and the taxing master had their offices in this area and the accountant general's department was located on the ground floor. The administrative staff, fairly small in numbers, constituted a self-contained branch of the public service, with its own promotion ladder and salary scales, before the institution of the court service. The attorney general and the chief crown solicitor and his staff occupied offices on the south frontage of the building. There was room in the building for the estate duty office at one end, and at the other the headquarters of the Law Society, where the secretary sat in state in the solicitors' library. Some offices of the ministry of finance were also located within the building. The effect of this centralisation was that little time was taken up in communication between offices, as they were all so close to each other.

Unfortunately the Treasury did not approve the original plan to accommodate the criminal courts within the Royal Courts of Justice structure, and they remained in the county court-house on Crumlin Road. This building was completed in 1850 to an original design by Charles Lanyon, but much altered in subsequent years. Its accommodation was not distinguished – Sir Charles Brett described the courtrooms as giving the impression of 'a cross between an anatomy lecture theatre and a Presbyterian church'.[1] As far back as 1861 McComb, in his glowing account of the architectural glories of the building, was constrained to admit that the courtrooms were 'decidedly defective in acoustic properties'. That had not improved to any significant degree by the time I appeared there as a barrister and later sat as a judge. The building, although historic and atmospheric, was by then downright dingy and gloomy and the standard of the accommodation and the court furniture, for both bench and bar, was lamentable. Criminal trials at the Belfast city commission and quarter sessions were held there, involving a significant waste of time and energy in travel and

---

1 Charles Brett, *Buildings of Belfast, 1700–1914* (London: Weidenfeld & Nicolson, 1967), p. 26.

communication, which was considerably exacerbated by the exponential increase in criminal work following on the civil disturbances from the late 1960s onwards. This state of affairs persisted until the closure of Crumlin Road court-house in 1998, as it had become unsafe for use, and the erection of the Laganside court building, which opened its doors for business in 2002.

The recorder of Belfast sat in the Crumlin Road court-house until 1967, when the petty sessions court-house was opened opposite the Royal Courts of Justice in lower Chichester Street. Until then the magistrates' courts were held in the old town hall building facing Victoria Street, a rather dim red brick building dating from 1871. It would be difficult to attribute any architectural merit to the petty sessions court-house, a severe rectangular construction designed in-house by the Ministry's architects' department, which was an unhappy reflection of the utilitarian style of public buildings of its era and was described by Brett as a 'judicial office-block'.[2] It nevertheless fulfilled its purpose as a home for the magistrates' courts and the recorder's court, though the recorder later moved for a time into refurbished quarters in the old town hall. Both buildings had seen better days by the time that the ambitious plans for the Laganside building were prepared. When this became operational in 2002, it contained sixteen court-rooms, housing the recorder's court and the magistrates' courts in modern accommodation. The building was originally designed to face the Royal Courts of Justice across Chichester Street, but unhappily it was found necessary to swing the alignment round so that it faces Oxford Street and presents its less prepossessing side façade to the older building. The accommodation is generally good, but there were some early errors in the layout of the courts and their furniture – some, it has to be said, because the writer's advice to copy the measurements of the seating in the nisi prius court across the road, one of the most comfortable courts in the country, was not accepted.

The administration of justice was carried on in a motley collection of court-houses round the province, many of which had remained unchanged for generations. Some of them have been refurbished or replaced in recent years and a number have been closed in a process of rationalisation. I had occasion during my early years of practice to appear in many of these courts, at sittings of the county courts or at petty sessions. Maurice Healy said somewhat dismissively:[3]

---

2 Charles Brett, *Court houses and market houses of the province of Ulster* (Belfast: Ulster Architectural Heritage Society, 1973), p. 50.
3 Maurice Healy, *The old Munster circuit* (London, 1940), p. 67.

> I think that all County Courts in Ireland were built from a single plan in the Office of the Board of Works. Some were smaller and some larger than others; but they reproduced the same standard of discomfort in every county town.

Healy's strictures are in fact contradicted by the variety of architects who designed the several court-houses,[4] but it would be difficult to disagree with their substance when considering the facilities in most of the court-houses in use when I was going the rounds. There were some notable exceptions such as the splendid court-house in Armagh, designed by Francis Johnston at the beginning of the nineteenth century, extensively renovated in 1965, badly damaged by terrorist action in 1993 and sympathetically restored and reopened in 1999. Some of the court-houses had, however, considerable historic atmosphere. The crown court in Omagh, with its curious little well in which the lawyers sat, had remained unchanged since Sub-Inspector Montgomery was tried there in the 1870s for the Newtownstewart murder. Its replacement, like that of several other courts, though certainly more comfortable to work in, has none of the same character. The old Newtownards court-house suffered a similar fate. Although it was hardly a distinguished building and not well laid out, the design of its successor built in 1969 (again to an in-house Ministry design) has been excoriated by Brett in particularly vitriolic terms.[5] Some of the magistrates' courts were held in rather unusual surroundings: in Crossmaglen, where I did a motoring case once about 1960, the resident magistrate sat on the stage of a cinema (wearing his overcoat, as the auditorium was so chilly), looking down at the lawyers in the stalls below.

I have written so far almost exclusively of the bar and bench, because that was the centre of my professional experience. We, of course, had plenty of contact with solicitors, who were our clients and in many cases valued personal friends. I think it best to leave an account of the development of the solicitors' profession and the impact of changes upon it to those who were more closely concerned, but I naturally have many recollections of the work of solicitors in earlier days and its interaction with ours as barristers. My main impression of the changes since then is of the scale of firms of solicitors. Most, even the leading firms in terms of amount and quality of practice, were very small by today's standards. The increase in size of the major firms and the

---

4 See Brett, *Court houses, passim*
5 Ibid., p. 76.

number of mergers, some with firms from outside Northern Ireland, have changed the landscape of practice. With the exception of a few firms, mainly in Belfast, practitioners did not specialise. The typical firm, especially in country towns, contained a small number of partners, not infrequently members of the same family, and there were many sole practitioners. In consequence there was a greater tendency to seek the opinion of counsel on matters on which solicitors' firms are today readier to advise their clients themselves.

The pace of life was slower in those days throughout the legal profession, and I remember my mentor, when I did work experience in a solicitor's office during my student days, meeting his friends twice a day for a leisurely tea or coffee break in a nearby café. When one conducted a case in a country town, one could on occasion find it difficult to get away afterwards without socialising for some time. One country solicitor at least had the reputation that when he came to Belfast he was ready to make a day of it and expected counsel he instructed to accompany him. Some of the local solicitors were well-known characters, and one might be regaled by the hour with their stories – there was not much else to do in a country court-house while we waited for an interminable title dispute about a pocket handkerchief of land to wend its way to a conclusion. Some of them were links with a vanished age. One of my clients, Fred Mullan of Newry, who was well up in years when I was a young junior, told me once that he could remember sitting in Dundalk court-house very many years before, watching Tim Healy shred the plumage of a quill pen.

Some of the more cost-conscious practitioners exercised a substantial degree of economy. A few solicitors, for this or other reasons, were in the habit of sending files to counsel instead of making up cases to advise, and I recollect one leading senior counsel hurling a file across the Bar Library in exasperation at the diffuse untidiness of his instructions. One rather unusual country solicitor used to recycle large envelopes sent to him by turning them inside out, writing the address on the hairy side and posting them and their contents off to counsel.

These were no doubt the colourful exceptions who stick in one's memory. In my own practice, once I was well established, I was fortunate to be instructed by a number of firms of highly competent practitioners who had deservedly built up solid practices. One of my clients regularly prepared cases to advise which could have been a model in any jurisdiction in their completeness and clarity and the quality of their appreciation of the legal issues and the questions posed for counsel's opinion – which not infrequently merely confirmed the provisional conclusion reached by the draftsman. Solicitors in those earlier days still tended to have experienced unqualified clerks, who handled segments of their practices very effectively – the admiralty clerk of one leading firm was reputed to be the most reliable authority on shipping and admiralty matters in the province.

A visitor to the Royal Courts of Justice in 2013 who remembered them from 1957 would see the differences at once. The building itself looks very similar at first glance, apart from the addition of a reception desk at the entrance, movable seating in the Great Hall and various information signs and notices. But the observant visitor would soon see that some of the courts opening off the hall have been re-designated and that more courtrooms have been opened on other floors. He might then examine the court lists displayed on the boards in the hall and would find, if he happened by chance to have in his possession a list relating to the day's business in the late 1950s, that the amount of work being done by the courts has grown enormously in the interval. He would see a rather bigger throng of people in the hall and many more barristers and solicitors about than had been the case on his earlier visit. If he had access to the original Bar Library, he would see that it is no longer the working headquarters of the bar, but a much tidier and quieter reference library, which is deserted much of the time. He would look in vain for the Law Society's rooms and, if he wondered where the Department of Public Prosecutions, established in 1972, might be, he would not find it there. The bar, now some six hundred in number, are housed in a fine new building next door, opened in 2003, where some members share rooms on the upper floors and others have desks on the ground floor. The building is of an interesting design and the bar has assembled in it a good contemporary art collection. The rear half of this building, with a separate entrance, is home to the DPP and his staff. Our visitor, if he wished to call on one of the judges, would have to be admitted through the security door to the judges' corridor operated from the reception desk. Once inside the corridor, he would find that there are now fourteen judges and fourteen sets of chambers, with an elegant common room at the southern end. The administrative and legal assistants to the lord chief justice, multiplied in number and designation, have offices on the first floor.

This augmentation of the judiciary, administrators and bar reflects a considerable change in the quantity and nature of the work of the courts over the years. When I entered the profession there was a balanced but fairly light diet of high court and appellate litigation, which occupied the bar reasonably comfortably but without undue strain. There was a fairly steady stream of county court and petty sessions cases, which was not highly remunerated but provided essential employment for young junior counsel. Earnings were rather modest but sufficient for the lifestyle of the times. A member of the bar could expect, given a moderate degree of forensic ability, industry and good fortune, to advance in a few years to take silk and be eligible for further preferment in due course at some level, always desirable in those days because of the relative inability of practitioners to make adequate provision for a retirement pension. That pattern has changed substantially over the years. The numbers at the junior bar are such that the competition for work is keen and there appears to be greater disparity between those who succeed and those less fortunate. Those junior counsel who take silk tend to do so at a more advanced age, and are not inclined to seek appointment to the bench until later in life than before. Quite a few able juniors have declined to take silk and some talented queen's counsel have opted to remain at the bar until retirement. It would not be surprising if some were deterred from seeking either category of appointment by the cumbersome and long drawn-out process of application and consideration for the posts.

The pattern of judicial work has changed in equal degree over the years. It was relatively leisurely fifty years ago, at high court, county court or magistrates' level. The pressure to complete hearings and produce reserved decisions was materially less than in latter days. Judges had, and took, more time to research the law and write their judgments, which before the days of word processors meant long-hand composition. They had from time to time to engage in bursts of more intensive activity: the need to give a proper charge to a jury in a long and complex criminal or civil trial required concentrated effort, the more so since hearings tended to be more telescoped than today – the celebrated trial in 1953 of Ian Hay Gordon for the murder of Patricia Curran commenced on a Monday morning and ended at 10.45pm on the Saturday of that week. But this was the exception rather than a constant occurrence and both professional and judicial life proceeded at a more measured pace. Barristers' fees were low by comparison with today, even after taking full account of the change in the cost of living. Judicial salaries had remained unchanged for generations and were only commencing to increase to keep pace with inflation.

The number of judges has steadily increased over the years, until there are now fourteen members of the court of judicature, the lord chief justice, three lords justices of appeal and ten judges of the high court, who staff the chancery division, family division and queen's bench division. They are appointed by the Queen, but no longer on the sole advice of the lord chancellor. The appointment process changed after it was taken over by the judicial appointments commission (JAC), which was set up by the Justice (Northern Ireland) Act 2002 but did not commence operation until after my tenure of office as lord chief justice. The previous process was constantly criticised in a long campaign by the advocates of transparency as perpetuating the 'old boy network' and the 'tap on the shoulder'. I feel that a great deal of the criticism has come from those who have little idea how the system actually worked and the meticulous care with which those entrusted with the responsibility of selection carried out their task. The lord chief justice furnished the lord chancellor with detailed information about each person reckoned after consultation to be a serious candidate and a full assessment, based on the opinions of consultees and his own knowledge, of the merits of each, culminating in a recommendation. The lord chancellor gave thorough consideration to this material and quite commonly discussed it with the lord chief justice before reaching his conclusion. The person selected would then be asked to accept the post, and on his agreement the lord chancellor would forward his recommendation to the Queen.

The process of appointment to judicial posts at all levels is now in effect in the hands of the JAC. It invites applications from persons qualified for appointment, who have to complete a lengthy and complicated application form. It considers references and other documentation, conducts interviews of candidates and allots points to different qualities assumed to be relevant. The process takes very considerably longer than before, during which a candidate's practice may suffer. The length and complexity of the process have not escaped criticism, nor have its results in every case, but it is not the function of this paper to discuss the validity of the criticisms. The former process may not have satisfied the desires of those who pressed for change, but I can say from experience that it produced well-qualified appointees who have done sterling work on the bench.

One of the major changes in judicial life has been the need for enhanced security. Following immediately on the assassination of a county court judge and a resident magistrate on the same day in 1973, judges of all courts were given armed police protection. It became a part of daily life for judges to be accompanied by police escorts and ferried in armoured vehicles whenever they left their homes or the courts and to have an armed guard stationed twenty-four hours a day at their residences. This requirement persisted for many years during the troubled times and has been relaxed to an extent only in very recent years. The security issue, that is to say, the degree of risk to judges and their families and the necessary restrictions on their lives, has undoubtedly had an effect on the willingness of some practitioners to consider appointment to the bench. It may well have deprived the public of the services of some able people who in other times would have served as judges.

The weight and pressure of judicial work are undoubtedly greater than in the 1950s. Judges' salaries are substantially higher, but relative to the earnings of leading barristers they do appear to have fallen some way behind (though this is nothing new, as when I went on to the bench high court judges' salaries were very much lower than the earnings of a QC in a good practice). Moreover, the pension situation has changed dramatically: practising barristers can now make provision for a sizeable pension pot and are not so dependent on obtaining a judicial appointment to secure a pension, while the judges' pension contributions now to be levied put them further at a disadvantage. These factors are likely to have an influence on barristers' decisions whether to seek judicial appointments. Many are still ready to accept appointment, feeling that judicial work would be satisfying and worthwhile; a judge's lifestyle is certainly less pressurised than the life of a barrister with a heavy practice, and some feel that the change of pace is not unwelcome; while there is also the factor of duty, being willing to undertake judicial work for the benefit of the public. The fact does remain, however, that a noticeably larger proportion of experienced barristers now remain in practice until retirement without going on to the bench.

Two of the most significant changes in the administration of justice in Northern Ireland in the last fifty years have been the establishment of the post of director of public prosecutions (DPP) and the institution of the court service. Before the appointment of the first DPP prosecutions were instituted by the police and conducted under the aegis of the attorney general, who gave directions for the prosecution of indictable offences, a laborious task involving the consideration of numerous police files and reports. When the DPP took up office in 1972 he established a department which took over this function. Inevitably some complained of bureaucratic decision-making or delays, but the founding of the department was a timely development, for the number of criminal prosecutions increased very substantially over the next few years. Moreover, with the assumption by the English attorney general of the functions of the AG for Northern Ireland, following the prorogation of the parliament of Northern Ireland in 1972, it became even more crucial that there should be a department responsible for public prosecutions, for it would not have been practicable for the AG to continue to direct their institution. Under the founding legislation the director of public prosecutions was to work under the superintendence of the AG. That proved to be a fruitful relationship, largely due to the diplomacy and integrity of the first DPP Sir Barry Shaw QC and his successor Sir Alasdair Fraser QC, both of whom established a reputation for impartiality and judgment which has benefited their department.

The department was reconstituted by the Justice (Northern Ireland) Act 2002, under which the English AG has ceased to be AG for Northern Ireland, being replaced by a local appointee. The AG for Northern Ireland now appoints the DPP, but the latter has a greater degree of autonomy than under the previous legislation. They interact to a degree in consulting each other as required, but subject to that the DPP is independent and is now solely responsible for the conduct of all criminal proceedings in Northern Ireland.

The Northern Ireland Court Service was set up by the Judicature (Northern Ireland) Act 1978. Its constitution has followed the pattern set by the court service in England, rather than that adopted in the Republic. It is responsible for the building, maintenance, staffing and running of the courts at all levels, its function being described in the 1978 Act as being 'to facilitate the conduct of business' of the courts. It originally operated under the aegis of the lord chancellor, who appointed the staff, gave directions from time to time and even had statutory power to abolish it. Following the devolution of policing and justice to the Northern Ireland Assembly in 2010, it became an agency of the Department of Justice and its remit extended also to tribunals. The lord chief justice has to be consulted about the appointment of the statutory officers, that is, his principal secretary and legal secretary and the masters of the court of judicature, but otherwise the judiciary have no direct role in the operational matters entrusted to the court service, though they are represented on the court service agency board.

Needless to say, the system would not work smoothly and harmoniously without a considerable amount of discussion and consultation between the lord chief justice, the presiding judges of the county courts and district courts and the court service. There were periods in the earlier days when relations were not as easy as they should be, but by my time as LCJ it was working well, assisted by regular meetings with the director of the court service. This proved to be an essential element of an administrative system that was not judge-led. It was facilitated by the provision of sufficient and timely information to the judges about matters of current concern and the understanding by all parties of the needs of the others. As part of this interplay it was clearly understood that the function of determining the listing of matters in the courts remained a judicial responsibility. The administrative task of arranging the lists is delegated to officials, but their content must always be a matter for the judges to decide.

The changes that I have outlined in the legal profession and the administration of justice reflect the changes in the content of litigation, of which they are a consequence. Most notable is the large increase in the work of the courts in the last fifty years, which has necessitated the increase in the number of judges and practitioners. The amount of work tends to fluctuate from time to time, but the overall increase has been marked and seems unlikely to diminish.

Probably the most striking change is in the number of criminal trials and the way in which they are conducted. When I started in practice murder cases were rare, generally not more than one or two per year, and were the subject of great interest among members of the profession. If a heavy case came into the list at assizes it would commonly be adjourned for hearing in Belfast. The city commission was in session for only part of the year. Most trials were short in duration and in the absence of disclosure of documents there was little in the way of preliminary proceedings. Indictable offences were all tried by juries. High court judges presided at all trials of serious offences and quite a lot of less significant ones.

The amount of criminal work was beginning to increase before the civil disturbances, but since their commencement it has grown very considerably. When non-jury 'Diplock' trial of terrorism-related offences was at its height in the 1980s, about forty per cent of indictable offences came before judges sitting without juries. That ratio steadily dwindled until by 2004, when I ceased to be a judge in Northern Ireland, it was down to about seven per cent. The time spent by high court judges on crime increased steadily until in fairly recent years it occupied several of them at any one time. A very large proportion of all criminal cases is now heard before county court judges, some of whom are now authorised to try cases of murder, attempted murder, wounding with intent and rape. High court judges now try relatively few, all involving serious offences, and a substantial proportion of those are non-jury trials.

The format of criminal trials has undergone a number of quite profound changes. For a number of years following the introduction of non-jury trial in 1973 the prosecution case in most cases depended on confessions by defendants – the reason was distressingly simple, the widespread reluctance to testify on the part of witnesses other than police and military personnel. In consequence very many Diplock trials centred round a 'statement fight', in which the admissibility of confessions was challenged in a *voir dire*, lasting on occasion for several weeks and even months. This has declined substantially since the introduction of sophisticated recording of interviews of defendants in police custody. Although they could sometimes be diverting in the sheer ingenuity of the allegations of ill-treatment, they were a very tedious part of criminal trials and their decline is little regretted. The much-criticised 'supergrass' trials, founded upon the evidence of an accomplice, have waxed and waned – though one attracted some attention not long ago – but their virtual disappearance has given some relief to judges, if not to those lawyers for whom it was a dependable source of income for long periods at a time. The growth industry in recent years has been based on the requirements of disclosure of crown documents and of defences in modern law. The process of satisfying these requirements can lead to substantial delays in bringing cases to trial and the judges have instituted a structured system of intensive case management in a strenuous attempt to keep them moving at a satisfactory pace.

A similar development has taken place on the civil side of litigation. It commenced with the institution of the commercial list, designed to improve arrangements for the hearing of commercial cases, which as the non-jury list had tended to be the Cinderella of civil trials. They were usually listed after the jury actions, which meant that they too often failed to get a slot for hearing and consequently were at times neglected by practitioners. Strong representations had been made that business clients and their litigation required better service from the courts and I set up the list in 1992 to implement a report recommending it. It proved to be a successful way of bringing such cases to trial and litigants came to feel that disputes which thitherto had gone to arbitration could be heard expeditiously and effectively in the courts. The process is labour-intensive, in that it requires a good deal of judicial time and trouble, and is assisted by strict insistence by the administrative staff that parties adhere to the timetable laid down by the court. The example spread to medical negligence cases, where case management proved beneficial, and has now been adopted widely throughout the high court. Discovery of documents in civil cases has become more universal and more complicated, and burdensome, and the volume of documents in the average civil action has grown considerably. The requirement to submit skeleton arguments setting out each party's case on issues of law has revolutionised appeals and cases involving legal argument. It has to be said that some purported skeletons tend to become rather chubby, but most practitioners have become more proficient at summarising their cases, allowing the judges to acquaint themselves in advance with the issues and facilitating the dispatch of cases, which in the court of appeal occupy a materially shorter length of time than in my earlier years.

During my whole time at the bar most civil actions, and certainly all claims for damages for personal injuries, were heard by juries, and a large part of one's working life was spent in addressing juries and shaping cases in such a way as to appeal to them. This changed in 1987, when a provision was brought in whereby all civil cases, with a few exceptions such as defamation and the occasional case of false imprisonment, were to be heard by a judge alone. Concerns were expressed about the change before it occurred, but the profession accepted it with a good grace and came to grow comfortable with it. The number of personal injury cases soared from the 1970s onwards and at one time some thirty cases a day were listed and there was a backlog awaiting trial of some 8,000 actions. The pattern has changed to an extraordinary extent since then, with the reduction in civil legal aid and the much increased early settlement of claims, so that the number coming into the trial list is, by comparison, minuscule.

Other types of litigation have filled the vacuum. Judicial review cases were almost non-existent when I went on to the bench in 1984, but their numbers and importance have grown exponentially since then, to the extent that fairly recently two high court judges were engaged full time on deciding them. One judge is assigned exclusively to commercial work, with occasional assistance from others. The chancery division is considerably concerned with cases arising out of insolvency, both personal and corporate, fuelled by the credit crisis, and with disputes arising out of family provision and claims by wives and partners to equitable interests in dwelling-houses. Another significant expansion has been that of family cases. Fifty years ago the matrimonial work consisted mainly of a few undefended divorce cases. Now, in addition to a hugely expanded divorce list, the judge assigned to the family division is very heavily engaged in issues involving children, adoption and the division of matrimonial property. There has been a correlative increase in the work of the court of appeal, and its judges are much more confined to appellate work than in previous years.

The courts have taken a number of steps to make the progress of litigation easier and speedier and reduce the cost, for example, the use of television links and telephone conferencing and the provision of documentation by way of computer disc. Pre-hearing meetings of expert witnesses are regularly directed, in order to have their evidence focus on real points of difference. Another significant development is the encouragement of recourse to mediation.

The rules of the supreme court in operation up to 1980 were descended from those that applied in the old Irish courts, and frequent recourse was had to the commentary and cases cited in Wylie's *Judicature Acts*. It was decided to bring the rules closely into line with the English rules of the supreme court, a major task undertaken by the rules committee. When the new rules came into operation it was possible to make regular use of the English White Book in arguing and deciding matters of procedure. This worked well, but was relatively short-lived, for in 1998 the English system underwent a fundamental change-over to the Civil Procedure Rules, which have not been adopted in Northern Ireland – so old White Books are carefully preserved in our jurisdiction.

Outside the high court, the county courts have continued at a steady pace. The jurisdiction, limited to claims for £300 in the 1950s, was increased by stages to the present level of £15,000, and is due to be further enlarged, which will no doubt conduce to the growth of litigation in that forum. Costs scales in my early days were low – counsel's maximum fee on a civil bill was nine guineas, with an extra guinea if the hearing took place more than 25 miles from Belfast. Costs scales have been increased substantially since that time, and procedures have become more elaborate, so it may be more difficult to regard the county court as the cheap and simple tribunal that it once was. Claims for criminal injuries to the person and criminal damage to property escalated from the commencement of the civil disturbances and at a time formed a considerable source of income for many lawyers. Another area of huge growth has been the development of tribunals hearing cases arising out of claims of discrimination in employment, both sexual and religious. These have tended to be very long drawn-out – a fact on which the court of appeal made very critical comments on more than once occasion – and to generate appeals involving large quantities of documentation.

Appeals to the house of lords had been brought at fairly regular intervals before the Second World War, but they became rare after the war until a successful appeal was brought in 1956 in an employment case. Although the requirement of leave to appeal to the house of lords was imposed in 1960, the flow of appeals recommenced and proceeded steadily thereafter. The practice changed significantly, giving rise to a shortening of oral hearings – and the consequent increase in the numbers of appeals heard and the weight of work descending on to the shoulders of the law lords. During my time in practice, applications for leave were heard orally in the house of lords and allowed or dispatched on the spot. The practice was later instituted of a sub-committee considering the applications on paper (a time-consuming and tedious but important labour), only rarely requiring an oral hearing. The parties' printed cases have become very much longer and more elaborate since I appeared as counsel in the house of lords. A direction was given about 1980 that they were to set out only a synopsis of the argument for the party, with no recital of the progress of the case below and the finding of the lower courts. I recollect that in one fairly major appeal involving industrial derating my printed case consisted of eight pages. Now it is not uncommon for each party's case to exceed one hundred pages and the lawyers and law lords have to do an immense amount of pre-reading for each appeal. In a typical week a law lord would sit on two appeals, each lasting two days, having done the necessary pre-reading of printed cases and authorities, then have to prepare opinions on cases previously heard and start in to the next week's work – far from a sinecure.

The citation of authority in the house of lords has also been transformed. When I was at the bar each party was required to star his six most essential cases. The leather-bound volumes containing the report of each such case would be to hand for each member of the appellate committee, and the other authorities cited in the printed cases would be held in readiness, again in the form of volumes of law reports. The parties had to have all these volumes at hand at the hearing, and it was usual for solicitors in Northern Ireland appeals to have London agents, who would arrange for the books to be provided. In recent years it has been the universal practice for reports to be photocopied and bound in comb binders. The number of these has multiplied and it was not uncommon for the law lords to have forty or even more such binders in bookcases beside their seats. Information technology is starting to make a difference now in the supreme court and privy council and much more material is being provided and disseminated in paperless form. Until 1963 decisions of the house of lords were given by the law lords reading their judgments (technically speeches) *in extenso*, which could take up considerable time. In recent years the practice was for embargoed copies of the judgments (which became termed opinions) to be given to the parties' lawyers the day before judgment was given. The hearing itself, held on a morning before the main sitting of the house, consisted of a brief summary by each member of the appellate committee of his or her decision and a resolution of the skeletal house disposing of the appeal.

This account of the changes in legal practice over one practitioner's lifetime has necessarily been selective, but I hope that it has given a flavour of how it has developed over those years. Society itself has changed, and the practice of the law must change with it if the legal system is to fulfil its proper function of serving the public. The practice of the law, in both branches of the profession, has come to take more account of economics, or, as some would put it, is more mercenary. Such changes may be necessary in order to enable practitioners to provide a more effective service to their clients, but it is undeniable that client loyalty has declined with them. The bar has less of a club-like feel about it, an inevitable consequence of its immense augmentation, though an admirably friendly atmosphere still prevails and its sports and social clubs continue to flourish. Happily, the traditional camaraderie has survived the many stresses and strains of the intervening years. It is said at times that solicitors have less of a personal relationship with their clients than before, but with larger firms and greater specialisation that would have been hard to avoid. Those who are in practice today have to take the world as they find it and make their way accordingly. One who has known both worlds might, however, be forgiven for harking back a little and indulging in a hint of nostalgia without being classed as being a mere *laudator temporis acti* (a praiser of past times). Alas, the fleeting years roll on, as Horace said; the survivors of that past age are wont, no doubt like the elder statesmen of every generation, to aver that their world was a better time in which to practise, and I hope that from the foregoing account our successors can at least understand that view. However advanced the world may now be, we may feel in our hearts that things can never be quite the same. But then they never are.

The changing role of equity in the Irish courts in the twentieth century

RONAN KEANE

Although my subject is the role of equity in the Irish courts in the last century, I will begin with a case decided as far back as 1856 but which is particularly illuminating in the light of those later developments. In *O'Fay v. Burke*,[1] the plaintiff or petitioner, Dr O'Fay, was a parish priest in County Galway who was anxious to obtain a lease of a cottage and some adjoining land, which was in a poor state of repair. He was prepared to spend substantial sums on effecting the necessary improvements but understandably wanted some greater security of tenure than that offered by a periodic tenancy and it was proposed by him (or on his behalf) that he should be given a lease for three lives and thirty-one years. The landlord, James Burke, lived nearby in a house called St Clerans, which, as far as I can ascertain is the beautiful house at Craughwell designed by Gandon and the Irish home nearer to our own time of the film director, John Huston. He was happy to accommodate Dr O'Fay, but was advised that because of the settlement under which he held the lands, he could not make such a lease. He wrote to Dr O'Fay saying:

> I find I have not the power to execute the lease you propose. If you choose to take the farm in the usual way, I will allow you twenty pounds to get up the cottage and a lease for your own life.

Dr O'Fay went into possession of the farm and cottage and paid an agreed rent. James Burke died without executing any lease and was succeeded by his son, John, the remainderman. Dr O'Fay asked John Burke's agent for an extended lease and was told that, 'I handed your letter to Mr Burke who requests me to acquaint you that he will not make a lease on any part of his property.' At a later stage, the agent served notices to quit on all the tenants on the estate, including Dr O'Fay, with a view to getting the rents increased. He wrote to the agent,

[1] (1858) 8 I Ch R 225, 511.

enclosing the letter he had received from John Burke's father agreeing to give him a lease for life, and adding:

> However, as a friend, in justice to all parties, I leave my case in your own hands at present; therefore there is no necessity of making a further proposal, particularly as a lease will not be granted on any part of his property and hence no necessity of notices [to quit] ...

John Burke, who was a major in the British Army, never received this letter; he had left for the Crimea. No action was taken on foot of the notice to quit and over the next two years Dr O'Fay spent £543, obviously a substantial sum at the time, in significant improvements to the property.

After Major Burke's return from the Crimea, relations between him and Dr O'Fay deteriorated, principally as a result of a ram escaping from the latter's property and doing damage on the adjoining land. A further notice to quit was served and this time ejectment proceedings followed with both parties adopting an intransigent attitude. Dr O'Fay issued his own proceedings in the then separate court of chancery, claiming specific performance of what was alleged on his behalf to be an agreement to grant a lease. When the case came before the master of the rolls, he had no difficulty in refusing to grant that relief, holding that there was no enforceable agreement for such a lease. He was, however, more impressed by an alternative argument that it would be inequitable for the landlord to be given possession of the land on which the tenant had spent substantial sums in the belief that he had been given an assurance that he would be granted a lease. Sir Thomas Smith MR explained the law as follows:

> If a tenant holding from year to year or for any other term makes permanent improvements on the land which he so holds, this raises no equity as against the landlord, although he may have looked on and not given any warning to the tenant. ... But if the landlord, knowing that the tenant believes he holds under a valid lease or contract for a lease, looks on at the expenditure without warning the tenant that he means to impeach the contract, such a proceeding is a fraud ... and the tenant has a remedy against the landlord (although he be a remainderman) if he seeks to turn the tenant out without compensation.

He added:

> There are many cases at Law and in Equity in which a person who looks on when a third party acts on the assumption of a particular state of affairs and remains silent as to his rights is estopped from insisting on such a right.

Here, eight years before the celebrated house of lords decision in *Ramsden v. Dyson*[2] – normally seen as its *fons et origo* – is an acceptance of what was to emerge as the doctrine of proprietary estoppel. But it was of no avail to Dr O'Fay: Smith MR concluded that, since Major Burke was unaware of his father's promise to give him a lease or of the substantial improvements that he had made to the property, there was no equity on which Dr O'Fay could rely to defeat the landlord's legal right to possession. Although the master of the rolls lamented the state of the law which had brought about what he regarded as an unjust and oppressive result and hoped that his judgment might be set aside on appeal, it was not to be: the lord chancellor and Blackburne LJ were agreed that the petitioner could not succeed. The former, indeed, also deplored the result but hoped that Major Burke as 'a British officer and a gentleman' could see his way to ensuring that Dr O'Fay would be left in undisturbed possession of the holding for the rest of his life.

Whether that happened, I do not know, but the law under which tenants of agricultural land had neither security of tenure nor the right to a fair rent was, of course, subsequently swept away following the campaign led by Davitt and Parnell and the enactment of the Land Purchase Acts. The doctrine of proprietary estoppel, however, confirmed in *Ramsden v. Dyson*, was to result in decisions in Ireland and England which demonstrated that the difficulties encountered by the Irish judges in arriving at what might seem a fair result persisted in a very changed social milieu.[3]

The first important strand in the decision was the acceptance that the courts when exercising the equity jurisdiction required litigants to act 'in good conscience' unlike the common law courts. The second important strand was the recognition that equity did not replace but rather supplemented the common law and that, in particular, while the application of equitable principles could result in the requirements of

---

2 (1866) LR 1 HL 129.
3 *Plimmer v. Wellington Corporation* (1884) 9 App Cas 699; *Siew Soon Wah v. Yong Tong Hong* (1973) AC 836 PC; *Cullen v. Cullen* (1962) IR 268; *McMahon and Another v. Kerry County Council* (1981) ILRM 419.

conscience being upheld, that could not justify setting aside the law as to the ownership of property. Major Burke's conduct in evicting his tenant without compensating him in any way for the improvements he had made to the land, however unattractive, was perfectly legal under the law as it was and equity could not be successfully invoked to prevent it by the tenant.

In *Ramsden v. Dyson*, Lord Kingsdown said,

> if a man, under a verbal agreement with a landlord for a certain interest in land, or, what amounts to the same thing, under an expectation created or encouraged by the landlord, that he shall have a certain interest, takes possession of such land, with the consent of the landlord, and upon the faith of such promise or expectation, with the knowledge of the landlord and without objection by him, lays out money upon the land, a court of equity will compel the landlord to give effect to such promise or expectation ...

This passage, repeatedly cited in later cases, fits the facts in *O'Fay v. Burke* perfectly, with one crucial qualification, that the landlord did not know of his father's promise or of the expenditure on the land.

In the same case, Lord Cranworth LC said,

> if a stranger begins to build on my land, supposing it to be his own and I, perceiving his mistake, abstain from setting him right and leave him to persevere in his error, a court of equity will not allow me afterwards to assert my title to the land on which he has expended money on the supposition that it was his own.

Again this statement of the law has been cited in many later cases, although it was to prove less far reaching in its application than that of Lord Kingsdown.

All of this law was carried over into the law of the Irish Free State by Article 73 of the Constitution of the Irish Free State and into our present law by Article 50 of the Constitution. In the meantime, although the Judicature (Ireland) Act 1877 had abolished the separate courts of common law and equity and provided that the principles of law and equity were to be applied in every case, with the rules of equity prevailing in the event of a conflict, there was no fusion of the two bodies of law.

It is true that in a house of lords decision in 1978, *United Scientific Holdings Ltd v. Burnley Borough Council*,[4] Lord Diplock said that the two bodies of law had been fused as a result of the Judicature Act, and that decision was followed by the supreme court in *Hynes v. Independent Newspapers Ltd.*[5] But his remarks were *obiter* and were received with little enthusiasm in other common law jurisdictions with the exception of New Zealand. While the issue does not seem to have arisen in the Irish courts since then, it seems likely that, if it does, it would be held that the significant distinctions between the two systems of law remain of relevance.

This is well illustrated by cases where the most important of equitable institutions, the trust, and its associated principles, are invoked. In those cases, common law areas, such as negligence and contract, will continue to be of only limited relevance. As McClachlin J (subsequently chief justice) explained in the Canadian case of *Canson Enterprises Ltd v. Boughton*,[6]

> My first concern with proceeding by analogy with tort is that it overlooks the unique foundations and goals of equity. The basis of the fiduciary obligation and the rationale for equitable compensation are distinct from the tort of negligence and contract. In negligence and contract, the parties are taken to be independent and equal actors concerned primarily with their own self interest. Consequently the law seeks a balance between enforcing obligations by awarding compensation and preserving optimal freedom for those involved in the relationship, contractual or otherwise. The fiduciary relationship has trust, not self interest, at its core and where breach occurs the balance favours the person wronged ... In short equity is concerned, not only to compensate the plaintiff, but to enforce the trust which is at its heart.

Under Articles 73 and 50, the corpus of equity law was only carried over by both constitutions insofar as it was consistent with them. In practice, this has been of limited significance in the case of equity, since the major developments in constitutional jurisprudence have on the whole been of significance in the area of public rather than private law. But it is the case, as the supreme court has made clear on a number of occasions, that if a right guaranteed either expressly or by implication by the Constitution is attacked, the absence of an established statutory, common law or equitable remedy will be immaterial. In such cases, the courts are required to take whatever steps are necessary to protect and

---

4 (1978) AC 904 HL.   5 (1980) IR 204.   6 (1991) 5 DLR (4th) 129.

vindicate the right.[7] Thus, in 1987 in *AG (SPUC) v. Open Door Counselling Ltd*,[8] the equitable remedy of an injunction was granted to the attorney general acting at the relation of the Society for the Protection of the Unborn Child restraining the defendants from disseminating information as to abortion facilities in Britain, in breach under the then law of Article 40.3.3.[9] The most widely used of equitable remedies would not normally have been available to plaintiffs in such a case where they had suffered, or would suffer, no damage themselves.

In cases concerning the possible illegality of conditions attached to trusts, the Constitution had also some role to play. Thus, in *Re Burke's Estate, Burke v. Burke*,[10] Gavan Duffy P refused to enforce a condition that the testator's nephew was to be educated in a Roman Catholic school to be selected by the trustees. Conditions of this nature had been held to be void in England on a public policy ground, i.e., that they weakened the tie between parent and child. But the learned president also regarded the condition as invalidated by Article 42.1 of the Constitution, containing an acknowledgment by the State of the role of the family as 'the primary and natural educator of the child' and a guarantee that the right and duty of parents to provide for the education of their children would be respected. A similar view was expressed by Dixon J in *Re Blake*.[11] In *Maguire v. AG*,[12] Gavan Duffy J, as he then was, invoked the language of the Preamble to the Constitution in upholding a gift for the founding of a convent for the perpetual adoration of the Blessed Sacrament as a valid charitable gift.

It is, of course, also the case that decisions of the courts of the United Kingdom prior to 1921 are not generally regarded as binding on Irish courts.[13] But where such decisions have become so entrenched in the law and frequently acted on that departing from them would have wide and complex ramifications, it has on the whole been left to the Oireachtas to remove any difficulties associated with them. In the case of equity, that power has not been exercised on many occasions. One recent example is the Charities Act 2009, which, although preserving Lord Macnaghten's celebrated four classes of charitable trusts, has also made significant changes in the law, nearly all of which have still to be brought into force at the time of writing.

7 See *Meskell v. CIE* (1973) IR 12, SC.   8 (1988) IR 593, 610.
9 The article was subsequently amended to permit the dissemination of such information subject to such conditions as might be laid down by law.
10 (1951) IR 216.   11 (1955) IR 89.   12 (1943) IR 238.
13 *Exham v. Beamish* (1939) IR 336; *Attorney General v. Ryan's Car Hire Ltd* (1965) IR 642; *Irish Shell Ltd v. Elm Motors Ltd* (1984) IR 200.

The doctrine of proprietary estoppel which, as we have seen, was anticipated in *O'Fay v. Burke* was thus applied by Irish courts in accordance with the principles laid down in the English decisions. But Irish law in this area also took some less predictable turns. An example of the orthodox approach was the decision of the high court in *Haughan v. Ruttledge*.[14] The plaintiffs, who were the trustees of an association engaged in the promotion of harness racing, hoped to lease the defendant's land with a view to holding races. The defendant agreed to let the lands to them for a trial period. If, at the end of the period, the plaintiffs left the land, they would pay no rent but the defendant would be entitled to the benefit of the works carried out. In the event, the plaintiffs with the consent of the defendant carried out works of a more permanent and expensive nature than was originally envisaged. The parties subsequently fell out and the defendant sought possession of the land. The plaintiffs claimed that the defendant had agreed to give them a lease for twenty years but Blayney J found that there was no such agreement. They also claimed that the defendant was estopped from denying them a proprietary interest in the land, but the learned judge rejected that claim, holding that there had been no representation by the defendant on which they could rely. He applied to the facts the following passage from the seminal speech by Lord Kingsdown in *Ramsden v. Dyson*:

> if a tenant, being in possession of land, and knowing the nature and extent of his interest, lays out money upon it in the hope and expectation of an extended term or an allowance for expenditure, then, if such hope and expectation has not been encouraged by the landlord, the tenant has no claim which any court of law or equity can enforce.

Cases of proprietary estoppel must, of course, be distinguished from cases of promissory estoppel. While both are usually regarded as subspecies of the generic doctrine of equitable estoppel, they are significantly different. The former is a remedy normally giving rise to proprietary rights, whereas the latter prevents or modifies the enforcement of contractual rights.

There have also been a number of cases from the middle of the last century onwards in which the proprietary estoppel doctrine has been successfully invoked where there was a close relationship between two

---

14 (1988) IR 295.

people, sometimes resulting in the sharing of a home, and the court was able to find that there had been an expectation of a benefit encouraged by one of them, on which the other had relied to his or her detriment. Again, Irish and English law have tended to move in the same direction in this area, an example being the decision of Costello J in *Re JR, a Ward of Court*.[15] In that case, an elderly man had formed such a relationship with a woman, significantly younger than him, whom he had met while they were both patients in the same hospital. She ultimately went to live in his house and he had assured her on more than one occasion that it would be all hers at some stage and that he would leave it to her in his will. The learned judge found that she had acted to her own detriment in leaving her home and going to live with him. When he subsequently became a patient in a psychiatric hospital and was made a ward of court, his committee asked for leave to sell the house, which was now in a dilapidated condition. The learned judge found that a case of proprietary estoppel had been established and that, while it was in the ward's interest that the house should be sold, her equity should be satisfied by the purchase of a smaller house in which she would be entitled to reside for the rest of her life.

Another Irish example is *Smyth v. Halpin*.[16] In that case a son had asked his father for a site on which to build a house. The father persuaded him instead to build an extension on to his (the father's) house, since he said it would ultimately come to the son. The father's will, however, left the house to his wife for her life and thereafter to the daughter. Geoghegan J applied the earlier English decisions and held that the son was entitled to a reversionary interest in the house after the expiration of the mother's life estate.

However, the recurrent dilemma presented for judges in cases such as *O'Fay v. Burke* was resolved in a manner notably different from that mandated by the mainstream of Irish and English authority in *McMahon and Another v. Kerry County Council*.[17] The defendants sold a plot of land to the plaintiffs in 1964 in the belief that the latter would build a secondary school on the site. In 1965 the plaintiffs abandoned this plan and did not visit the site again until 1968 when they discovered that the defendants were preparing to build on it, whereupon they complained and the building stopped. The plaintiffs never fenced or marked off the site, upon which the defendants subsequently built two houses, the work beginning in 1972. In 1973 the plaintiffs discovered this for the first time and began proceedings, after some delay, claiming

15 (1993) ILRM 657.   16 (1997) 2 ILRM 38.   17 (1981) ILRM 419.

possession of the site. The defendants, after the proceedings began, put two tenants in the houses.

The defendants relied on the principle in *Ramsden v. Dyson* but were, of course, in the difficulty that the plaintiffs had not acquiesced in any way in the building on their property and indeed had protested against it at an early stage. Finlay P, while acknowledging that it was a novel application of the doctrine of equitable estoppel, said that he considered that the court should have regard not only to the plaintiffs' conduct but also to that of the defendants. He also pointed out that the site had no intrinsic or sentimental value for the plaintiffs. In these circumstances, he considered it would be 'unconscionable and unjust' for the plaintiffs to recover possession of the site with the two houses which were being used by the defendants to meet the housing needs of their area. He accordingly granted an order for possession but, having assessed compensation for the loss by the plaintiffs of their land, he put a stay on the order which in the event of the compensation being paid within a specified time was to become permanent. This undoubtedly could be regarded as a just result in the particular circumstances, but was difficult to reconcile with the fundamental principle laid down in *O'Fay v. Burke* that the law as to the ownership of property could not be set aside to prevent a result which might seem unjust or oppressive.

There have been some other Irish decisions from the same period of which the same could be said, but these were cases in which, unlike *McMahon*, the court followed English decisions in arriving at such a conclusion. This was when Lord Denning, then the master of the rolls in England, was propounding some novel equitable doctrines which have not lasted too well. It had long been accepted that the law recognised the variety of trust known as constructive trusts which come into being because it would be unconscionable for the legal owner to deny another's equitable entitlement to the property. The circumstances in which such constructive trusts arose were reasonably clearly defined, but Lord Denning sought to widen them radically by holding that the trust was to be imposed 'wherever justice and good conscience require it'.[18] These 'new model' constructive trusts, as they came to be called, were recognised in a number of Irish decisions of which *Kelly v. Cahill*[19] is an example.

In that case, a man instructed his solicitor that he wished to alter his will so that his wife would inherit all his assets and his nephew, who was

18 *Hussey v. Palmer* (1972) 1 WLR 1286, 1289.
19 (2000) IR 56. See also *HKN Invest Oy v. Incotrade PVT Ltd* (1993) 3 IR152 and *Murray v. Murray* (1996) 3 IR 251.

a beneficiary under the will, would not receive anything. The solicitor advised him that, because of tax considerations, the best way to do this was by transferring his assets to himself and his wife as joint tenants so that she would inherit them all by survivorship. The solicitor, however, mistakenly omitted from the transfer certain land of which the deceased was also the owner. Consequently it passed under the terms of the will to his wife for life and after her death to the nephew absolutely, subject to the wife's legal right share to one half of the lands. Barr J considered that the question he had to decide was whether the evidence established a clear, positive intention on the part of the testator that his wife should inherit all his property on his death. He accepted that the nephew was neither aware of nor had any responsibility for the mistake, but said that 'justice and good conscience' required that the nephew should not be allowed to inherit any part of the deeased's property. He accordingly held that the nephew held his interest in remainder on a constructive trust for the wife.

There now appears to be a general acceptance in common law jurisdictions that deciding cases solely on the basis of what 'justice and good conscience' requires is an unduly simplistic approach and the 'new model' constructive trust has lost favour as a result. There has also been little enthusiasm either on the bench or in academic commentary for another radical reshaping of equity by Lord Denning, which would have replaced the doctrines of undue influence and setting aside of unconscionable transactions by an all embracing doctrine of 'inequality of contract'.[20] The reaction was understandable: the formulation of rules that protect the consumer while ensuring that the conduct of business is not unduly hampered is best dealt with in legislation.[21] That approach does not preclude the courts from laying down guidelines in particular areas where litigation is frequent, as the house of lords did in cases where wives had acted as sureties for their husbands in transactions with banks and issues arose as to whether the guarantees in question should be set aside as being procured by undue influence.[22]

In family law cases, the dilemma facing courts that sought to reconcile a fair result with the requirements of principle and precedent arose again. The greatly increased number of such cases in the Irish courts in the closing decades of the last century included many that required the resolution by the courts of disputes as to the ownership of

20 *Lloyds Bank v. Bundy* (1975) QB 326.
21 See the comments of Lord Scarman in *National Westminster Bank plc v. Morgan* (1985) AC 686.
22 *Royal Bank of Scotland v. Etridge* (No 2) (2002) AC 773.

property in cases of marital breakdown. These called for the application of principles as to the equitable ownership of such property – almost invariably the matrimonial home – in a context very different from that in which such principles had originally evolved in the courts of equity. Although in some cases the purchase price was paid by one of the parties – usually the husband – in other cases both parties made contributions. The property might have been conveyed to the party who provided the purchase money or into the joint names of both parties. The courts applied the equitable doctrine of the resulting trust to such cases and this meant that, where the property was in the husband's name, but both parties had contributed to the purchase price, they were entitled to the beneficial interest in proportion to the amounts which they had contributed. But if the property was purchased in the wife's name, there would be no resulting trust in favour of the husband, even if he had contributed the whole or part of the purchase money. This was because of another equitable doctrine, i.e., the presumption of advancement, under which it was presumed that the husband intended a gift to his wife. Moreover, if the property was conveyed into their joint names, it was presumed that they were entitled to it jointly, even if all the purchase price had been contributed by the husband. The presumption of advancement could, however, be rebutted by evidence that a gift was not intended.[23]

The application of such equitable principles to relatively modern cases of marital breakdown was rendered more complex by the fact in such cases that the bulk of the purchase money was normally paid by a bank or building society on the security of an instalment mortgage. The fact that one party had paid the deposit was obviously not a satisfactory basis for holding that person entitled to the beneficial interest where the other party had either paid or contributed to the repayment instalments. Even if there had been no direct contributions, but there had been other financial contributions to the usual domestic outgoings, thus facilitating the mortgage repayments, the question arose as to whether they could ground a claim to a beneficial interest. (It was ultimately held that they could.[24]) Moreover, in such cases the parties usually had not at the outset entered into any agreement as to the shares in which they were to own the matrimonial home. The concept of the 'prenuptial' agreement lay far into the future.

In England, it was held that the presumption of advancement, dating from the days before the Married Women's Property Acts when women

---

23 *RF v. MF* (1995) 2 ILRM 572.
24 *McC v. McC* (1986) ILRM 1.

could not own property in their own right, had little if any relevance to modern conditions and it was largely discarded in that jurisdiction.[25] But it continued to be applied in Ireland, although the case for abandoning it was even stronger here, since it was clearly difficult to reconcile with the guarantee of equality in Article 40.1 of the Constitution.

Ultimately, many of these difficulties were removed by legislation enabling the courts to make property adjustment orders in such cases, where the parties were obtaining either a judicial separation or a divorce, so that the rights of the parties to the matrimonial home and other property were no longer necessarily determined by the cumbersome application of such equitable rules.[26] Problems remained, however, in the increasing number of cases where the parties were living together but were not married or were in a same sex relationship. These have been recently addressed by the granting to the courts of a similar jurisdiction in cases involving such couples by the Civil Partnership and Certain Rights and Obligations of Cohabitants Act 2010. There remain cases, however, where such issues will continue to arise, for example, where the entitlement of a deceased spouse or partner to property is in issue or in litigation by a third party against a spouse or partner involving property. It can also arise in annulment cases, since there is no provision for property adjustment orders in such cases. Under the existing Irish law, those questions will continue to be determined by the application of the resulting trust doctrine and (in the case of married couples) the presumption of advancement.

In England, where there has been no equivalent to the 2010 Act, the courts have abandoned the concept of the resulting trust in such cases and replaced it with what has been termed a 'common intention, constructive trust'. That is something of a legal oxymoron, since the essence of the constructive trust is that a party is bound in conscience to acknowledge the title of another party to property and the actual or presumed intentions of the trustee and beneficiary are not the determining factor. The resultant jurisprudence has become increasingly confused and contradictory. In *Stack v. Dowden*,[27] the house of lords held that, in the case of property held in joint names by

---

25 *Pettitt v. Pettitt* (1970) AC 777. It has been abolished in Northern Ireland by the Law Reform (Miscelleaneous Provisions) (Northern Ireland) Order 2005, art. 16, and in England by the Equality Act 2010, s.199, but the latter provision has not yet been brought into effect.
26 Under the Family Law Act 1995 and the Family Law (Divorce) Act 1996.
27 (2007) 2 AC 432, HL.

unmarried cohabitants, the court could not only infer an agreement between the parties as to the shares in which the property was held but could 'impute' such an agreement between the parties. That seemed to suggest that the court could simply impose what it considered to be a fair answer to the question as to the shares in which the property was to be held, although such a proposition was expressly disclaimed by Lady Hale in the leading speech for the majority. More recently, in *Jones v. Kernott*[28] a majority of the newly established supreme court reaffirmed that position, but the minority, although concurring in the result, said that the court, in imputing the relevant intention to the parties, was imposing what was a fair and reasonable determination as to the shares in which the property was to be held.

In such cases, a more attractive solution might be what has come to be called 'the remedial constructive trust'. This was a remedy developed in other common law countries – notably Canada and Australia – to deal with cases of 'unjust enrichment'. A person who entered into a contract which a court found to be void might have paid money or transferred property to the other party without obtaining any benefit. Unless the court could devise a remedy, the result would be that the other party was unjustly enriched. Hence the development by the courts of the concept of restitution which could result in the court ordering the payment by the party concerned of a sum sufficient to reverse the unjust enrichment. That was a common law remedy which did not rest on the premise that the plaintiff had a proprietary interest in the money he had paid or the property he had transferred.

But in Canada it was held that in such cases the courts could impose a constructive trust on the money or property transferred which in turn might be binding on third parties who acquired an interest in the funds. A remedial constructive trust of this nature has been availed of in Canada and Australia in cases of disputes between couples as to the ownership of property where the court was satisfied that it would be unconscionable of the legal owner to deny that the other party had an equitable interest[29] but has received little judicial support in England. However, while it departs from the orthodox view of trusts by effectively creating one where the supposed beneficiary never had an equitable interest in the property, it has been pointed out in one of the Australian cases that the trust itself began life in medieval times as a

---

28 (2011) UKSC 53.
29 *Pettkus v. Becker* (1980) 117 DLR (3d) 257; *Atlas Cabinets & Furniture Ltd v. National Trust Co. Ltd* (1990) 68 DLR (4th) 167; *Muschinski v. Dodds* (1985) 160 CLR 583, HC.

remedy and only gradually assumed the form of an equitable estate.[30] While the rights of third parties with existing interests in the property could be protected by the court declaring that the trust only came into existence when it made its order, problems could still arise if there was a subsequent insolvency. It has been pointed out in England that for a court to declare a party to be entitled under a constructive trust as a remedy rather than to give effect to an existing proprietary right would be to allow the court to substitute its own discretion for the statutory rules applicable on an insolvency.[31]

It remains to be seen what attitude the Irish courts ultimately adopt to the concept of the remedial constructive trust. In this, as in other areas, the dilemmas which arose in cases such as *O'Fay v. Burke* will continue to cause problems for the courts as they seek to reconcile conflicts between the preservation of legal rules for the ownership of property and contractual rights and the search for a just result in the cases before them.

---

30 *Muschinske v. Dodds*, above, per Deane J.
31 Per Mummery LJ in *In Re Polly Peck International (No. 2)* (1998) 3 All ER 812, 827.

The changing face of the circuits during the past twenty-five years

HUGH GEOGHEGAN

'He had an extensive practice on the western circuit.' This was one of the favourite obituary clichés which Myles na gCopaleen (otherwise Brian O'Nolan) liked to lampoon in relation to judges and barristers. It is no accident that such a sentence in a similar context would nowadays be unusual. For centuries in Ireland, the circuits and circuit life were of great importance in the barristers' profession. This was partly because most indictable crime and most civil cases on the common law side in the high court were dealt with by judges sitting on assize with juries outside of Dublin. By the time of the foundation of the Irish Free State, the importance of the assizes had somewhat declined and the high court work had become more centralised in Dublin. Nevertheless, the assizes and circuits remained an important part of the system. In addition, as far as the junior bar was concerned, there were the county courts and their criminal jurisdiction opposite number, the 'quarter sessions' – both largely serviced in advocacy by the bar.

After the foundation of the new Irish state, there were from time to time a number of structural changes not necessary to detail in this short article. It is sufficient to observe that with the higher jurisdiction of the newly established 'circuit court' over that which had pertained in the old county courts and in quarter sessions, the circuit collegiality and culture remained, despite some name changes.

The important difference was that, by the end of the 1920s, there were two different sets of circuits as far as the structure of the courts was concerned; one relating to the high court and the other relating to the circuit court, but the old circuit collegiality and loyalties effectively transferred themselves to the circuit court circuits set out in the schedule to the Courts of Justice Act 1924.

Although the circuit court was nominally an invention of the Oireachtas of the Irish Free State and embodied in that Act of 1924, its historical roots go back to the invention in the early eighteenth century of the document which to this day is the initiating document for civil proceedings in the circuit court, namely the civil bill. It all started with the judges on assize being willing to hear small local claims at the assizes and was founded on the simple document known first as an 'English bill' but subsequently as a 'civil bill'. These were supplied in the local shops and filled in, but the beauty of them was that they were in English and not in Latin like the writs issued from the superior courts of common law.[1] The uneducated could therefore understand what was involved. The civil bill cases grew in such popularity that the assize judges could no longer cope and a statute was passed in 1796 permitting the barristers at that time assigned to give legal advice to the lay magistrates in quarter sessions to hear the civil bill cases on their own. Those 'Civil Bill Courts' manned by 'assistant barristers' were later converted by statute to 'County Courts' manned by permanent county court judges. The county courts, in turn, became converted into the newly established circuit court by the 1924 Act. I mention this because barristers had a right of audience in the civil bill courts and county courts and, broadly speaking, they would have been members of the same bar and circuit as would have attended the nearest assizes. When the assizes were effectively abolished and the county courts became the circuit court with the same judge administering justice in several counties instead of one or two, it was natural that the circuit bar system, although under different names, continued. This was especially true as the assizes were effectively abolished and the current system of the 'high court on circuit' introduced much later.

Historically, the discipline of the bar was largely controlled by the bars of the circuits. Although the Bar Council pre-dated the independence of the state, it, nevertheless, did not come into existence until early in the twentieth century. For centuries a barrister's ethical behaviour was effectively kept in control by his colleagues on his circuit. I have not added the word 'her' as there was no female barrister in Ireland until 1921.

Although the Bar Council formally took over those functions, nevertheless the circuits continued to perform an important role in maintaining standards. The members of the Bar Council, as such, or in more modern times the members of the disciplinary bodies formed by that council, were not in a position to monitor the behaviour of any particular barrister in his or her day to day work outside of Dublin. Such standards were often more effectively maintained through moral pressure coming from circuit colleagues. I can best describe how that

---

[1] See F.H. Newark, *Notes on Irish legal history* ([Belfast], 1960). Newark was professor of jurisprudence at Queen's University Belfast.

came about by reference to my own experience from 1962 to 1977 as a junior counsel on the midland circuit taking in the counties of Roscommon, Longford, Westmeath, Offaly and Laois. Different circuits had slightly different traditions but the differences were not significant.

My typical week was as follows. The circuit judge did not sit on Mondays, which meant that we were able to stay in Dublin and attend to whatever work we might have in that city, especially the various motion lists in the high court. The remaining four days were spent or, at least, were potentially spent, on circuit but there were differences. Although we travelled by day to and from the nearer towns of Mullingar, Tullamore and Portlaoise, in the case of Roscommon, Boyle, Longford, Athlone and Birr, we stayed overnight in a local hotel. All members of the circuit stayed in the same hotel, and had dinner together at the same hour – excluding from attendance any outsider and, especially, any solicitor. If a barrister had behaved out of line that day, some gentle teasing and adverse comments at his or her expense were often as effective as any censuring by the Bar Council. There was a fierce sense of belonging. The occasional circuit dinner when a member either took silk or became a judge was attended by those of the senior bar who had been juniors on the circuit, the most senior of them presiding and making the necessary speech. He had and still has the affectionate title of 'father of the circuit'. In another more practical sense, the seniors who had previously been juniors on the circuit retained their links with it because the solicitors in the counties in which they had practised tended more often than not to brief them for their high court cases.

A great deal of this culture still remains. Nevertheless, there has been quite a degree of profound change during the past quarter of a century. The change has been inevitable and should not be bemoaned with any sense of either antiquarianism or sentimentality. In some respects, the change is a natural consequence of more modern and efficient ways of providing legal services. There was a time when it would have been a highly relevant question to ask any one of, say, the ten leaders of the bar 'What circuit did you come from?' even if one or two of them had remained in chancery practice in Dublin for most of his or their working life. Such a question would no longer make sense. The growth of commercial life, the ever-increasing rates of serious urban crime, the breakdown of marriages resulting in a 'family law bar', new areas of law such as human rights, immigration, extradition in the context of the European Arrest Warrant and judicial review have added hugely to the

Dublin court workloads. One good effect of this is that it has made room for much more specialisation at the bar which is to the benefit of potential clients, even though it diminished one attractive feature of being a circuit barrister in my time. One's regular solicitors tended to avail of one's services in all their cases no matter what branch of the law was involved. As a consequence, one acquired some knowledge and experience of every branch of the law. Nowadays, much more importance is attached to specialised knowledge when a solicitor is choosing the right barrister to brief for any particular case.

All of this has had practical effects on the circuits where admittedly the cases are still of a more general nature. But even within the territory of these circuits, there are in practice quasi-specialist divisions within the circuit bars. For one thing, it is no longer the case that the entire circuit follows the same judge, as I did, in my time, around the different towns. While there is still one judge in charge of each circuit, he or she is flanked by at least one back up judge who will normally be sitting in a different town at any given time. One, but not the other, will be dealing with crime with the effect that a specialism in criminal work grows up within a circuit itself. To some extent, the same is true of family law. From discussions with modern circuiteers, it would seem that this considerably breaks down the overall collegiality of the circuit. The culture of everybody staying in the same hotel and dining together, which I have described, is something of the past. With the growth of the new motorways and the increasing tendency of circuit barristers to live in marriage or partnership on the circuit itself, the tendency is to travel home each night.

Many of the traditions of comradeship from the circuit remain which I have little doubt are still a help to the maintenance of standards. Perhaps sadly though, inevitably, they do not remain as significant to the barristers' profession as they once were.

Judges of the midland circuit, 1924–94

AN EDITORIAL ADDENDUM

Between 1924 and 1994 the following were judges of the midland circuit: John Wakely, George A. Moonan, William J. Gleeson, Michael Binchy, Michael J. Sweeney, Conor P. Maguire, Peter O'Malley, Kevin O'Higgins and Matthew Deery. Aspects of their careers are recalled below.

1924–30   John Wakely (1861–1942).
Eldest son of John Wakely JP, DL, of Ballyburley, Rhode, King's County (now Co. Offaly) and Mary, daughter of the Revd Richard George of Kentstown, Co. Meath. Graduated TCD 1882. Called to the bar in 1885, he assisted Richard Cherry in the completion of the latter's widely used volume on Irish land law and the land purchase Acts that appeared first in 1888.[1] He took silk in 1899 and became a bencher of King's Inns in 1902. For some time he was crown prosecutor for Co. Waterford. Appointed judge of the Roscommon and Sligo county courts in 1904. It is said that, 'A lucrative practice preceded Judge Wakely's elevation to the bench.'[2] His brother William George was 'a man of frail physique' who, nevertheless, served as secretary of the Incorporated Law Society for fifty-four years from 1888 to 1942, and is said to have been 'a walking encyclopaedia'.[3]

In 1908, it was noted that,

> The family of Wakely, who still retain their ancestral home, was seated at Ballyburley as far back as 1550. Its representative at the beginning of the eighteenth century was John Wakely, M.P. for

---

1   Richard R. Cherry, *The Irish Land Law and Land Purchase Acts, 1881, 1885, and 1887: with a complete collection of the rules and forms issued under each Act in the land commission, high court of justice, and county courts respectively; and appendix of incorporated statutes, edited, with full notes of the various cases decided under each section and rule and an index* (Dublin: J. Falconer, 1888).
2   Obituary notes, *ILT & SJ*, lxxvi (1942), 186, 190.
3   *Irish Times*, 27 March 1942.

Kilbeggan, who built Ballyburley Church in 1686, and was High Sheriff of the King's County, 1695. He married Elizabeth Lambert, niece of the Earl of Cavan, and was succeeded by his eldest son, Thomas, who was High Sheriff, 1726. This Thomas Wakely, of Ballyburley, who died 1751, had three sons: John, of Ballyburley, High Sheriff, 1763, whose male descendants expired in 1842; James, who died unmarried; and Francis, great-grandfather of His Honour Judge Wakely, the present owner of Ballyburley.[4]

The Wakelys farmed about 1,700 acres at Ballyburley. During the civil war, '[o]n one occasion when his house was raided by armed men looking for guns Judge Wakely, anticipating what was going to happen when aroused from bed in the dead of night, secured his favourite shotgun and while he was interviewing the raiders he kept the gun cunningly concealed underneath his dressing gown. In view of the circumstances of the time his courage was rather unusual.'[5] About this time one of his gardeners claimed from the county council's malicious injuries fund £440 in compensation for the loss of his wife, who had died of heart failure that the gardener attributed to 'shock caused by raids by armed men'. Early in 1923, anti-Treaty forces gave Wakely and his family an hour to get out of their home before burning it to the ground. The raiders wanted to burn the stables too, but the judge remonstrated with them and said that he would have no place to put his horses, and that a number of men would be put out of employment. So the stables were spared, although a large quantity of hay was burned.[6]

The Wakelys had previously rebuilt Ballyburley after an accidental fire in 1888 and, once the Troubles ended, John Wakely set about rebuilding it again. When in 1924 the newly independent Irish state replaced the old county courts with eight circuits, Wakely was appointed the judge of the midland circuit. This was comprised of the counties Longford, Leix (Laois), Offaly, Westmeath and Roscommon and had a total population of 388,000. At his first sitting in Tullamore, he responding to various compliments from members of the legal profession by declaring that, 'He wanted to say, too, that he did not

4   F.R. Montgomery Hitchcock, *An account of the early septs and settlers of the King's County and of life in the English Pale* (Dublin: Sealy, Bryers and Walker, 1908), p. 297.
5   David Clarke, 'Times past in Longford', *Longford Leader*, 2 Dec. 2012.
6   Nicholas Carlisle, *A topographical dictionary of Ireland* (London, 1810), at Ballyburley; *Irish Times*, 16 Sept. 1922, 10 March 1923; *King's County directory* (1890), p. 181, p. 270; J.F. Fuller, *Omniana: the autobiography of an Irish octogenarian* (London, [1920]), p. 169.

think himself a great judge; as he said the other day in Birr, he was a judge who tried to live and learn by experience as he went on.'[7] In April 1930, one writer extended his sympathy to Wakely 'in the illness which necessitated the sudden abandonment of his court at Maryborough [now Portlaoise]; for he is a very popular judge, and has a wide circle of legal and other friends.' His health did not recover and he retired on 31 December 1930. He moved thereafter to England. Back in Dublin for a ceremony in his honour in the Solicitors' Building at the Four Courts, he was presented with a tea and coffee service of silver, and an inscribed salver and illuminated address. The signatories declared of Wakely that, 'To a profound knowledge of the law and scrupulous impartiality he united a deep knowledge of his fellow countrymen, and an intimate acquaintance with the agricultural pursuits upon which most of them had been engaged.' He died at 'The Birches', Redditch, Worcester, on 15 July 1942.[8]

1930–1   George A. Moonan (1872–1945).
Second son of Richard Moonan of Drogheda, Co. Louth, and Mary Anne Tiernan. In May 1930 Moonan was appointed deputy circuit court judge during the absence, through illness, of Judge Wakely. He was called to the inner bar the following month. He had earlier worked from 1896 as a temporary minor staff officer in the registry of deeds in Dublin and at the war office in London before being admitted a student of King's Inns in 1908. He was called to the bar in 1911. Maurice Healy recalled him appearing soon afterwards on the Munster circuit.[9]

An enthusiastic Irish scholar and prominent member of the Gaelic League from 1893, Moonan founded the Leinster College of Irish in 1906 and served variously as its honorary secretary, honorary manager and chairman. Lectures that he gave there were incorporated into a work that he wrote with the professor of modern Irish history in the

---

7 *Offaly Independent*, 18 Oct. 1924, cited at length at Michael Byrne, *Legal Offaly: the county court-house at Tullamore and the legal profession in County Offaly from the 1820s to the present day* (Tullamore: Esker Press for Offaly Historical and Archaeological Society, 2008), pp 173–7.
8 Courts of Justice Act 1924, Section 37 and schedule; *Irish Times*, 12 April 1930 (with photograph), 13 May 1932; Obituary notes, *ILT & SJ*, lxxvi (1942), 186, 190.
9 Government Servants (Courts of Justice) (Ireland). Return to an order of the house of commons Wednesday 27 April 1910, p. 13. Ordered to be printed by the house of commons, 21 July 1901 <http://eppi.dippam.ac.uk/documents/21602/eppi_pages/606201> (accessed 4 April 2013); Maurice Healy, *The old Munster circuit: a book of memories and traditions* (London, 2001 edition with biographical introduction by Charles Lysaght), p. 61.

National University of Ireland. This was well-received by critics and became widely used as a text book.[10] The Gaelic League also published as a pamphlet the text of an address entitled 'The spirit of the Gaelic League' that he had delivered to its Athlone and Blackrock branches. He was a foundation member of and held high rank in the Dublin branch of the Knights of St Columbanus. He acted as counsel for the state in the Central Criminal Court, Green Street, Dublin. He and the chief justice conducted in the Irish language his ceremony of appointment as deputy circuit court judge. In January 1931, persons in 'well-informed quarters' tipped off journalists that Moonan was likely to be appointed permanently to the midland circuit, but this did not in fact happen.[11]

1931–50 William J. Gleeson (1878–1953).
Eldest son of Joseph Gleeson of Frankfort Lodge, Inchicore, Dublin, and Frances Nolan. He first qualified as a solicitor and practised for some time with his father, who was a solicitor in Dame Street, Dublin. However, he continued his studies and in 1908 was called to the bar, where he built up a substantial practice, especially in criminal and common law. He took silk in June 1927, and one year later was appointed deputy circuit court judge during the illness of Judge Edward McElligott. He subsequently deputised for both Judge Bernard Roche and Judge Cahir Davitt before being appointed, in January 1931, judge of the midland circuit in succession to Wakely.

In 1932, at Longford, he welcomed Miss Violet Kempton BL to the midland circuit. Both he and Mr Delany, a solicitor, congratulated her 'on her able advocacy of her clients'.[12] The *Irish Times* also deemed it newsworthy to report, when he married in 1935, that Gleeson was presented with a radio gramophone and a cabinet in cutlery by the barristers, solicitors, county registrars and court officials of the midland circuit. Accepting the gift,

> Judge Gleeson said that it was unusual to pay such a compliment to a judge unless he had made up his mind to take his departure. When, as in this case, he had no intention of doing anything of the sort, it showed that those who made the presentation had a great

---

10 Mary Hayden and George Moonan, *A short history of the Irish people* (Dublin, 1921; London and New York, 1921); James J. Fox in *The American Historical Review*, 27:4 (1922), 783–85.
11 *Irish Times*, 27 May 1930, 13 Jan. 1931; *ILT & SJ*, 79 (1945), 308.
12 *Irish Times*, 20 Jan. 1932.

appreciation of him. During his whole time as Judge of the Midland Circuit there had not been an unpleasant incident of any kind with any member of the legal profession practising in his Court, and, so far as he was concerned, he hoped that there never would be. He had the most loyal Bar that any Judge could wish to have. Having had the experience he now had of the Midland Circuit, nothing could persuade him to leave it, if he had any choice in the matter.[13]

Two years later he welcomed to his circuit at Roscommon one Nevin Griffith, the son of Arthur Griffith, commenting that 'he felt proud that the Midland Circuit had been chosen by the son of one of Ireland's most distinguished citizens.'[14] An occasional visitor to Gleeson's court was Patrick MacKenzie, a practitioner on the eastern circuit who in 1987 was appointed as a high court judge. MacKenzie thought that the midland circuit was then 'a hard-living, hard-drinking establishment' and 'extremely formal'. He wrote that, 'a Circuit dinner was held every night, presided over by the longest-serving barrister, known as the Father. Unpunctuality, or some other breach of convention or etiquette, was punished by a fine – usually the presentation of a case of wine. As a result of the fines, the mess in each town had a good collection in the cellar of whatever hotel was used.'[15]

Gleeson made his last appearance on the bench at Birr, Co. Offaly, on 5 December 1950, having reached the age for retirement. He died on 3 Feb. 1953. According to an obituarist, he was 'one of the best-known members of the legal profession in Ireland.' Recalling him in 1982, on the sudden death of Mr Justice E.M. Walsh who had appeared before Gleeson a number of times, 'Noll' (Oliver D.) Gogarty SC wrote that Walsh 'would recall with great delight the few cases I asked him to do many years ago before our genial Midland Circuit court judge William Gleeson, KC, whose wit allowed us all to enjoy appearing in his court.'[16] Tom O'Higgins appears not to have shared this memory of Gleeson as genial. O'Higgins, later to become chief justice, practised on the midland circuit between 1938 and 1948 and has left us an account of his experiences that includes a lengthy description of Gleeson and his manner of conducting business in court.[17]

13 *Irish Times*, 28 Jan. 1935.   14 *Weekly Irish Times*, 13 Feb. 1937.
15 Patrick MacKenzie, *Lawful occasions: the old eastern circuit* (Cork & Dublin, 1991), p. 75.
16 *Irish Times*, 12 Jan. 1931, 18 Dec. 1932, 28 Jan. 1935, 4 Dec. 1950 (photograph at Leopardstown Race Course), 4 Feb. 1953; *ILT & SJ*, 79 (1953), 63.
17 T.F. O'Higgins, *A double life* (Dublin, 1996), pp 75–97.

1950–60 Michael Binchy (1893–1971).

Second son of James Binchy, solicitor, Charleville, Co. Cork, and Katie Fitzgibbon. Called 1916. He had an extensive practice on the Munster circuit. He was a first cousin of two barrister brothers, these being Daniel Binchy (1899–1999) who served as Irish minister to Berlin and was an expert in Brehon Law, and William Binchy (1907–71) whose erudite reading habits feature in Lee's account of the south-western circuit.[18] Michael took silk in 1930 and was elected a bencher of King's Inns in 1937. Between 1934 and 1940 he was official arbitrator under the Road Traffic Act 1933, in which capacity he assessed compensation for businesses taken over by the railway and then tramway companies. Chairman of the Mining Board 1949–50. In 1950 he was appointed judge of the midland circuit. In 1960, he and two judges of the high court, George Murnaghan and Thomas Teevan, constituted a visiting committee that investigated recent appointments in UCD. The investigation followed a private petition to the government by John Kenny SC, who was then also described as an 'assistant in the Law Faculty' of UCD and who claimed that the appointments of a number of lecturers and professors should have been made by the senate of the National University of Ireland. Binchy and his fellow visitors found that UCD, under its charter, had no power to appoint lecturers and assistant lecturers. Also in 1960, Binchy was transferred to the Dublin circuit.

In 1963, reaching the age of 70, and thus obliged to retire, he made one last appearance in Dublin circuit civil court where members of the profession gathered to pay him tribute. On behalf of the senior bar, Tommy Doyle SC said that they felt that they were suffering a great loss with his departure. Doyle added that Binchy had brought to his practice 'three great old-fashioned virtues –probity, learning and skill in the law, and great courage ... There is something wrong with a system that removes, in the plenitude of his powers, a man who has given such signal service.' Desmond Collins, solicitor and vice-president of the Incorporated Law Society, described Binchy as 'a gentleman of the old school'.

After his retirement he was appointed a member of the Censorship of Publications Board. Died at Kilcroney Convalescent Home, Co. Wicklow, 20 Feb. 1971.[19]

---

18 Gerard A. Lee SC, *A memoir of the south-western circuit* (Dublin, 1990), pp 15–16
19 *Irish Times*, 6 Dec. 1950, 21 Jan. & 29 April & 6 May 1960, 1 Aug. 1963; *Irish Independent*, 23 Feb. 1971; *ILT &SJ*, 105 (1971), 83–4.

1960–6 Michael J. Sweeney (1896–1981).
Eldest son of James Sweeney of Kells, Co. Meath, and Julia Nolan. Said to have been the first Kells man to become a judge. 'He inherited neither wealth nor influence', but in 1915 won a Meath County Council scholarship to study science at UCD. While at college, he contributed to the *Meath Chronicle* from 1917 to 1919 a weekly column expounding the Sinn Féin philosophy. He was an active member of the Irish Volunteers. A fluent Irish speaker, he became a science master at St Malachy's College, Belfast. Also for some years on the staff of the *Freeman's Journal* and the *Irish Independent*, and a member of the General Headquarters Staff of the National Army who is said to have given it its official name 'Óglaigh na hÉireann'. He stood unsuccessfully as a Dáil candidate for Fine Gael. Called to the bar in 1933. Appointed to the circuit court for the northern circuit in May 1956, he was in 1960 transferred to the midland circuit to replace Binchy. The northern circuit, compromising Leitrim, Cavan and Monaghan, was at that point amalgamated with the north-western circuit, then comprising Sligo and Donegal. His brother James was vice-chairman of Kells Urban Council. Many warm tributes were paid to him at Birr court-house in Co. Offaly on the occasion of his last sitting, and he reciprocated by praising the profession and the press, ' – the fourth Estate to which he had the honour of belonging for quite a considerable time'.[20]

1966–73 Conor P. Maguire (1922–2009).
Eldest son of former Chief Justice Conor A. Maguire of Ashurst, Mount Merrion Avenue, Dublin, and Nora Whelan. He visited the Nuremberg war crimes trials with his father. Called 1945. Took silk 1959. Practised on the western circuit until 1960. Then practised in Dublin until appointed a judge of the circuit court in October 1963. In 1961 he became a commissioner of charitable donations and bequests, and served from 1965 until 1973 as chairman of the Censorship of Films Appeal Board. In May 1966 he was permanently assigned as judge of the midland circuit. In November 1973 he resigned from the bench and, 'to the amazement of some of his colleagues' it is said, took up an appointment in the legal department of the Directorate-General for Competition of the European Communities. He had earlier taken a course in EEC law at the Europa Institute of the University of Amsterdam. In early life a member of the Fianna Fáil National

---

20 *Irish Independent*, 6 May 1960; *Irish Times*, 30 April 1966; *Meath Chronicle*, 14 May 1966; *Westmeath Examiner*, 28 May 1966; *Meath Chronicle*, 23 May and 27 June 1981.

Executive, in retirement he turned back to an interest in broadcasting that he had developed as a student and for over a decade before his death presented a popular big band recorded music show on RTE Radio 1.[21]

1973–86 Peter O'Malley (1921–2002).
Second son of Michael George O'Malley, a surgeon, of Barna in Co. Galway, and Christina Mary Ryan. Called 1944. Took silk 1963. Already a temporary judge, in December 1973 he was appointed permanently and assigned to the midland circuit court to replace Maguire. He was president of the circuit court from 1990 until 1991. After retiring from the bench at the age of seventy, he accepted an invitation from minister for justice Máire Geoghegan-Quinn TD to act as the competent authority to deal with appeals against refusals to grant recognition of refugee status. After his death, tributes were paid to him at the commencement of a sitting of the high court in Mullingar by Mr Justice Hugh Geoghegan and other members of the legal profession. He was remembered as 'an excellent and a very understanding judge' and, that encomium that still matters, 'an absolute gentleman'.[22]

1986–7 Kevin O'Higgins (b. 1946).
Fourth son of Niall B. O'Higgins, psychiatrist, of Elmhurst, Mulgrave Street, Limerick, and Joan O'Shea. Nephew of Kevin O'Higgins, the minister for justice who was assassinated in 1927. Called 1968, he specialised in criminal law. Appeared in the Arms Trial, and in the Senator Billy Fox murder case, as well as the case of Rose Dugdale among others. Took silk 1982. Represented the DPP and attorney general in the complex public inquiry into the handling of investigations into the death of a baby in 1984. It was said that 'His gentle and humane manner struck a sane note in the bizarre Kerry Babies tribunal proceedings'.[23] He became a judge of the circuit court in 1986, serving first on the Dublin circuit, then on the midland and lastly on the south-western circuit before his appointment to the high court in 1997. He was the Irish representative on the consultative council of European judges (2000–8). Appointed to the court of first instance of the European Communities (now the European general court) in July 2008 for the period until 31 August 2013, there succeeding Judge John D. Cooke.

21 *Irish Times*, 30 Apr. 1966, 27 Oct. 1973 and 17 Jan. 2009; *Sunday Independent*, 15 Feb. 2009.
22 *Irish Times*, 6 Dec. 1973; *Westmeath Examiner*, 9 March 2002.
23 *Irish Press*, 26 Feb. 1986.

1988–94 Matthew Deery (b. 1944).
Second son of John Deery, GNR engine driver, of 3 Brook Street, Dundalk, Co. Louth, and Brigid Quigley. He worked as a clerical officer for Monaghan Co. Council for over three years before resigning to go to university. Called 1972. Appointed a judge of the circuit court in May 1988, he was sitting in Listowel in October of that year when *The Kerryman* newspaper reported that he was being 'hotly tipped to be given the vacant position of Circuit Court Judge on the famous South Western Circuit of which Kerry is part'. In welcoming him at Listowel, Dermot Kinlen SC said that it was the wish of the bar that he be appointed to the south-western circuit: 'We think it is the best circuit in the country.' The press reported that the judge noted that Kinlen had led Deery in a number of cases when the latter was in practice as a barrister. However, it transpired the following month that he was in fact to serve as judge of the midland circuit, transferring from 1994 to the northern circuit. In 2005 he was appointed president of the circuit court. This, according to the Dundalk *Argus* newspaper, was 'a remarkable achievement for the Dundalk-born judge considering the absence of a legal background in his family and the fact that he never worked as a senior counsel'. He succeeded as president Judge Frank Roe, another Louth man and the signatory of Deery's admission papers for King's Inns. According to one account of Deery's appointment, 'his approval by Cabinet was seen as a recognition of the manner in which he handled a number of awkward and controversial cases in the north-west and for his sound judgment both in the special criminal court and the circuit courts'. He also served as chairman of the Garda Síochána complaints appeals board.[24]

OTHER JUDGES

Among those who have practised on the midland circuit and subsequently become judges elsewhere have been Raymond Groarke, appointed president of the circuit court in 2012, Sean Gannon, Eamonn Walsh and Kevin Lynch who were elevated to the high court in 1972, 1981 and 1984 respectively, Tom O'Higgins and Thomas Finlay who each became chief justice in 1974 and 1985 respectively, Hugh Geoghegan who joined the supreme court in 2000 and Susan Denham, chief justice of Ireland since 2011.

24 *Irish Press*, 18 May 1988; *The Kerryman*, 14 Oct. 1988; *Leitrim Observer*, 26 Nov. 1988; *The Argus*, 27 May 2005.

Fifty years in a rural law practice

ROBERT PIERSE

> Mastering the lawless science of our law,
> That codeless myriad of precedent,
> That wilderness of single instances ...
> Alfred Tennyson

IN MY MASTER'S TIME

Apprenticeship

It was on the 14 December 1956 that I entered into an indenture of apprenticeship with my master, James Fitzjames Raymond, in the small town of Listowel in 'The Kingdom of Kerry'. The population of the town was then about 3,500, with approximately 16,000 in its agricultural hinterland. There was no industry as such in the area, other than the creamery. The situation was the same generally, per my master, as when he had entered into his apprenticeship with his master Matthew J. Byrne, who had been a noted classical scholar as well as a brilliant lawyer. He had been admitted as a solicitor in 1887, and Mr Raymond was admitted in 1912. I was admitted in 1960.

The office of my master was full of history. Both Matthew Byrne and James Raymond had lived through British occupation, the Troubles and the civil war; and of course the British courts, the Sinn Féin courts and the Irish Free State courts. They both remained in touch with their landlord clients and had a well known 'Sinn Féiner'/Republican as a clerk. He used to keep a revolver in the deeds box. One day during my apprenticeship we were searching for old landlord files, when the Head Clerk and I found that revolver in a file. We were advised to give it to the gardaí. Mr Raymond had been aware of its probable existence because of an event during the Troubles. The Black and Tans had raided the office, with some regular British troops, searching for weapons. Matthew Byrne shook hands with the commanding officer. He expressed surprise that his office was being raided. He told the officer that a client of his, Lord Listowel, would be visiting the office in fifteen minutes accompanied by Mr Sandes, a local middle landlord. They would be very disturbed if they thought these soldiers were searching through their papers. He, Mr Byrne, said that perhaps the officer should go to Mr Sandes' house, where Lord Listowel was, and explain the need for this. The officer apologised saying that he was misinformed about the office and about what was alleged to be going on in it. The Black and Tans left.

My master

Mr Raymond, my master, was a Protestant beloved of the town for his wit and music. There was no religious discrimination in town by the ordinary people. When James died we thronged into the Protestant church, in the hope we might be all excommunicated!

My apprenticeship deed is a very interesting document nowadays in view of the changes in the approach to apprentices – sorry 'trainees'. The main portion reads:

> Witnesseth that the apprentice HATH and by these presents DOTH put and bind himself as an apprentice to the Master to learn the business, profession and art of a solicitor and with the master to serve as an outdoor apprentice for the space and term of five years to commence and be computed from the day of the date hereof during which time the apprentice shall and will well and faithfully serve the said Master and keep the secrets of the said Master and of his clients and gladly and willingly keep, observe and obey his lawful commands and write, engross, transact and do the business of his said Master and of his clients at all times with care, attention, fidelity and dispatch and shall and will attend in such offices and houses and within such hours and times as shall be appointed by his said Master for the constant dispatch of his said Master's business AND also shall not and will not embezzle, waste, mutilate, destroy, injure and dispose of or give away the money, goods, papers or documents of his said Master or of his clients nor suffer it to be done by others and shall not during the said apprenticeship absent himself from the office or business of his said Master for any space of time whatsoever without the previous consent of his said Master but in all things as an honest, good and faithful apprentice, behave, conduct and demean himself towards his said Master and his said family during said apprenticeship and shall and will provide himself with find and defray during his apprenticeship diet, lodging, washing, clothing and other

> expenses whatsoever AND the said Master on his part and in consideration of the premises, promises and agrees to teach and instruct the said apprentice in the business and profession of a Solicitor and at the end and expiration of said apprenticeship to certify and do all other acts, matters and things, on his part necessary to the admission of the said apprentice as a solicitor but at the proper costs and charges of the said apprentice.

Not only did I have to provide my own diet, lodging, washing etc., but my mother had to pay my master the sum of £300. My mother, who was chief negotiator in the family, felt this was a legacy from the bad old days. I took a different view, which I still hold, that a master who does give time teaching is entitled to be paid. I still find it hard to accept that the pupil/apprentice/trainee solicitor has to be paid.

Personally, I consider the research necessary for the successful practice of the law as an exercise of science as well as an art. We are in a way detectives seeking precedent and setting parameters for the future. My master, when he saw I liked litigation, gave me many cases to research. I felt like a detective trying to match facts to principles and precedents.

The office

Working in that office in the 1950s was akin to much that one reads about in Charles Dickens' novels. There was a tall special desk at which a clerk, known as a 'scrivener' and using a special black ink, was writing by hand parchment memorials. This was to comply with a statute of the reign of Queen Anne of 1707. Registration of deeds was introduced in Ireland, in the context of the Penal Laws. These memorials were for the Registry of Deeds as the town of Listowel and some landlord property was and still is 'unregistered' land. Indeed the scrivener, a male clerk, used to prepare conveyances and leases also in manuscript in copperplate handwriting. The typewriter was viewed with suspicion, as was the phone – it being tucked in a corner so that it would not breach the peace.

Conveyancing and probates dominated the work in the office. There were only about twenty law books, of ancient vintage, including Clerk and Lindsell on tort, Chitty on contract, Cherry on land law, etc. The office still acted for Lord Listowel. The local farms were registered in the land registry but the titles were all subject to 'equities'. A sale of such land meant going back on the old tenancy titles, often with very interesting material in family history of the clients. This continued in my own time. In one local area I discovered that, often, marriages took place only after the 'heir' arrived. Also, in other cases half the 'fortune' was held until the heir arrived.

As outlined in Professor Wylie's book on Irish land law (chapter 24), the registration system under the Land Purchase Acts proceeded on the basis of vesting the fee simple in the person *ostensibly* the tenant working the farm in question subject to burdens and equities held by third parties. However, the land commission administering the land purchase scheme did not carry out an investigation of the title of the 'tenant' and so was in no position to register all these burdens and equities, which were preserved as if no registration had occurred. It might thus be necessary on any transaction to trace the title back to and prove the original fee farm grant, lease or tenancy held by the tenant prior to his purchase of the freehold under the Land Purchase Acts.

A good probate was always welcome. It required the completion of great yellow revenue forms, full of irrelevant questions. These were stored in the lower drawer in the big 'form cupboard'. There would be much tut-tutting about iniquitous death duties of various kinds in the occasional large estate. Also, this justified good fees.

As to probate, in chapter 26 of Dickens' *David Copperfield* David's master explains the value of a good probate:

> I asked Mr Spenlow what he considered the best sort of professional business? He replied, that a good case of a disputed will, where there was a neat little estate of thirty or forty thousand pounds, was, perhaps, the best of all. In such a case, he said, not only were there very pretty pickings, in the way of arguments at every stage of the proceedings, and mountains upon mountains of evidence on interrogatory and counter-interrogatory (to say nothing of an appeal lying, first to the Delegates, and then to the Lords), but, the costs being pretty sure to come out of the estate at last, both sides went at it in a lively and spirited manner, and expense was no consideration.

Many in the profession regarded litigation as somewhat beneath the dignity ('*infra dig*') of a lawyer's position, really, especially when such matters as affiliation orders had to be dealt with. Circuit court cases and the very rare high court case were sent to counsel immediately. The fact that all high court work was in Dublin meant that while I was in UCD as a student I often attended on counsel. My master would otherwise have had to travel by train – a whole day each way. He did not like leaving his comfortable office.

Books of account were massive ledgers, leather-bound in the back, and were double-entry. There was a petty-cash book and petty-cash box with a float of five pounds, made up of pennies, sixpences, shillings, half crowns, ten-shilling notes and the odd one pound note. These were a mixture of English and Irish coins and notes as we had a common currency with the UK. Staff wages ranged from three pounds to six pounds a week.

I enjoyed my master, his office and my apprenticeship, meeting 'fee simples', 'springing and shifting uses', 'fee farm grants', 'leases for lives renewable for ever', 'entail males' all over the place! Well not all over the place but in some of the old titles of the landed gentry.

Legislation and cases

The legislation being enacted in the years of my apprenticeship (1956–60) reflected the legal problems that seemed to infringe on society. Forty-eight Acts were passed in 1956. Most of them were financial (for example, two finance Acts and three imposition of duties Acts) and administrative, that is, ministers and secretaries, central fund, appropriation, tea importation and distribution. The main Acts that affected legal practice were the Fatal Injuries Act 1956 (repealed by the Civil Liability Act 1961) and the Gaming and Lotteries Act 1956.

My master did not get the Acts as published but when he saw relevant Acts mentioned in the solicitors' *Gazette* he wrote for them. These Acts cost a few shillings each – very expensive, as always, to get material from within the Pale, he'd grumble!

The digest of law cases was got in the office – usually published in every decade about three years after the period covered. The annual Irish law reports were not obtained. The *Irish Law Times and Solicitors Journal* (with its reports) was received and then tied together with pink ribbon (as opposed to red tape) at the end of each year.

Harrison's *Irish digest, 1949–1958* was not in the office by the very end of my apprenticeship, so I bought a copy myself. It had about 400 pages but under the heading 'Constitution of Ireland' only six cases were mentioned. There was no copy of the 1937 *Constitution of Ireland* in my master's office.

IN MY OWN TIME

Writing this in 2013 it seems the past fifty-three years practising law in a rural town have flown as the law is so challenging and interesting. By 2011 the population of Listowel had risen, but only to 4,200, with approximately 20,000 in its rural hinterland. All of human life is there. I still put my head in my hands and ask how will I solve this problem? It is great to be a lawyer!

UCD

I qualified in 1960, complete with Hons. BCL and Hons. Ll.B. The university years were genuinely academic – arts courses, such as philosophy, ethics, psychology, with wide legal courses in jurisprudence, canon law, Roman law (with Professor John M. Kelly – what a treat!). At a time when few law books were published, and virtually none on Irish law, there was great importance in attendance at lectures. The identity and skills of lecturers, as a means of learning what would otherwise be potentially inaccessible law, were vital. Students appreciated particularly good lecturers. We had only part-time lecturers – mainly practising barristers – so lectures had to be at 9 a.m. or 5 p.m. I remember being rather surprised by the lack of interest in the Constitution of Ireland of 1937. That Constitution had come into operation two days before myself, that is, on 29 December 1937. That connection gave me a reason to be interested in the Constitution and also the fact that my granduncle, Michael Collins, had played a considerable role in the drafting of the 1922 Constitution. The extent of his role (with H.J. Kennedy KC and others) became clear to me in 2004 when I was researching in a case the 1922 Constitution on judicial independence and impeachment. Constitutional law as understood and taught in the 1950s was about Dicey's view of the British unwritten constitution and Professor Ivor Jennings criticising it. Thank heavens that some years later Professor John Kelly illuminated the Constitution of Ireland for us – in 1961 his *Fundamental rights in the Irish law and Constitution* appeared – what a joy! However, I had been taught constitutional law by the Paddy McGilligan SC, who did not give any real consideration to 'Dev's Constitution'. McGilligan also lectured from *Kenny's outlines of criminal law*, a UK book. When he came to the chapter on sexual offences, he gave a cough, and skipped the chapter saying 'that never comes up in exams'. I read the chapter with shock, coming across terms such as 'buggery' and 'homosexuals' which I had never heard of. There was also a small Irish book on criminal law and procedure (first published in 1930) written by Robert Lindsay Sandes, a member of the bar who was the son of a man from Newtownsandes, a village eight miles from Listowel. The name of that village has been changed to Moyvane.

First job

My first job was in Dunmanway, Co. Cork, in a small sub-office, where I was the only solicitor. There was only one other solicitor in the town. I had the great good fortune to have a wise and genuinely learned district justice, James Crotty. He was one of the first district justices to have been appointed in 1923, when he was a comparatively young man. He had qualified as a solicitor in 1918. In 1960 he published a book on practice and procedure in the district court, described by Chief Justice Cearbhall Ó'Dálaigh as the first comprehensive work on the subject under our own government. Justice Crotty would say in any difficult case, 'Mr Pierse, what is the law on this?' This, and appearing later in Listowel before a careful and dedicated circuit court judge, Barra O'Briain, has made me a law 'bookaholic'. I have now two libraries in the office and three rooms full of law books in my home – my wife is very patient! She refers to the law as my 'mistress'.

In Dunmanway I was paid nine pounds a week, which was the best salary in the class. Some of my class earned only five pounds a week, as jobs were scarce. I paid six pounds each week for full-board for seven days a week, and thirteen shillings and four pence for a Tax and Social Welfare stamp, and had about £2.6.8 left for myself. It cost six pence to go to the films once a week, the only entertainment as I have never drunk alcohol. No TV then.

I became familiar with prosecutions for making poteen, for failure to cut noxious weeds, the odd assault, marriage settlements, probates, will-making – often late at night, and with the basic decency of West Cork people. The district court sat locally one day a month and rarely went on for more than two hours.

My late father used poteen as a rub for his greyhounds. I got a supply for him from the gardaí usually!

My own office

In 1504 Thomas More wrote to his friend John Colet, dean of St Paul's Cathedral, as to why he stayed to practise law in London, the city of his birth, even though it was a place of wickedness: 'Wherever you turn your eyes, what will you see but confectioners, fishmongers, butchers, cooks, poulterers, fishermen, fowlers, who supply the materials for gluttony and the world's lord, the devil'. His view of the country where Colet lived was where simple people can live who do not know the deceits of the city. Out there 'wherever you cast your eyes, the smiling face of the earth greets you, the sweet fresh air invigorates you. There you see nothing but the generous gifts of nature and traces of our primeval innocence'. I do not know what Kerry was like in 1504 but in 1962 it would not coincide with More's idea. I often wonder how did Thomas More qualify for sainthood – a lawyer who espoused free speech but condoned the burning at the stake of so-called heretics! However, I liked country living. I used to feel suffocated in cities, even in my student days.

On 5 February 1962 I set up on my own in Listowel, having converted my parents' sitting room into an office. The first six weeks were scary – not even the postman knocked. I then got a break, winning an (alleged poaching) fishery case on an old bye-law of 1911. The bye-law read that it was prohibited to snatch or attempt to snatch salmon or trout from the River Feale with a line and hook. I won a direction in the district court on the basis that the bailiff had not given evidence there was a hook on the line. The Fishery Board appealed. My counsel on appeal was Richard Johnson BL (later president of the high court, now retired). We won the appeal again on a direction. The bailiff (sorry, water-keeper) had remembered there had been a hook on the line. However, counsel pointed out to the judge that he had not proved that there were salmon or trout in the river or that our decent client was attempting to snatch them. I remember counsel's fee for the appeal was £3.3.0 (three guineas) and my fee taxed at £10. The local paper, *The Kerryman*, gave it great publicity, as did the late John B. Keane, the Listowel writer and publican. No one, it was claimed, had beaten the bailiffs for twenty years.

The result was in that first year I made £37.10.0, but was single, living at home. In 1963 when I made a profit of £375, I got married, to a courageous woman. I make a bit more now in 2013 but not anything like six years ago! Our economy has gone from boom to bust with the International Monetary Fund (IMF) and the European Central Bank dictating our lives and money. Also, of course, the number of solicitors in Kerry has quadrupled from about thirty-five when I set up to over 150 in the county now.

Mentioning John B. Keane shows the value of a small-town living. Under the Statute of Frauds (Ir) Act 1695,[1] I had a great case about a

1   7 Will. III, c.12.

field near the town. John B. Keane attended the hotly contested case and his play *The Field* appeared shortly after about that field and a murder not far away. I immediately recognised the witness in my case as the basis for 'Bull' McCabe in the play. The late William Binchy, senior, was my counsel. We produced a 'power of law' for the very interested judge. There was high drama and local politics involved.

Fight

While the jury was out in a personal injury case I was in, John A. Costello SC, the leader of the bar and former taoiseach, advised me in his gruff way: 'Pierse – you're in Kerry. When in court fight, fight. If you lose the case the clients will blame the judge. If you do not fight they will blame you.'

That advice was very valuable to a young man in Kerry.

1960s

The practice I developed was mainly civil litigation. None of the other solicitors in town, whom I regarded as ancient, being all over fifty years of age, were interested in spending days in courts in Dublin, so I got to within the Pale reasonably often. The 1960s were tough years. The criminal law was, in modern terms, very petty – no lights on bicycles, not cutting noxious weeds, fishery cases, hushed up sexual cases, and a growing number of drink-driving and dangerous driving cases. Fees ranged from ten shillings to ten pounds. By the end of the 1960s serious motorcar accidents began to come my way. I used to head off at 5 a.m. to Dublin in my Volkswagen Beetle. I had by then employed a secretary.

My master used to come to tea sometimes to our home. He once said to my wife, 'your husband's interest in the law is his hobby, as well as his means of earning his livelihood'. This helped her to cope with my long work days: a five-and-a-half-day week and ten hours of legal research and reading I do every week – still doing it fifty years on! The late William Binchy BL put another slant on it one hot day after a difficult day in an equity suit we won. He said, 'Please, Robert, put aside all those books and stop looking for a *scintilla juris* [a spark of legal right] in a boghole!'

Surprisingly interesting civil cases came my way. I got UK books, linked up with Frank Duggan BL. We also got a great engineer, Tony O'Keeffe.

I fought successfully the might of the GAA about natural justice in *Ahern v. Molyneaux* [1965] Ir Jur. Rep. 59. That was a pretty sacrilegious thing to do in the Kingdom of Kerry, that is, take the GAA to court and beat them. A player had been suspended without a proper opportunity to put his case, and this denial of natural justice and due process was set aside by the circuit court. I fought discrimination about Travellers by my local authority in *Listowel UDC v. McDonagh* [1968] IR 316. My great friend, the late Dermot Kinlen SC (later Mr Justice Kinlen of the high court), enjoyed both cases, acting as my counsel. I later got elected on that Urban Council and stayed on it for fourteen years.

There was a good deal of law reform in new legislation. The Civil Liability Act 1961, inspired by Professor Glanville Williams, opened the door to much litigation with a new concept of division of responsibility for loss, through contributory negligence. Also the Road Traffic Act 1961, which came in with a mass of statutory instruments in 1963, brought a lot of district court work. I was eventually to write a book on this. I had maintained careful notes of all decisions dealing with road traffic over the years. I had bought the UK, Canadian and even a Hong Kong book on road traffic. As mentioned in section 7.9 of that book (1989 edition), 'many [technical and specialist definitions] are forged from the history of experience, and were introduced to change or modify abuses that developed or court decisions which were seen to allow loop-holes to emerge.' I had been buying books from Professional Books in the UK due to the absence of Irish books. They rang me one day saying that I seemed to be their best buyer of books in Ireland; would I consider writing a book on Irish law and suggest a subject? I suggested road traffic law pointing out that 70 per cent of the then district court cases were about road traffic. Oddly, it turned out to be a bestseller in Irish law book terms.

Another very reforming Act was the Succession Act 1965 which put an end to the despicable practice of disinheriting spouses – usually the wife who had 'married into' the farm, especially if there were no children.

Conveyancing was growing, especially of sites as the town was growing and farmers' children who worked in towns were getting sites from their parents. District court criminal and civil cases, wills, probates, farm transfers, tax problems were the common fare. I used to do a fair bit of tax work but in the 1970s the accountants took over that work from the legal profession generally.

1970s

In the 1970s I was busy enough to employ an assistant – the first lady solicitor employed in Kerry. At first the reaction was very mixed. As one farmer commented, 'What would that girl know about drains and rights of way or bulls crossing ditches?' In 1972 I earned £4,272, so things were improving. I paid £943.95 tax on that. No VAT then.

A partner, Paddy Fitzgibbon, joined me in 1975 and we named our firm Pierse and Fitzgibbon. Paddy did conveyancing and probate mainly. This let me free to deal with the new phenomenon of industrial accidents. He was also a great 'ideas' man as to how to get into new areas of law. He retired only a few years ago.

Equipment

I always was interested in equipment and communication infrastructure. In the mid-1970s I got the first dictaphone (battery-charged overnight) in the area. One older colleague remarked that these 'new fangled gadgets' would never replace his secretary, who corrected his mistakes! I then got a photocopier complete with its black powder and photosensitive paper (two types). Then I got into computerised accounts systems, electrical typewriters, and in due course word processors. The legal traditionalists thought I was mad.

Clients

I just loved my clients, especially my small farmer clients – still do! My wonderful father, a vet, always told me they were the salt of the earth. So they were. They spent little on themselves and had high standards of morality. I was never left unthanked or unpaid by them. The family farm transfer deed and agreement dealt with the transfer to the son; the 'fortune' of the wife coming in (to go out with a daughter); the rights of the parents to residence and to a private bedroom (usually at the back of the fire), the joint use of the kitchen, full support and maintenance. These invariably worked well due to a high standard of community support, that is, public morality. It was a shameful thing not to look after your parents properly. I met a similar attitude in China, Japan and the Philippines. I was delighted when the EEC (now EU) improved their lot in the 1970s, as its agricultural policy boosted farm income and hence land values. After that 'fortunes' began to die out. I got the transfers into the joint names of the husband and wife. There was some resistance to this. I myself bought a small piece of land near my house in the early 1970s. I put it my wife's sole name. My neighbour when he heard of it said 'Robert I am surprised. It is bad to give the women too much power!'

1980s

The 1980s were tough again – the banks were squeezing people with high interest rates. It's odd that twenty-five years later a further collapse was due to too much money being given out at low interest, bad banking practice and poor government decisions. We had about nine staff by this time (1980s) and we kept them all. I have always believed it is better to keep people on. Unemployed people at this time had few opportunities and lost their skills. We just drew living expenses – there were no profits.

I did, however, open another office in Tralee, a neighbouring town, which was unusual. I had a view that to grow the practice I should open an office in a bigger population and business centre. Paddy did not join me in that practice. Coleman Sherry, now in Gort, joined me in Tralee.

However, a large industrial plant started in West Limerick – Aughinish Alumina – with lots of cases out of it. I had a team of Ralph Sutton SC, Richard Johnson SC and Frank Duggan BL. I remember, some years after the building there started, coming back to Paddy at the end of a two-week session and saying, 'it is almost immoral the amount of money we made in two weeks'. Frequently, afterwards, he would urge me to go away and make more immoral amounts! It did not happen really again. I extended the office – concentrating on more colour and more light. We had grown to four solicitors and six other staff.

From the 1980 period onwards the law was complex and difficult to keep up with. My library was increasing and a stream of Irish law books flowed. It was necessary to get in two more assistants, who became partners. Both came from Galway. Michael Fitzpatrick came when I was in the midst of my only general election effort. He was very funny about the chaos of the courts and canvassing. Hugh Joyce joined us later in the 1980s. Both are still with us.

1990s

The 1990s saw beneficial changes such as an increased number of high court sittings in Limerick and Cork, within an hour or two of the office. Industrialisation had reached the area. This brought the prosperity of regular wages. Young people were not emigrating in huge numbers. Then the tide turned completely and the Irish were coming back. My sons were in the office, and a new generation of clients poured into the office. We were extending our staff on an annual basis. My eldest son, Risteard, took over my Tralee office. Another son, Riobard, came into

Listowel and is now the managing partner there. It was a wonderful time – still is!

The basic problems of our society changed, as did the area of law we practised. We were specialising and dividing into teams. I employed an industrial psychologist to set up and monitor our teams. New computers, especially word-processing, were helpful.

I had nice challenging cases, even about the beautiful Blasket Islands. For fifty days in the high court in Dublin we fought a greedy government about an Act, promoted by Charlie Haughey's government, dispossessing some of his neighbours of their island (*Blascáod Mor Teo v. Commissioner for Public Works*, [1994] 2 IR 372). I remember when my late colleague, Peter Callery, asked me to act for the landowners I read the Bill. I immediately said that the Act if passed in that form would more than likely be unconstitutional. It had a central discrimination in that it gave certain descendants of former islanders the right to retain their lands. We referred to these later in court as 'the people of the blood'. I remember saying to Peter that I thought that type of practice ended in 1945.

It was great to be before a caring and courteous Mr Justice Declan Budd. I exercised my own right of audience acting for a plaintiff, making my own written and oral submissions at one stage. Mr Justice Budd duly found the Act unconstitutional, on the 27 February 1998. The supreme court dismissed an appeal against the high court decision ([2000] 1 IR 6). The learned judge, and he *is* learned, gave a number of subsidiary decisions in the course of the proceedings which were important but never reported – a pity!

In the 1990s I also began to introduce some art into the office. Clients and staff do find it interesting. The problem now in 2013 is that I have more pictures, statues and works of art than walls. The solicitors' *Gazette* did a feature article on it some years ago. I got a lot of telephone calls about it. I said I did not like the Dickens-type images. Of course, I had extended the office back through my parents' turf house, horses stables, cow house and my mother's chicken house. I always bought these buildings as my father said you never appreciate anything unless you paid for it.

Family law was and is an area I find most difficult, as I get upset about the children in particular. In my opinion everyone ends up at a loss really when the fundamental constitutional value of the family is shattered. Fortunately, for my first thirty years in practice we did not get too much of this type of law in a rural or semi-rural community. Regrettably, since the late 1990s and now we get too much of it.

Also the legal aid scheme was changing the criminal side. Much disjointed criminal legislation was passed. I had many difficult cases during the Troubles. The gardaí had too free a hand altogether, in my view.

European laws were pouring down on us – and coming up the estuaries as Lord Denning said:

> The Treaty [of Rome] does not touch any of the matters which concern solely England and the people in it. These are still governed by English law. They are not affected by the Treaty. But when we come to matters with a European element, the Treaty is like an incoming tide. It flows into the estuaries and up the rivers. It cannot be held back, Parliament has decreed that the Treaty is henceforward to be part of our law. It is equal in force to any statute.[2]

In the 1990s we took on young assistants. It was necessary to specialise as I mentioned above but only to a limited degree as in a country town there was a personal loyalty to the client's 'own' solicitor in the office. Also, new communication technology enabled us to begin to 'break our geography' – to get clients from outside the radius of twenty miles of the town. Telexes, faxes and much improved telecommunication systems were coming in.

Books and cases

My ever-present interest in books drove me to write law books and articles. My *Road traffic law* book grew and became two volumes. It is gone into its fourth edition and seems to be well regarded. This most recent edition, published in 2012, takes into account the two Road Traffic Acts of 2011.[3] These Acts increase the 'ungodly jumble' that now pertains in this important area. Oliver Cromwell used the phrase 'ungodly jumble' about the law of property. There are now fourteen Acts that I deem part of the ungodly jumble.

Industrial 'accidents' and road traffic civil cases led to my book on damages. This book has faded due to the Personal Injuries Assessment Board (PIAB) and its mysterious assessments. I consider this legislation is loaded against a plaintiff. I hope someone will consider updating the book as to what judges are doing on damages.

2 *H.P. Bulmer Ltd v. J. Bollinger SA* [1974] Ch 401 at 418.
3 R. Pierse, *Road traffic law: the 1961–2011 Road Traffic Acts: annotated legislation* (Dublin, 2011).

We have a wonderful array of books now on Irish law, although this has slowed down recently. Legal publishers are being hit by the recession.

I loved my constitutional and administrative law cases. So much depends on having a good judge. You will remember that Harrison's *Irish digest, 1949–1958* had only six constitutional cases. There was a massive growth in constitutional law in the 1990s. The 'Clancy' digest of 1994–9 has noted over 200 constitutional law cases. Just consider the size of Kelly's *Constitution*, now over 2,000 pages. I expect the next edition may be in two volumes. In the first decade of the current century it is judicial review that has mushroomed. There are really interesting cases, many of them both in civil and criminal law 'digests' that are now replaced by internet systems. We have these in the office: very useful, but I am still a book man – it's my age I suppose!

Judges

I often found the quality of some of the district justices (now judges) (and at other levels too) variable. I am critical of the political basis of the judge's appointment. I think judges should be able to 'spit in everyone's eye'. A wise and independent judiciary is an enormous power in a democratic state. They have to be seen to be moderate and providing long-term principles of justice and fairness. I always remember an old farmer who had lost a right-of-way case saying, 'Well the judge was a fair man, he listened carefully and maybe he was right.' A poor judge is a poor shield for a poor man against the powerful state and its prosecution process.

I find many judgments short on principles, – particularly on the issue of calculation of damages. The matter of general damages is still very much in the area of guess-work on the morning of the court. It often depends on the judge you draw.

IN MY SONS' TIME

I retired from the partnership when I reached the age of 70, in 2007. Fortunately two sons had joined the offices, one in Tralee and one in Listowel many years before then. Both had taken over as managing partners early on, as I found management rather time consuming. It had become a burden with huge statutory and regulatory obligations, often restrictive and unsuitable for small practices. I ceased working in reality in Tralee in 1998. It does well still T.G. [thank God], under the name Pierse McCarthy Lucey – its three partners. I have remained on in Listowel. I still am trying for the third time to retire or at least to get down to half-days. What I write about this period is really about what happened to the practice in Listowel and how it functions as we have entered the second decade of the third millennium

My son Riobard became managing partner in Listowel – largely because none of the other partners wanted the stress! He has turned out to be a superb, hard-working managing partner – not too tough on his father! He has a taxation degree and is married to a non-practising accountant. What an enormous help spouses are! He quickly grasped the limitation of our district of North Kerry. He developed further the concept of breaking our geography. He has with his partners doubled the staff and the size of the office, buying premises next door. We had been using technology and boutique practice areas within the practice and these continue to be developed. The firm has three other partners and we now have about forty other staff. The youngest partner is a lady barrister, Martina Larkin, who has become a solicitor. We have five young lady solicitors – of the nine solicitors in the practice. They are all married locally which brings great stability to the practice. We have a full-time office manager, accountant and computer expert employed. Such change from my apprenticeship days! So much technology and rapid communication! Do we have time to think?

Another son Paul joined us in 2009 and was helping expand the age profile of our clients. However, he is academically inclined so he has recently joined the teaching staff of Griffith College in Cork (legal section). The fact that his wife, Aisling O'Sullivan, is a practising solicitor in Barry Galvin's office in Cork probably was a considerable factor in the move to Cork.

The practice continues to be divided into teams. The litigation department still leads in earnings, but due to unemployment (over 20 per cent here in Listowel) this is suffering. Over 3,200 people 'sign on' in this small town – God help them! This is a nasty recession – there simply is not enough work to go around. We are the second-biggest employer in town.

Work

The conveyancing department has largely sunk under the waves of the recession and emigration. There are over 100 unoccupied houses in Listowel and forty unoccupied businesses, including five public houses, so there is no conveyancing of substance. About half of our income now is derived from 'supermarket' law, that is, low-cost, mass-produced legal services to non-Kerry based businesses. Of course, competition is severe. There are just too many solicitors for the limited work available in 2013. The government is steering traditional legal work away from the courts.

Surprisingly, even our probate practice has gone down. People are not taking out probate etc. They do not see it as an urgent need and of course asset values are severely reduced. Civil actions are still a fairly strong pillar of the practice but declining. From the clients' point of view we have been running these on a 'no foal/no fee' basis in most cases. This is difficult to continue especially in medical negligence cases where the outlay can be enormous. There is need for a workable civil legal aid system. Criminal law has increased somewhat. Family law is still high on the agenda but mostly in the district court and circuit court.

Remuneration

When I ceased to be a partner five years ago I made a deal that my salary would be one third of what I brought in. This has greatly reduced my earnings, but I think it is possibly a way forward in salaries in a recession. It would need fine-tuning if it is not to create internal imbalance. We are privileged to be in an interesting profession where there are rewards far beyond fees. There is always a need for cross-subsidisation within a practice, but a realisation of the values of interest, of serving your clients and community are important too.

Law Society

The Law Society is a good organisation but continues, in my view, to wear too many hats in the profession. It has had an educational, a representative and a regulatory role. When I started it gave you some basic training in things like bookkeeping. It gave you your annual practising certificate. I did some years on committees later on. I found and still find them a dedicated group of practitioners who give a lot and get little thanks for it. I thank them. The society's staff has grown enormously. I remember with pride that in 1977 I was the first person to give £1,000 towards buying their present headquarters in Blackhall Place – £1,000 was real money then.

I welcome many provisions of the current Legal Services Regulation Bill limiting some of the roles of the Law Society. I do worry about whether a strong independent profession will survive some of its draconian provisions.

The law

'Law' continues to grow like mushrooms. On a daily basis law books, statutes, statutory instruments, rules, case law, directives, magazines, etc., pour into the office or are accessed by computers. This continues to result in greater need for specialisation and management of resources. I simply do not know how sole practitioners can cope.

The rational emergence and development of broad principles of law seem to be replaced by the makeshift craft of massive statutes and procedural rules. We are being drowned in the detail of this Irish and EU tide of 'law'. There is a whole raft of legislation on financial matters such as insolvency, debt mitigation schemes that take a lot of time to understand.

Many young lawyers seem to be trained technicians now – with little or no insight into jurisprudence, no comparative law (other than EU law). I think many courses described above helped me to think out legal problems and solutions. Maybe I am being arrogant. We have a highly skilled staff – technically. I feel that lawyers should have more time for research, what I call legal detective and thinking time!

I have mentoring sessions in the office library each week where I bring up Plato, Aristotle, Cicero, Justinian, Blackstone, Hayek, Wittgenstein, Rawls, Finnis, etc., to try to see the larger picture. These sessions are a failure, in my view, if there is not strong disagreement and a good deal of laughter in the session – fortunately there is plenty of both!

I see that the next five to ten years will be difficult. I believe there will always be a need for good lawyers. They are needed to advise and protect their clients. They need to be reasonable, well-informed, objective advisers and courageous advocates.

The law continues to be interestingly challenging and to be challenged. At the end of the day our freedom and society's ordering depend to a considerable extent on good lawyers on and off the bench. I do not think the bar stands up to judges enough in the appropriate cases, but then many would disagree with me on that and many things I have mentioned here. The independence and ability of the courts and judges is of prime importance to our freedom and the rule of law.

Life in the law continues to be good, so (with apologies to Henry Wadsworth Longfellow's 'A Psalm of Life'),

> In the law's broad field of battle,
> In the bivouac of Life,
> Be not like dumb, driven cattle!
> Be an heroic lawyer in the strife!
>
> Let us, then, be up and doing,
> With a heart for any fate;
> Still achieving, still pursuing,
> Learn to be lawyers and for Judges wait.

Was there a criminal bar and what happened to any such tradition?

PATRICK GAGEBY

'Let us be merry before we go.' Perhaps the last line of John Philpot Curran's well-known poem[1] was in the minds of the members of the criminal bar who, on 11 January 2010, packed their briefs and papers in Gandon's Four Courts and trailed upriver and west to the Criminal Courts of Justice building in Parkgate St, Dublin. Having reached the capacious new facility of glass, Italian marble and round halls, abutting the Phoenix Park and the derelict buildings and outhouses of nineteenth-century military Dublin, perhaps the words of Psalm 137:1 were on the lips of some: 'By the rivers of Babylon, there we sat down, yea, we wept, when we remembered Zion.' The criminal bar in Dublin is now separately housed, along with the criminal courts, and it might be interesting to query how the criminal practice and its practitioners evolved – and who were the ancestors?

In 1798, at which time this review begins, the bar was small, perhaps 360 practising, of whom thirty-six were serjeants or silks.[2] Criminal trials were usually conducted at quarter sessions, assizes or commissions; counsel were more likely to be involved at assizes and commissions, the latter in Dublin sitting at Green St, the former with judges going on circuit to dispose of criminal and civil business. Criminal practitioners were naturally part of the common law bar at a time when juries sat extensively in civil matters. The extinct institution of serjeant as leaders of the bar is of some criminal relevance. Serjeants frequently led for the crown in crime, occasionally with the attorney general and solicitor general, but in addition serjeants were expected to and did sit as judges of assize when the necessity arose. Indeed Serjeant Sullivan, 'the last serjeant', who thought that the assizes were as thoroughly Irish as the mountain or the moor, was sitting as an assize judge under armed protection on the Connaught circuit when the truce

---

1 John Cooke (ed.), *The Dublin book of Irish verse* (Dublin 1915), pp 5–6.
2 A.R. Hart, *The king's serjeants at law in Ireland* (Dublin, 2003); Kenneth Ferguson, 'The Irish bar in December 1798', *Dublin Historical Record*, 52:1 (1999).

was declared in 1921.[3] Serjeants might expect judicial preferment. For obvious reasons, it is unlikely that a barrister in criminal practice only could make a living – or one equal to what proficiency in other branches might reap. Criminal practice was not highly respectable – in 1840 Joseph Napier, later lord chancellor, gave a lecture on criminal law in Dublin in which he opined 'a total ignorance of (criminal law) is not considered incompatible with a high professional character.'[4]

Legislative reforms of the nineteenth century were chiefly directed at jury laws, reform of complex rules on indictments, the lessening of offences attracting capital punishment and the growth and regulation of summary jurisdiction. A significant anomaly which prevented counsel making a full defence (essentially a closing speech on the facts) in felony was remedied by the Prisoners' Counsel Defence Act 1836[5] but by the close of the century the accused was still an incompetent in his own defence – even for not having a dog licence.[6] Many accused were unrepresented until the establishment of a legal aid scheme in 1965 and the decision of the supreme court in *State (Healy) v. Donoghue*.[7] But one overweening fact is the absence of a simple appellate procedure, not remedied until 1924. Professionally represented accused might have the benefit of arcane indictment points, challenges to the array, motions for new trial or to arrest judgment as O'Connell and others did,[8] but no court of criminal appeal existed. No layperson could deploy such arguments, most of which are so different to modern criminal law that they might be from the discipline of theology. The court for crown cases reserved could only be realistically reached with counsel. On a cursory review of the digests from 1867 to 1918, less than one per cent of the content relates to criminal matters.

For the century prior to the 1960s, the only constant legal aid apparent was that in capital/murder cases where the Crown might pay counsel. The dock brief system never applied in Ireland but the bench might appoint counsel for an indigent prisoner. The Cox Reports,[9] devoted to criminal matters in both islands, show that when Andrew Fogarty was indicted in 1851 before the Co. Down assizes for the

3 A.M. Sullivan, *Old Ireland, reminiscences of an Irish KC* (London 1927).
4 Colum Kenny, *Tristram Kennedy and the revival of Irish legal training, 1835–1895* (Dublin, 1996), p. 103; Desmond Greer, 'Crime, justice and legal literature in nineteenth-century Ireland', Ir Jur, NS, 37 (2002), 241.
5 Upon which O'Connell spoke in the house of commons, the greater part of which is occupied by some wrangle he had with Charles Phillips.
6 *R v. Sullivan* (1874) IR 8 CL 404.
7 *The State (Healy) v. Donoghue* (1976) IR 325.
8 *R v. O'Connell & Ors* (1844) 11 Cl & Fin.   9 5 Cox CC 161.

murder of his wife and could not employ attorney or counsel, Chief Baron Pigot asked William MacMechan, an able junior, to act, and was declined. Babington's report shows some conference among the bar, and the father, Sir Thomas Staples QC, addressed Pigot on the impropriety of counsel acting without an attorney, and also requested that the crown should pay a fee, which had been done heretofore. The chief baron opined that the bench could call on a barrister to give his honorary services, but not an attorney. After further observations by MacMechan, Pigot said he could not compel counsel but would appeal to the sense of feeling at the bar. A solicitor was found and MacMechan then consented to act. No good living from criminal practice alone was known until the modern day. Dr Webb protested much when he was assigned to defend Joseph Brady in 1883 for the Phoenix Park murders.

The memoir literature of the Irish bar has placed an enormous cachet upon its pre-Union composition – and accentuates the ascendancy of the bar in the Irish house of commons and its opposition to the Act of Union. Such a root of title was intimately connected with the rise of emancipation politics, the repeal movement and trials of cases which pivoted on party or religious lines. All this was against a backdrop of the limited class from which juries were drawn.

John Philpot Curran was the first Irish counsel to be lionised in literature. Whig, versifier, patriot and defence counsel, his work and speech is captured in the state trials and biography. He had a large and lucrative practice in civil matters from the early days. His first fee book was available to J.R. O'Flanagan[10] who easily disproved Phillips' assertions of Curran's poverty in his first years – in fact, in his fourth year Curran was earning in excess of £1,000. His oratorical skills are displayed in the cases of the 1790s[11] and notwithstanding his lack of success in those matters, including habeas corpus,[12] his reputation as an advocate and patriot survives. Karl Marx thought highly of him.[13] However, the reputation of Curran's able junior, Leonard MacNally, has suffered.

Perhaps an untypical way to examine the changing world of criminal practice is to start with the trial of two barristers, the Sheares brothers.[14]

---

10 O'Flanagan, *The Munster circuit* (London, 1880).
11 Hamill 25 St. Tr. 749, Jackson 26 St. Tr. 783, Weldon 26 St. Tr. 228, Early 26 St. Tr. 877, Finnerty 26 St. Tr. 901, Finney 26 St. Tr. 1020.
12 Wolfe Tone 27 St. Tr. 613. Tone's own legal career was short – he did three circuits and heartily disliked it. See Tone, *Autobiography*, abridged and edited by Sean O'Faolain (London, 1937), pp 22-4.
13 Ferguson, 'The Irish bar', 36.   14 27 St. Tr. 255.

The *dramatis personae* of the Irish bar walk the small stage. The proceedings commenced on 4 July 1798 in Green Street, the grand jury having found bills of indictment against both accused. Appearing for the crown were the solicitor general, John Toler (later Lord Norbury), the prime serjeant, James Fitzgerald (later dismissed for opposing the Act of Union), Saurin, O'Grady, Mayne, Webber and Ridgeway – the latter reported the trial, and five months later was secretary of a meeting of Irish lawyers who opposed the Union.[15] Curran, Plunkett, Ponsonby, MacNally and others appeared for the two prisoners. Henry Sheares' trial demonstrates some matters not too different from today – Curran and Plunkett arrive, not at the appointed hour of 9.30, but an hour and a half late, whether by design or not. In the interim, MacNally, junior counsel, made an argument to quash the indictment because one Ducluzeau, a Huguenot and thus possibly an alien, had sat on the grand jury which had found the true bill of indictment. Saurin was of similar descent, allusive references sometimes appearing in O'Connell's speeches in later years. After Curran's apologies for tardiness were made, a series of pleadings now extinct were reduced to writing and filed. The prisoner's argument was dismissed by Viscount Carleton who alluded to his annotated copy of *Hawkins pleas of the crown*.[16] The trial proper commenced and the first item on the agenda was an adjournment application by the defence, Toler pressing forward with some circumspection, which time seems to have been employed to have an affidavit sworn by the crown solicitor, suggesting that the defence were seeking to delay! Such applications were commonly made. At the Doneraile conspiracy trial in October 1829, when O'Connell had been retained the court refused a short adjournment on the morning of the trial to await O'Connell's arrival, Torrens J observing 'it was the business of the court to prevent delay and defeat artifice'.

In the Sheares' case, on 4 July 1798, the court granted an adjournment of eight days. On 12 July, proceedings continued with the empanelling of the petty jury, the prisoners challenging thirteen peremptorily, and fourteen for want of freehold; the crown stood by eleven and challenged one for want of freehold. Toler, who had been appointed attorney general in the intervening week, opened by adverting to the grief it caused him to have, as his first professional

15 Ferguson, 'The Irish bar', 40–1, 44.
16 Sitting in the same building 180 years later, Séamus Sorahan SC would always carefully marshal the Law Library copies of Hale, Hawkins and East into a neat row in front of him. While some of those books are commonly cited today, Joseph Gabbett's *Treatise on the criminal law* (published in Dublin in 1843) was occasionally cited into the 1970s.

duty, to prosecute two gentlemen of the profession 'to which I am linked by every tie of affection, regard and gratitude that can bind a man of honourable feelings'. He then called eight witnesses including Major Sirr, all of whom were cross-examined. Then Ponsonby made a speech for John Sheares and Plunkett for Henry, after which the prisoners called nine witnesses, three barristers among them. Most of the defence witnesses spoke as to the character of either the prisoners or the prosecution witnesses. No part of this class of evidence has realistically survived into modern practice. Cross-examination of the defence witnesses was to the point and well prepared. The proceedings caused Curran, who had foregone appearing for both accused and who had succeeded in making a closing speech for Henry, to complain at midnight of the sixteen-hour sitting; there followed a twenty-minute interval and some refreshments served in court. The presiding judge summed up.[17] The jury, after seventeen minutes, returned a verdict of guilty at about eight o'clock on the morning of Friday 13 July. MacNally then made a point on the indictment on account of 'the zeal which I feel for my client' which was shortly swept aside by the court.[18] Sentence was pronounced later that afternoon and effected on the following day. Carleton J, addressing both barristers when passing sentence, mentioned that 'I knew the very valuable and respectable father and mother from whom you are both descended.'

Roughly similar defence teams appear in the case of John MacCann,[19] for which the jury deliberated five minutes, in the case of William Byrne,[20] ten minutes and Oliver Bond,[21] seven minutes. Referring to Curran, Mr Justice Day, in sentencing Bond, observed that the prisoner 'had the assistance of as able, acute and zealous counsel as the bar of Ireland affords ...' Five years later, in 1803, Joseph Doran[22] was indicted for treason committed in New Street, Dublin, with MacNally the sole defending counsel. The prosecution, in a manner redolent of the present, stated 'it has been the uniform practice of the counsel for the Crown to confine themselves to a mere statement of the facts, without colouring or ornamenting'. More importantly, in a case which was substantially about visual identification, MacNally pointed out that were the indictment for *felony* he would not be entitled to the

---

17 See also Adrian Hardiman and Mark Radford, 'The (show?) trial of Robert Emmet', *History Ireland*, 13: 4, 25–30.

18 MacNally frequently made such points between 1795 and 1803 in the treason cases and later on the Leinster circuit in cases under the Whiteboy Acts. He published, in 1807, *The rules of evidence in pleas of the crown*, freely drawing on his experiences.

19 27 St. Tr. 400.   20 27 St. Tr. 455.   21 27 St. Tr. 523.   22 28 St. Tr. 1041.

aid of counsel on a matter of fact (i.e., that in treason the prisoner's counsel might be heard on the facts but not in felony[23]). MacNally called nine witnesses, mainly by way of alibi and good character. The solicitor general expressed a doubt about prosecuting the case further and Lord Norbury, noting 'the Crown have candidly given up the case', thought the jury should acquit, which they did.

On one view of the above proceedings, the roles of participants in and the conduct of criminal trials have not changed much – and counsel make speeches, which may even pass into history as literature. A number of academic authors[24] have pointed out that the *'lawyerised criminal trial'* with questioning and speechifying counsel is a comparatively modern phenomenon. And treason trials reported in the state trials series are themselves unrepresentative. Modern writers, mining the Old Bailey sessions papers, argue that in the eighteenth century an Old Bailey trial had few of the modern appurtenances of a trial. The prosecution was more likely to be represented, perhaps privately,[25] than the defence. Trials were conducted speedily, and frequently in batches; juries frequently gave their verdict without retiring, the judge could not only direct a verdict of guilty but was 'counsel for the prisoner' whether the accused was defended or not. It is said that the law of evidence was in its infancy.

Certainly the Caravat and Shanavest trials, discussed below, appear to have many such features; however, since judicial direction of 'no case to answer' was not available, the issue of guilt with some steer from judge was always committed to the jury.

After his arrest in 1803, Emmet sought to retain Curran for his treason case; he declined, and so Peter Burrowes defended. One casualty of the rebellion was Lord Kilwarden, Arthur Wolfe, the chief justice of king's bench who had directed the writ of habeas corpus for Wolfe Tone in November 1798. In 1803 Wolfe was murdered by a mob in Thomas Street during the Emmet Rising. Emmet's attachment to Philpot Curran's daughter Sarah forms a strong romantic story as evidenced in Thomas Moore's song 'She is far from the land'. Curran's

---

23 Altered by the Prisoners' Counsel Defence Act 1836.
24 J.H. Langbein, 'The Criminal trial before the lawyers', *University of Chicago Law Review* 45:2 (1978); J.H. Langbein, 'Shaping the eighteenth century criminal trial', *University of Chicago Law Review* 50 (1985); J.M. Beattie, 'Scales of justice, defence counsel and the English criminal trial in the eighteenth and nineteenth centuries', *Law & History Review* 9:2; and Allyson May, *The bar and the Old Bailey, 1750–1850* (University of North Carolina Press, 2003).
25 When Sam Gray, a notorious Orangeman, was tried for murdering Bernard MacMahon in 1824 the Catholic Association financed the costs of his prosecution.

Judges of Ireland, Four Courts, Dublin, 6 April 1921. Courtesy of the Bar Council of Ireland.

For further details of all illustrations see pp xv–xxi above.

'Britain's first women barristers', Frances Kyle (*left*) and Averil Deverell. Inset: W.B. Deverell (Averil's twin brother), called the same day. *Daily Sketch*, 3 Nov. 1921.

The Four Courts and Public Record Office explode and burn, 30 June 1922.
Courtesy of the National Library of Ireland (Hogan, HOG57).

Remains of the statue of Michael O'Loghlen in the Round Hall of the Four Courts, July 1922.
Courtesy of the National Library of Ireland (IND H245).

Above and below: Remains of the statue of Henry Joy in the Round Hall of the Four Courts, July 1922. Courtesy of the National Library of Ireland (IND H248 and Hogan HOG8).

Denis Henry (1864–1925), first lord chief justice of Northern Ireland 1921–5.
Courtesy of the National Portrait Gallery, London.

Thomas Molony (1865–1949), last lord chief justice of Ireland 1918–24. By William Orpen. Courtesy of the Honorable Society of King's Inns.

Note that each judge wears a ceremonial collar of 'SS'.

William Moore (1864–1944), lord chief justice of Northern Ireland 1925–37. *Irish Law Times and Solicitors' Journal*, 15 Dec. 1928.

Mary Dorothea Heron BA (Queen's University Belfast). The first woman to be admitted a solicitor in Ireland. Courtesy of the Bar Council of Ireland.

Averil Deverell BL. The first woman to practise as a barrister in the Irish Free State. Artist unknown. Courtesy of the Bar Council of Ireland.

Lord Glenavy (formerly Lord Chancellor James Campbell) with Hugh Kennedy, future chief justice, in the garden of Kennedy's house in Clonskeagh, Dublin, 1922–3. Courtesy of the National Library of Ireland (KEN8).

Mella Carroll (1934–2006). The first woman appointed as a high court judge in Ireland. Here in her robes as chancellor of Dublin City University, with its then president Prof. Ferdinand von Prondzynski (September 2001). Courtesy of the *Irish Times*. Photographer: Joe St Leger.

eminence and popularity declined after Emmet's death. He became master of the rolls in 1806 and might have slipped more were it not for his biographer, Charles Phillips, who, perambulating the round hall of the Four Courts in Dublin bagless and briefless, was invited by Curran to dine in the Priory, Curran's Rathfarnham house.

Charles Phillips, Curran's friend and biographer, was called to the bar in 1812 and seems to have gone on the Leinster circuit, then to the north west – where he disgraced himself by a lampoon on the 'father', and thence rapidly to the Connaught circuit in the same year. He was a noted orator before being called and had published verse and romance, which trait he shared with Leonard MacNally, author of the ballad 'The lass of Richmond Hill', Theobald Wolfe Tone who with Richard Jebb and Thomas Radcliffe wrote the novel *Belmont Castle*, John Philpot Curran and Richard Lalor Sheil. Phillips mentions being counsel in 1812 to Fenton, a solicitor, tried for the murder of Hillas, a barrister of the circuit, in a duel in Sligo. But Burke names no counsel appearing and places the date as 1814, noting that the two lawyers had quarrelled over the alleged non-payment of a fee. The solicitor was acquitted, the trial judge opining to the jury that he had never heard of a fairer duel.[26]

To historians of the criminal bar Phillips is a figure of interest, not least by virtue of a notoriety he acquired at the end of his practice in *R. v. Courvoisier* (below). His view of counsel's duty to the client may have been formed the year after his call, when he was appearing with O'Connell for Magee, indicted for criminal libel, where O'Connell's speech lacked nothing in its attack upon the administration and on Saurin, the attorney general. For good measure, Magee had O'Connell's speech published in full prior to his sentencing, which cannot have mitigated matters. Both O'Connell and his client Magee were denounced by Day J.[27] When passing sentence, Day observed that Magee had 'boldly' instructed his counsel

> to give the reins to all his powers of vituperation and calumny; and it must be confessed that the Gentleman fulfilled his instructions to the letter. The sluices of slander were opened wide and the mountain torrent roared and rushed along, sweeping viceroys, law officers, judges, jurors, the Church, the State, every thing revered and sacred in society, down its muddy and turbulent tide, without discrimination or decorum.

26 Oliver J. Burke, *Anecdotes of the Connaught circuit from its foundation in 1604 to close upon the present time* (Dublin, 1885), pp 195–6.
27 *Mr Justice Robert Day (1746-1841): the diaries and the addresses to grand juries, 1793–1829*, ed. Gerald O'Carroll (Tralee, 2004), p. 237.

He also deprecated counsel for 'using the shelter of a bar gown', forgetting his duty and turning his back upon his client. Magee apparently thought no less of O'Connell.

O'Connell had an ally in the industrious Richard Lalor Sheil, playwright, called in 1814 who, in 1822, commenced writing his vignettes of the Irish bar co-authored with William Henry Curran, subsequently published together in 1855 as *Sketches of the Irish bar*. Lalor Sheil was intimately associated with O'Connell in the Catholic Association, and was one of the first Roman Catholics admitted to the inner bar in summer 1830. Prior to that, he was prosecuted in 1827 for comments made on the publication of Tone's autobiography.[28] MacKenzie, who edited subsequent editions of Sheil, opined that 'his legal knowledge was limited as respects depth and extent'.

Following the Magee case Phillips prospered rapidly, but it was in a matter connected to his own circuit that he came to wide public attention. John Guthrie was the secretary of the Connaught Bar Society and had wisely married the only daughter of an eminent solicitor. The plaintiff returned home in July 1814 from a bar dinner to discover that his wife had departed with the defendant. In the ensuing action for criminal conversation, heard before Lord Norbury in the court of common pleas in Dublin, Phillips' opening drew criticism and passed into literature.[29] Norbury indicated to the jury his 'unmixed pleasure' at the speech, 'a speech which contained as brilliant a display of classical eloquence, and as fine effusions of manly feeling as ever fell from the lips of any counsel in these courts.'[30]

Two years later O'Connell and Phillips appeared together in *Blake v. Wilkins* for the defendant in a breach of promise action. The plaintiff was a youngish but impecunious lieutenant in the royal navy, the defendant a widow of some substance in her mid-sixties. Because O'Connell was hoarse, Phillips closed to the Galway jury, but ridiculing his client and commenting highly unfavourably on her age and appearance. Though he had secured to the defendant a favourable verdict, she obliged by horsewhipping him in the street outside so that Phillips had to retreat to the bar room. History does not record if he was there consoled by Mr Guthrie.

28 But a *nolle prosequi* was entered – see O'Flanagan, *Bar life of O'Connell* (Dublin, 1875).
29 *The speeches of Charles Phillips, esq., delivered at the bar and on various public occasions in Ireland and England, edited by himself* (New York, 1817), pp 90–116; Jan-Melissa Schramm, 'The anatomy of a barrister's tongue: rhetoric, satire and the Victorian bar in England', *Victorian Literature & Culture* 32:2 (2004), 290–2.
30 Burke, *Anecdotes*, p. 194.

Phillips continued to publish volumes of speeches of eloquence and oratory, and as Richard Lalor Sheil noted 'his florid oratory obtained him considerable practice in adultery, seduction and breach of promise cases'. It is unlikely that such oratory is extant in modern family law cases. Phillips' own speeches attracted, at the time, unfavourable attention from Brougham, subsequently lord chancellor, with whom he later formed a great attachment. In the *Edinburgh Review* of 1816 Brougham decried the 'intemperate love of luxuriant declamation to which all higher considerations are sacrificed'.

Although nearly forty years younger, Phillips formed an intimate friendship with John Philpot Curran, who retired in 1814 and lived away from Ireland until his death in 1817. The following year, Phillips published *Recollections of John Philpot Curran*, favourably reviewed in that year by Lord Brougham, to whom Phillips later dedicated *Curran and his contemporaries*. Phillips never saw Curran in action as an advocate but opined that William Garrow only approached his ability, though he could not have seen Garrow at his youthful best. Garrow became a legendary Old Bailey defence counsel almost as soon as he was called in 1783, took silk in 1793, and turned to civil work, politics and prosecuting. A vigorous cross-examiner, learned in the law, he was an aggressive advocate of clients' rights before the Prisoners' Counsel Defence Act was passed.

Phillips was called to the English bar in 1821 and had a criminal practice at the Old Bailey, the Middlesex and Oxford circuits. Burke put it that, 'Rather too ornate, the imagery of his fancy threw a charm over every case, however dull, in which he was engaged.'[31] Sheil thought that his peculiar style of eloquence 'did not please' in England. He acquired the nickname Counsellor O'Garnish. His name appears relatively frequently in the Cox Reports but without any indication of oratory. He was thought to be the model for Charles Dickens' Buzfuz in *The Pickwick papers* and there is much similarity between Phillips' published speech in *Guthrie v. Sterne* and that of Serjeant Buzfuz in the fictional breach of promise suit *Bardell v. Pickwick*.[32] The reason why Phillips dedicated his Curran biography to Lord Brougham was that Brougham, with Denman, had defended Queen Caroline before the house of lords in 1820. Brougham described counsel's duty to his client

---

31 Burke, *Anecdotes*, p. 202.
32 *Bardell v. Pickwick: the* [fictional] *trial for breach of promise of marriage held at the guildhall sittings, on April 1, 1828* ... Edited with notes and commentaries by Percy Fitzgerald, 'M.A., F.S.A., barrister-at-law; and sometime crown prosecutor on the north-east circuit (Ireland)'. (London, 1902).

as 'to save that client by all means and expedients.'[33] In apparent pursuit of this idea, Phillips later defended Lord William Russell's valet, Courvoisier, who murdered his employer.[34] Courvoisier privately admitted his guilt during the trial to Phillips who, notwithstanding, proceeded to defend, in a manner inconsistent with his instructions, by implicating others in the crime and alleging the planting of evidence. When these matters became public after the trial and execution of the accused, public comment as to the proper limits of criminal defence was loud, *Punch*, in particular, excoriating Phillips. Dickens was present at Courvoisier's execution on 6 July 1840.[35] The Dickens portrait of the bench and bar in *The Pickwick papers*, though mainly of the civil side, is uniformly hostile. In 1842 Lord Brougham appointed Phillips as a commissioner of the bankruptcy court but the Courvoisier matter resurfaced in 1849 and resulted in published correspondence.

Reverting to Ireland, some insight into workaday criminal practice can be seen in the case of Hugh Fitzpatrick of Capel Street, printer and publisher of MacNally's *Justice of the Peace*.[36] In February 1813, Fitzpatrick was prosecuted in the king's bench for a libel on the lord lieutenant arising out of a capital conviction at the summer assizes of 1809 of a Patrick or Philip Barry. In defence, O'Connell, led by Burrowes (a good friend of Wolfe Tone, one of Robert Emmet's defence team in 1803, and who as a student had debated with Garrow), called evidence from Campbell who had been counsel for the deceased prisoner. Counsel told the judges of the king's bench how he had attempted to move an adjournment for the accused on the opening of the assizes in August 1809 in Kilkenny, which was not apparently opposed but, the matter having stood over till the next day, it was then refused by Norbury at which Campbell 'told His Lordship he must defend the man himself', apparently having stipulated 'if the trial should be proceeded on, I would not defend the man, in the absence of his witnesses; and upon the motion being refused, I threw up my brief and left the court.' Campbell then detailed how he wrote to the trial judge post-conviction and included affidavits of those who would have been witnesses to an alibi. Upon cross-examination by the solicitor general he opined 'I conceived the trial was not irregularly had' and was 'contrary to law' and that he 'talked of it publicly in the hall of the Four Courts'. Current etiquette might be slightly different.

33 Thomas O'Malley, *The criminal process* (Dublin, 2009), p 478.
34 *R v. Courvoisier* (1840) 9 C & P, p. 362. The report is on another issue.
35 Schramm, 'Anatomy of a barrister's tongue', p. 293.
36 St. Tr. 1169. Some original papers and judge's notes are appended to the report.

So the criminal trial of the nineteenth century might be characterised as nasty, brutish and short. Unrepresentative juries, unsympathetic judges, the limited role of counsel, if any, and unconscionable speed of trials were part of the accepted order. Robert Day, who was a member of Curran's drinking club 'The Monks of the Screw', had much criminal experience before his appointment to the king's bench in 1798. His diaries show that when travelling on the Leinster circuit in the spring of 1808 the assizes were dominated by trials of faction parties going under the colourful names of Caravats and Shanavests. He records the following: 'Monday 7 March opened the assizes ... two convicted of a murder and arson and robbery. Tuesday 8th two more convicted of murder. Wednesday 9th one man convicted of a rape – dined with the Bar.' On moving to Waterford: 'Tuesday 22nd Ian Wilson acquitted of a barbarous murder, two men capitally convicted of mail robbery. 23rd two young men convicted of a burglary. Friday 1st April, finished the crown business in one day, two men convicted of burglary.'[37]

Three years later, Lord Norbury and Chief Baron O'Grady (both of whom had prosecuted the Sheares brothers) conducted a special commission over seven days in Clonmel, Waterford and Kilkenny to try about forty prisoners of the same 'banditti' who awaited trial. Most of the prisoners were represented by MacNally, usually on his own, and only three other defence counsel are named.[38] In two cases pleas of guilty were entered, one of them causing the solicitor general to observe 'no kind of compact whatever has been entered into'. A fair swathe of death sentences were recorded by the time the commission closed on 13 February 1811, but lesser sentences of transportation, imprisonment, or whipping were also passed. On a capital indictment in *R v. Corcoran & Ors*, both Norbury and O'Grady, lord chief justice and chief baron respectively, presided together and, at the close of the prisoners' case, the report indicates that, 'the Chief Baron observed a fatal error in the capital part of the indictment', upon which MacNally insisted the matter should go to the jury before a new indictment could be sent up; the court concurring, the prisoners were acquitted of the capital indictment. The technical approach of the courts to indictments (see also the observations of Pennefather J in O'Connell) is also alluded to

---

37 *Day (1746–1841): the diaries and the addresses to grand juries, 1793–1829*. For the factions see Samuel Clark and J.S. Donnelly, *Irish peasants: violence and political unrest, 1780–1914* (Dublin, 1983).
38 31 St. Tr. A person named Campbell is mentioned, perhaps the same who was called by the defence in Fitzpatrick's case.

by Vaughan[39] and is a feature in ballad literature, for example, 'I then did stand my trial, and boldly I did plead, A flaw was in my indictment found that soon had me freed.'[40]

In 1835 Alexis de Tocqueville visited Waterford, Kilkenny and Galway assizes. At Waterford between 22 and 23 July there were sixteen murder cases disposed of – all manslaughter; and the jury was unchanged for each one unless a challenge was made. In Galway he asked the assize judge why he saw in the lists so many rape cases. The judge informed the Frenchman that the accusations were a ruse to compel the accused to marry the complainant and that, 'If the marriage takes place, the case is stopped as our laws provide. This behaviour of the girls proves very rough manners, but not their inchastity.'[41] Bar literature makes the same point frequently.

The only consistently paid criminal practitioners in the nineteenth century were crown counsel, senior and junior, who after the 1840s were appointed to each county, and supernumeraries who might be called upon if criminal business was being transacted on assize in more than one court. William Nicholas Keogh, called in 1840, was a prominent member of the western circuit and pointed out to the house of commons in May of 1849 that the cost of payment to prosecuting counsel had risen from £12,000 in 1846 to £19,000 in 1847.[42] In fact, Keogh was crown counsel in Galway and that very year at the spring assizes, Lefroy J told the grand jury there were 423 prisoners for trial and 297 bills, of which 15 were murder or manslaughter, 24 burglary and robbery, 115 sheep stealing, 57 cow stealing and 86 larceny. The previous year, according to Burke, crown counsels' fees at the spring assizes 'amounted to thousands of pounds' while the dock lawyers were left almost unemployed, on account, it seems, of many pleas of guilty by a beggared peasantry that 'felt that imprisonment was preferable to the horrors of starvation'.[43]

Comparing the situation in the early to mid nineteenth century with 'the present and the late state of Meath', when 'during late years there has been very little ordinary crime' John Adye Curran KC would note in 1915 that

39 W.E. Vaughan, *Murder trials in Ireland, 1836–1914* (Dublin, 2009), pp 109–15.
40 From 'The lily of the West', O'Lochlainn, *Irish street ballads* (Dublin, 1939).
41 De Tocqueville, *Journeys to England and Ireland* (New Haven, CT, 1958 edition), pp 138–40, p. 179.
42 Hansard HC Deb 1 May, 1849.
43 Burke, *Anecdotes*, pp 270–1.

At the Trim Lenten Assizes for the year 1818 there were 58 bills sent before the Grand Jury against 108 prisoners. The cases numbered nearly every offence known to the law, including murder. At the Summer Assizes for the same year there were 62 bills sent to the Grand Jury against 89 prisoners for the same class of offence. At the Lenten Assizes of 1828 there were 44 bills against 77 prisoners, the cases being of a similar class, with some bad additions. At the Summer Assizes of 1828 there were 52 bills against 80 prisoners, with the addition of highway robbery and other offences. At the Lenten Assizes of 1838 there were 40 bills sent up against 61 prisoners, and that year Whiteboyism appears for the first time as an offence. In the year 1848 there were 52 bills against 79 prisoners. At the Summer Assizes there were 21 bills and 24 prisoners. Stealing food seems to have been a very common offence in this year – the year of the famine.[44]

In 1849, Keogh also informed the house of commons that on every circuit the leading crown counsel was the oldest member and most had held their offices for half a century – and each was thus known as the 'father' of the circuit. Burke, whose *Anecdotes* seem to have been drawn with the assistance of yearly records, noted that the crown prosecutor in the 1840s for the western circuit was George French QC, 'a very irritable old man, well grounded in the principles of the law, but who for forty years, it was said, had never troubled his head with reading the reports ... The English laws of evidence he looked upon (as a French lawyer would) as so much trash, and his only aim was to make out the truth, caring not a jot whether it was hearsay or not'.[45]

Replying to Keogh the attorney general for England and Wales assured the commons that prosecution costs were declining, multiple retainers were pruned, indictments were to be paid at three and two guineas for senior and junior, only one counsel was to be employed if a large group of similar bills were laid and counsel might not be briefed where a plea of guilty was entered and, more pertinently, 'the Crown is not to be at the expense of defending prisoners and ... should the court think right to assign counsel for a prisoner's defence such counsel should act gratuitously.' An appointment as counsel, even gratuitously, might, should the case or result be favourable, constitute a fillip to a young and rising counsel.

---

44 J.A. Curran (junior), *Reminiscences of John Adye Curran KC* (London, 1915), pp 251–2
45 Burke, *Anecdotes*, pp 275–6.

To contemporary views, the common attributes of a nineteenth-century trial seem odd, the rules on indictment being of a complex and arcane nature. The main centres of attack appeared to be (a) the formation of the jury, or the array,[46] (b) challenges to credit, especially in cases of accomplices formerly called approvers, (c) alibis, either Kerry type in which case everything is correct about the alibi except the date, or Tipperary or Westmeath alibis, in which it is the witnesses for the prosecution who are gifted with an alibi, or placed elsewhere for the relevant date.

Philpot Curran, O'Connell and the eminent leaders of the common law bar in the late eighteenth/early nineteenth century all appear to have done crime and are so recorded in the reports of the times. It is unlikely that an exclusively criminal bar existed. Even Thomas Lefroy, when appointed first serjeant of the Munster circuit, prosecuted regularly. But he resigned his serjeantcy when, for reasons of palliating O'Connell, Lefroy, an arch-Protestant, was not asked to sit on circuit as an assize judge. His acquaintance in 1796 with Jane Austen shows a lighter side.

It seems that the predominant ability in crime was jury work, or presentation of a case thereto. One name, as a journeyman barrister (and literary author) sticks out – that of Leonard MacNally who composed a rhyming alphabet of the bar: 'L stands for Lysaght who loves a good joke, M for Macnally [sic], who lives by the rope.'[47] MacNally was known 'as a good dock lawyer'. In fact, his legal output was not small. In *The justice of the peace for Ireland*, published first in 1808, he decried 'the ignorance in jurisprudence daily exhibited by the proceedings of the Magistrates, [as] a grievance calling loudly for remedy and [as] perhaps the principal cause of those disturbances which have repeatedly disgraced Ireland.' The subscribers were many, the alphabetical index appropriately ordered by precedence – so 'John, the Earl of Annesly, the Earl of Belvedere and the Rt Hon. John P. Curran'. The second edition of 1812 had an even more indignant introduction. At the same time, MacNally had contributed rules of evidence in pleas of the crown and two volumes on equity. Originally

---

46 For example, in *R. v. O'Connell & Ors* (1844) 11 Cl & Fin. and also in Daniel Crilly's pamphlet *Jury packing in Ireland* (Dublin, 1887). The custom was noted also in civil matters, on 24 July 1807, a jury list in a defamation action had been returned at the nomination of the plaintiff's attorney, which Day J. thought 'a most audacious and corrupt practice'.

47 J. Roderick O'Flanagan, *The Irish bar; comprising anecdotes, bon-mots, and biographical sketches of the bench and bar of Ireland* (London, 1879), p. 211.

from St Mary's Lane, possibly a grocer, he was Dublin Castle's 'most reliable and consistent source of information on United Irish developments'.[48] Of his many works of popular entertainment only the ballad 'The lass of Richmond Hill' is still known.

Daniel O'Connell's legal career is well recorded in bar literature, but O'Flanagan has it right in suggesting that discretion was the best quality a prisoner's advocate could have, along with an abundant caution in cross-examination. He thought that O'Connell's greatest quality was 'his oblivion of himself' and that, 'no lust of oratorical display even tempted him to make a speech dangerous to the party by whom he was retained'.[49] O'Connell's success in civil and criminal matters is apparent from the Limerick summer assizes of 1813 when he held twenty-six record briefs and was counsel for the prisoners in almost every crown case. With two courts sitting, one wonders how it was done. He had an enormous practice on the rest of the Munster circuit and enjoyed the title 'counsellor'. O'Connell swapped the front seat for the dock when he, his son John and others stood trial for conspiracy in the Four Courts in 1844 on an indictment of counts said by O'Flanagan to be ninety-seven feet long and by MacDonagh to extend to one hundred yards of print but, in any event an indictment of such length that Denman J described it as 'an abuse to be put down, not a practice deserving encouragement' – 'a Behemoth' according to Richard Lalor Sheil, counsel to John O'Connell, in his closing speech.[50] Daniel O'Connell defended himself, defying the adage that a man who defends himself has a fool for a client. After conviction, he was defended by counsel. Just as O'Connell's address in Magee, thirty-one years earlier, had been a political harangue, just so was Sheil's closing speech, for which he was brought out of retirement. He did not appear on the motions and writs thereafter. O'Flanagan, who attended the trial as a reporter, thought 'his ear was charmed with ringing phrases, and his imagination delighted in novelty'. Ever conscious of popular matters, Sheil excoriated the attorney general not on account of his having called out a defence counsel to duel, but as the 'artful dodger' of the State, an observation which brought great applause.[51] Further applause greeted his comparison between the monster meetings and

---

48 Marianne Elliott, *Partners in revolution: The United Irishmen and France* (New Haven and London, 1982), p. 73.
49 O'Flanagan, *The Irish bar*, p. 253.
50 Michael MacDonagh, *The life of Daniel O'Connell* (London, 1903), p. 333
51 *Report of the Irish state trials 1844* (Dublin, 1844); P.M. Geoghegan, *Liberator: the life and death of Daniel O'Connell, 1830–1847* (Dublin, 2010), pp 166–79.

those of Protestants/Orangemen, and he mentioned the notoriously lucky criminal defendant, Sam Gray: 'Here is Mr Samuel Gray/The Protestant hero of Ballibay'.[52] Whatever the length of the indictment, the jury made a forensic hash of the conviction by their findings of partial guilt on some counts.

Of interest in the O'Connell case is the extraordinarily full frontal legal assault by the traverser's counsel in the application for a new trial and arrest of judgment conducted over nine days before the very judges who had just presided at the trial. The judicial language in riposte was that 'learned counsel has deceived himself and much misrepresented, no doubt unintentionally'; and 'the court was also taught not only what was defective in the present charge but what in other hands it should have been.' Many of the points were characterised as 'ingenious sophistry' and further that 'we were taught, in emphatic language what were the duties of a judge presiding and the duties of counsel were also dwelt upon and admonished that the Judge was Counsel for the prisoner.' This provoked Crampton to state that, 'As learned counsel has been so good as to remind the judges of their duties ... learned counsel has said the advocate's first duty was to his client, the second to himself and the third to the public or that he be a mouthpiece of his client ... such is not the office of an advocate. He will ever bear in mind that if he be the advocate of an individual and retained and remunerated (often inadequately) for his valuable services, yet he has a prior and perpetual retainer on behalf of truth and justice'. Burton J referred to O'Connell as 'The principal traverser as well known to be a gentleman of first rate talent, peculiarly versed in criminal law.' Pennefather, who had extensive criminal experience, quoted Hale that 'more offenders escape by the over easy ear given to exceptions in indictments than by their own innocence and many serious and crying offences escape by these unseemly niceties.' On a writ of error from the queen's bench in Ireland to the house of lords, the law lords themselves sought the opinion of eight judges which were given, trenchantly adverse to the accused's arguments and deploying a vast array of authority. But by three to two the law lords held for the traversers on at least three major grounds, Denman starting with the famous observation that if the practice in the current case passed without remedy, trial by jury would be a delusion, a mockery and a snare. The special jury list, amounting to about 717 persons, had omitted fifty-nine names.

---

52 D.S. Johnson, 'The trials of Sam Gray: Monaghan politics and nineteenth century Irish criminal procedure', *Ir. Jur. N.S.* 20 (1985), 88.

A more workaday practice was that of John Adye Curran, senior, who was called in 1833 and practised extensively in crime, on circuit and in Green Street where he himself, as a young man, had been sentenced to six months imprisonment for matters connected with the tithe agitation. After solving difficulties with the benchers he was admitted to practice.[53] His son, John, was called in 1860, a friend and companion to Constantine Molloy, a fond recounter of the history of the home circuit where Palles had his first brief at Mullingar assizes in a criminal matter. In Adye Curran's time two permanent crown counsel were briefed in each county and supernumeraries were given briefs at 'the sweet will' of the crown solicitor. He noted a particularly lengthy trial in 1873, *R v. Moore*, which lasted seven weeks – seven days of which were taken by the solicitor general in reply. He appears to have done much work at the commission court in Green Street where there were many strong prosecutors who rarely omitted replying, a contrast to the 1970s when such a right was not always exercised. Adye Curran was retained in *R v. Parnell*, the conspiracy trial, and whatever fee he negotiated on the brief, he got the highest refresher among the many juniors, that of fifteen guineas per day on a constant attention basis.

Unjustly neglected, the works of Roderick O'Flanagan, barrister and friend of O'Connell, are a good source of bar lore from the eighteenth and nineteenth centuries. O'Flanagan published three volumes, *The bar life of O'Connell* (1875) followed by *The Irish bar* (1879) and *The Munster circuit* (1880). O'Flanagan did not thrive at the bar and throughout his life interested himself in antiquarian matters and the writing of novels.

In his recent book on Irish murder trials between 1836 and 1914, which was cited above, W.E. Vaughan has marshalled a formidable amount of material.

By late Victorian times the bar literature changes. The year 1798 was well in the past and so also the more florid oratory, usually deployed in cases where the composition of the jury made the verdict readily foreseeable. However the land agitation marked an upswing for criminal business as had Whiteboyism, tithe agitation, repeal and all forms of land discontent in the past. While a busy criminal assize might profit crown counsel, the same could not be said of the defenders. The composition of juries was a matter refreshed in the public mind with the ascent of Peter O'Brien, later immortalised under the soubriquet 'Peter (or Pether) the Packer', whose burgeoning crown practice enabled him to take silk in 1880, deviate to defend T.D. Sullivan for seditious

53 J.A. Curran (junior), *Reminiscences*, pp 1–2.

conspiracy but move into the junior crown prosecutorship in Green Street in 1881 and senior prosecutorship in 1883. He prosecuted both the Invincibles and the Maamtrasna murder cases and many unpopular causes, ably assisted by Edward Carson. When appointed lord chief justice in 1889 he directed that there be printed in book form the case law around the Criminal Law and Procedure Act 1887, a coercion measure which cast a large net, mainly on the summary side but which brought forth a torrent of cases stated and prerogative orders – judicial review criminal matters. Some barristers appear prominently in these cases, O'Brien and Carson, usually for the crown; Healy, D.B. Sullivan, O'Shaughnessy and others for the various applicants among whom Dillon, O'Brien, Redmond and many Sullivans appear. I conjecture that the fondness of the Irish bar for judicial review and its ability in that area may date from this time.

By the end of the century the incompetence of the accused as a witness was removed in England and Wales by the Criminal Justice Evidence Act 1898 but not in Ireland, mainly on account of the opposition of Irish nationalist members of the commons, chiefly T.M. Healy who opined the government ought have advanced grounds for changing the wholesome practice of two or three centuries. Carson argued for the application of the legislation to Ireland but opponents may have thought that crown counsel's cross-examination of the accused would not be helpful to the prisoner. The prevalence of the alibi in Irish trials may well support such caution.

The opening of the twentieth century marks a torpid time in bar history, and it was reported in May 1903 that, 'Not one solitary recruit for the profession of the law put in an appearance at the opening of the Easter Sittings in Dublin. There was not a single call to the Bar ...'[54] Not surprisingly, few new legal texts were being published at the time. A plethora of books on justices of the peace had issued in the previous century, of which Nunn & Walsh, MacNally, Levinge and Molloy were probably the better. But the criminal text books of Hayes and Gabbett were hopelessly out of date and even William G. Huband's enormous tome on juries was, with its postea, demurrer, challenge to the array, the array of the tales and its eighty five-pages directed to challenges, teetering on the verge of extinction. Archbold seems not to have been as prevalent as it might have been. James O'Connor's *Justice of the peace*, first published in 1911 and again in 1915, notwithstanding its great age, was frequently deployed well into the 1990s.

54 *ILT & SJ*, xxxvii (2 May 1903), 184, cited at *King's Inns barristers, 1868–2004*, ed. Kenneth Ferguson (Dublin, 2005), p. 77.

With the foundation of the state the crown apparatus withered, the clerks of the crown and crown solicitors were pensioned off and the grand jury mothballed. Crown counsel moved on, Serjeant Sullivan opined that 'Old Ireland was dead' and packed his bags.

The nascent court of criminal appeal did not establish a vigorous jurisprudence, perhaps the judges of the old court for crown cases reserved had more experience. As *McKnight*[55] has shown the court had few appeals – 27 in 1925, 32 in 1929, 42 in 1933. The rate of quashing was on average 25 per cent, but retrials ordered in 75 per cent of same when such a power was given. The first case concerning the 'shield' provisions perhaps demonstrated one reason why opposition to the accused being competent in his own defence had been voiced in the 1890s, as Kennedy CJ opined that the accused 'thinking himself a more powerful advocate than his counsel' had dropped his shield.[56]

Prosecution practice on circuit can be seen in *Armitage*, in which the accused had apparently been prosecuted in Nenagh for threatening to murder his mother-in-law.[57] The proofs were deficient, and the court thought the prosecution 'should come into court having the proofs in order and not proceed as if they were conducting some trifling case in the former County Court ... and if the prosecuting solicitor ... feels that it is beyond him to present it adequately, the proper course for him is to have the authority of the Attorney General to obtain counsel to present the case ...'[58]

The early reports paint a picture of the disturbed times following the foundation of the Irish Free State, the murder cases demonstrating no great parity in representation. In *AG v. Murray*[59] the attorney general, Carrigan KC, Costello KC and Bewley were opposed by Gleeson in a case which reeked of a forensic trap sprung when the accused gave evidence concerning 'one of the usual unofficial executions'. Cornelius and Hannah O'Leary fared better having two king's counsel and a junior.[60] The following year McCabe was represented only by Alexander Lynn, called in 1921, the court dismissing the appeal on the third day, noting the applicant's argument about the previous statements while in 'illegal custody'.[61]

---

55 Michael McKnight, 'The Irish court of criminal appeal', *Ir. Jur. N.S.* 4 (1969), 91–118.
56 G.L. Frewen (ed.), *Judgments of the court of criminal appeal, 1924–1978* (Incorporated Council of Law Reporting for Ireland, Dublin, 1979), for Campbell's case.
57 Ibid., for Armitage.
58 Not dissimilar at all to what the attorney general mentioned in the house of commons on 1 May 1849 – see Hansard HC Deb 1 May, 1849.
59 *Murray* [1926] IR 266.   60 *O'Leary* [1926] IR 445.   61 *McCabe* [1927] IR 129.

In *McGann* the court of criminal appeal noted the appellant was without means to procure solicitors or counsel and 'no provision has been made in this country for the defence of poor prisoners at the public expense (save in capital cases) ... but the want of professional aid is not a legal ground of appeal.'[62]

Five weeks earlier, Christopher Smith, a bread man, was luckier.[63] He complained that, 'if I had been able to employ a barrister, I am sure I would not be here today', appeared in person on appeal and had his conviction quashed. But the disparity in representation is highlighted in *Healy*[64] where on a case stated about the illegal importation, a revenue matter, of five ladies' dresses, the attorney had two king's counsel and a junior, the accused a king's counsel and a junior. In the same year a mandamus suit concerning Seán MacBride (called to the bar in 1937) suspected of conspiracy to murder Kevin O'Higgins (called 1925) had Lynn as his counsel.[65] In 1963 MacBride went on to argue the last case on the Whiteboy code, which figured so largely in the early nineteenth-century trials. On a habeas corpus he carried only O'Dálaigh CJ but the learning of the Irish judges of the preceding century, in the court for crown cases reserved or elsewhere, is well displayed.[66]

Even in the early 1960s unrepresented defendants on indictment were common – in the circuit criminal court in 1960–1, of 143 convictions sixty-four were unrepresented; in the central criminal court, of nineteen, eight were unrepresented.[67]

The criminal bar of today could not have grown without the passage of the Criminal Justice (Legal Aid) Act 1962. This, for the first time in all indictable matters, provided for legal aid at trial. When launched in 1965 the anticipated budget was £20,000, declining to £18,000 in 1969–70. Keane noted the arrival of the scheme with the unqualified cooperation of the bar and wrote that 'the level of fees proposed was below what might reasonably have been sought'.[68] For senior counsel – in murder cases thirty guineas and all other indictable matters fifteen guineas, and juniors two-thirds *pro rata*.[69] On such modest rewards, the modern criminal bar was founded.[70]

62 *McGann* [1927] IR 503.   63 *Smith* [1927] IR 564.
64 *Healy* [1928] IR 460.   65 [1928] IR 451.
66 *The State (O'Connor) v. O'Caoimhanaigh* [1963] IR 112.
67 Desmond Greer, 'Legal services and the poor in Ireland', *Ir. Jur. N.S.*, 4 (1969), 270.
68 Ronan Keane, 'The future of the Irish bar', *Studies*, 54, no. 216 (1965), 374–84.
69 SI 12/1965
70 The author acknowledges the assistance of Mr Richard Donald, a researcher, in the preparation of this essay.

The Honorable Society of King's Inns: developments in legal education, 1988–2013

MARY FINLAY GEOGHEGAN

The focus of this article is to consider the developments, some radical, to the legal education delivered by King's Inns during the lifetime of the Irish Legal History Society, that is, during the twenty-five years since 1988.

The Honorable Society of King's Inns ('the Society' or 'King's Inns') was established in 1541. Since 1850, it has been providing educational courses leading to the qualification of persons as barristers in Ireland. It is not the purpose of this article to refer to either the history of King's Inns in general or the history of its provision of legal education prior to 1988. This is well documented elsewhere.[1]

The society in 1988, and now, comprises benchers, members (who include all those admitted to the degree of barrister-at-law and not disbarred) and those who are, for the time being, students of the society. All judges of the supreme and high courts (including former solicitors), the Irish nominated judges of the court of justice and the general court of the European Union, and the European court of human rights are *ex officio* benchers. In addition, benchers are elected from among the practising bar.

King's Inns is ultimately governed by the benchers. In 1979, the council of King's Inns was established, to which the benchers delegate the management of King's Inns, including the provision of education. However, the benchers retain the jurisdiction to admit persons to the degree of barrister-at-law and to disbar and remove persons from the roll of barristers. The members of the council are elected from the

---

1 See *inter alia* Colum Kenny, *King's Inns and the kingdom of Ireland: the Irish 'inn of court' 1541 to 1800* (Dublin, 1992); Colum Kenny, *Tristram Kennedy and the revival of Irish legal training 1835 to 1884* (Dublin, 1996); Daire Hogan, *The legal profession in Ireland, 1789–1922* (Dublin, 1986); Marcella Higgins, 'Developments in professional legal education at the Honorable Society of King's Inns' in Thomas Mohr and Jennifer Schweppe (eds), *Thirty years of legal scholarship* (Dublin, 2011).

judicial benchers, bar benchers, the bar council, practising bar and non-practising bar.

In Ireland the qualification of barrister has long been described as the 'degree of barrister-at-law'. However, it is not a degree in the academic sense but rather a description of the status of the holder.[2] In Ireland, unlike in England,[3] the degree did not of itself grant a right of audience as a barrister before the courts. Historically the right to practise before the courts in Ireland was granted in court by the lord chancellor through 'the call to the bar'. Since 1924 the chief justice has exercised this jurisdiction, which was recognised but not conferred by statute in section 3 of the Legal Practitioners' (Qualification) Act 1929 (now repealed).[4]

The chief justice calls to the bar only persons admitted by the benchers to the degree of barrister-at-law. The degree is also a representation by the benchers to the chief justice that the holder is qualified to be called to the bar.

In 1988, the course of education provided by King's Inns leading to admission as a barrister ('the degree course') was a two-year, part-time course principally delivered on weekday evenings and comprising, for the most part, lectures delivered in traditional theatre-style to the entire class on a mix of substantive law, practice and procedure, ethics and other topics relating to practice at the bar. Admission to the course was by one of two routes: either by being the holder of an approved Irish university law degree (having passed certain core subjects) or by being the holder of the King's Inns Diploma in Legal Studies.

In 1982, King's Inns had established a two-year evening course in substantive law leading to the award of the Diploma in Legal Studies ('the diploma course'). The primary aim of this diploma course was and

---

2 *Halsbury's Laws of England* (5th ed., LexisNexis 2008), vol. 66, para. 1033 states '[T]he term "barrister" is the name of a degree and refers to a person who holds that degree.' *Jowitt's Dictionary of English law* (3rd ed., 2010), p. 670 states 'Degree ... the state of a person, as to be a barrister-at-law'.
3 See *Re S a Barrister* [1970] 1 QB 160.
4 *Section 3:* No person shall be admitted by the Chief Justice to practise as a barrister-at-law in the Courts of Saorstát Éireann unless before such person is so admitted he satisfies the Chief Justice, by such evidence as the Chief Justice shall prescribe, that he possesses a competent knowledge of the Irish language: provided always that nothing in this section contained shall prevent the Chief Justice from admitting to practise as a barrister-at-law in the Courts of Saorstát Éireann any member of three years' standing at any other Bar who has been admitted to the degree of barrister-at-law by the Benchers of the Honourable Society of King's Inns, Dublin, pursuant to a reciprocal arrangement whereby members of the Bar of Saorstát Éireann may be admitted to practise at such other Bar.

is to provide knowledge and understanding of substantive law and legal skills to enable those who wish to practise at the bar to fully participate in the course leading to the admittance to the degree of barrister-at-law. For a minority of students it is a stand-alone qualification. From the outset, admission to the diploma course was open to either those holding a degree in any discipline from a third-level education institution (including abroad) approved by King's Inns or those who were at least 25 years old (now reduced to 23). In assessing the latter category of so-called mature applicants, King's Inns considers academic and professional qualifications and occupational experience. From 1982, King's Inns has encouraged persons who do not have a third-level qualification to participate in the diploma course and continue and qualify as barristers. This has contributed to an increase in diversity among barristers. Mature non-graduate students on the diploma course comprise on average approximately 20 per cent of the students on the course. Most have continued to qualify as barristers.

DEVELOPMENTS SINCE 1988

In 1988, there was no entrance examination to the degree course in King's Inns. King's Inns had ninety to one hundred places each year on the degree course, available to those holding its Diploma in Legal Studies and university law graduates. The places for university law graduates were awarded in order of merit on the applicants' degree results. However, there was concern in King's Inns about such method of allocation of places by reason, in particular, of potentially differing standards among universities in the awarding of first class honours and upper second class honours (2:1) law degrees. By the end of the 1990s, due to increasing numbers of applicants, a 2:1 degree in law did not guarantee a place on the course.

In 1998, a committee was established under the chairmanship of the late Mr Justice Peter Shanley to examine and make recommendations on the entrance requirements to the degree course. The committee consulted widely and, in particular, with law schools in the Irish universities. It proposed a common entrance examination and that the entrance requirements be modified to require a combination of either an approved university law degree or the King's Inns diploma (to include specified core legal subjects) and the entrance examination in five other core legal subjects. The common entrance exam has the merit that King's Inns can be satisfied that all students meet a minimum standard and have an up-to-date knowledge of substantive law in at least five core subjects. Limiting the exam to five subjects permits all to be taken at one sitting (usually held in August) and allows prospective students progress immediately after completing their degree or diploma to the professional course. This combination of entrance requirements was, at the time, unique to King's Inns.[5] The council of King's Inns accepted the proposal and the first entrance examination under the new scheme was held in 2002. Since that year, all those who hold a qualifying university degree or postgraduate diploma and pass the entrance examination have been offered places on the degree course in King's Inns.

The entrance requirements to the degree course have been reconsidered on a number of occasions since 2002. While there have been some changes made, the combination of an approved degree or postgraduate diploma, which includes certain specified legal subjects, and a common entrance examination in only five core subjects, subsists. The entrance exam is currently in Irish constitutional law; contract; criminal law; evidence and torts. The specified core subjects are: land law (including the law of succession), company law, equity, law of the European Union, jurisprudence and administrative law. In exceptional cases holders of a degree without one of these subjects may be permitted to take the society's diploma exam in the subject to supplement their degree. The nature of the exams and pass mark has been changed over the years.

THE VOCATIONAL DEGREE COURSE

In 2001, the council of King's Inns established a further working group to review and report on the future of professional education to be provided by King's Inns for barristers in Ireland. It was chaired by Dermot Gleeson SC.[6]

The Gleeson working group sought and obtained information from a range of institutions involved in the professional training of advocates, particularly in the common law systems worldwide. These included the Institute of Professional Legal Studies of Queen's University Belfast,

---

5 The committee did consider the Law Society system, an exam for all including law graduates in approximately eight subjects, but taken by most students over more than one sitting.
6 The members comprised Mr Justice Finnegan, then president of the High Court, Frank Clarke SC, Mary Finlay Geoghegan SC, Brian Murray BL.

the Faculty of Advocates in Scotland, the Bar Council of England and Wales, the Inns of Court law school in London and bodies engaged in advocacy training in Australia, Hong Kong and the United States of America. It also obtained information about and considered the professional course then delivered by the Law Society of Ireland for the training of solicitors. The working group concluded that a remarkable consensus had emerged worldwide over the two previous decades that the concluding phase of professional training for advocates in the common law world should comprise intensive, full-time and largely practical instruction concentrating on the vocational skills of the advocate and that the course should last approximately one full year.

The Gleeson working group reported in October 2002 and recommended that the then current two-year degree course, delivered in the evenings, should be changed to a full-time, one-year vocational degree course with emphasis on course work, practical instruction and training in the working techniques that are required of barristers in the course of their professional work. It made clear that this recommendation was enabled by the entrance requirements, which permitted King's Inns to be satisfied that all those admitted to the degree course already had up-to-date knowledge to a requisite standard in the substantive law of the five entrance examination law subjects and a knowledge of substantive law in the other requisite core legal subjects to degree standard.

King's Inns decided to adopt the recommendations and to establish a new, full-time vocational course leading to admission to the degree of barrister-at-law and for that purpose established the new position of 'Dean of the Law School' of King's Inns. Both decisions made a radical change to the subsequent delivery of education by King's Inns. In 2003, the society appointed as dean, Sarah Macdonald, an English barrister with prior experience of designing and delivering a bar vocational course in England and Wales.

During 2003 and 2004, the new vocational course was designed; working materials drafted; a new assessment and examination regime established; tutors appointed for the delivery of the new course and requisite tutor training carried out. There was considerable involvement of both benchers and barristers. Members of the practising bar were surveyed. Approximately fifty-five judges and practising barristers were involved in the preparation of the design of and materials for use on the new course. As the course was to be a full-time course simultaneously taught in small groups of approximately sixteen, it also required many new facilities to be available daily in King's Inns. Considerable work was done by all members of staff in King's Inns to achieve the commencement of such a radical new course in a relatively short space of time.

The new vocational degree course commenced with 177 students in October 2004. During the academic year 2004/5 the society also had approximately 110 students completing the last year of its previous two-year course which had commenced in 2003. The new course was and is radically different to the previous one. It is a professional course, designed to be delivered to persons who have demonstrated an up-to-date knowledge in substantive law to enable them acquire the additional knowledge and skills required of a practising barrister. Fundamental to the design of the course is the integration of the learning of knowledge and skills so ensuring that the skills are always learnt in context and students understand the knowledge they have acquired through consistent application. Most classes are interactive in groups of approximately sixteen and the students are expected to undertake numerous different types of exercises including advocacy, negotiation, drafting and consultation.

The teaching on all aspects of the course is almost exclusively delivered by experienced practising barristers. During the course, students are expected to behave in accordance with the professional standards which will be expected of them as barristers. Attendance at the course is compulsory. Students are required to approach their work, colleagues and teaching staff in accordance with the standards of professional responsibility which would be expected of them as barristers. Throughout the course they receive lectures in professional ethics and, in addition, ethical issues are introduced in teaching of other aspects of the course.

At the heart of the vocational course are the civil practice course and criminal practice course. The civil practice course is structured to take students through the process of civil litigation from the beginning, when instructions are first received by a solicitor, to final appeal stage and enforcement of the judgment. The students learn the law and procedure applicable to each stage of the process and, at the same time, through the interactive exercises, the legal skills of advocacy, consultation, negotiation, legal research, case analysis, opinion writing and drafting. In recent times, alternative dispute resolution has also been introduced as part of the civil practice course.

The criminal practice course is similarly structured to take students through the process of criminal litigation from the investigation of offences by the gardaí, through arrest and detention of suspects, the first appearance of the suspect in court and all the stages in the court process through to sentencing and appeal. Similarly, learning and teaching legal skills (in particular of advocacy, consultation, legal research and case analysis) is integrated into the procedural part of the criminal practice course so these skills are learnt in context.

During the course, the students participate in mock civil trials and mock criminal summary trials in a courtroom in the Four Courts, and recently the Criminal Courts of Justice, before a judge or an experienced practicing barrister acting as a judge. Students are also obliged to attend court and prepare reports on what they have observed.

At the commencement of the vocational course each year, there is what is termed a 'foundation course'. This is a short course which gives an opportunity to the students to revise core substantive law subjects through a focus on remedies and quantum. It also gives students their first opportunity to tackle problems which contain a number of different legal aspects and may cut across different substantive law subjects. It is aimed at helping students to understand the need to shift their emphasis away from a purely academic discussion of law towards the application of their knowledge and analytical skills in the giving of practical and useful advice. This is a difficult bridge for some to cross.

Towards the end of the course, students are given the opportunity to take a short course in the law and practice of two potential areas of practice, the 'option courses'. In 2011/12, the options available were employment law; company litigation; immigration and asylum; advanced family practice; landlord and tenant and conveyancing; planning and environmental law; advanced Irish and alternative dispute resolution. The option courses are delivered for the most part in small groups, although the precise teaching methods vary in accordance with the requirement of the particular option.

At the end of the year, students are examined in their knowledge primarily by two multiple-choice exams in civil litigation; remedies and evidence; and criminal litigation sentencing and evidence; and a written assessment in ethics. The skills are assessed both orally and in writing. In general, students must pass each assessment to successfully complete the vocational course. There is very limited scope for passing by compensation. The view taken is that to admit a person to the status of barrister the King's Inns must be satisfied that the person has reached a requisite standard in all aspects of practice reflected in the vocational course. There are repeat assessments each autumn.

From the outset, student reaction to the vocational course has been extremely positive. Feedback from students is obtained as part of the quality assurance procedures in King's Inns. Each year the dean presents a report which is then reviewed by the Development Committee of King's Inns. In general, the students consider the course to be challenging but practical, enjoyable and worthwhile.

MODULAR DEGREE COURSE

When King's Inns introduced the new full-time vocational course in 2004, it made a commitment to consider the provision of the course on a part-time or modular basis to facilitate those persons who wished to study for the bar while continuing to work. Historically, a significant number of people working in the public service and in private employment qualified as barristers. The prior degree course delivered in the late afternoons over two years had facilitated this.

Following careful examination of how the new vocational course could be delivered in a manner consistent with its core objectives to those who wished to take it outside of normal working hours, it was decided to deliver it on a modular basis at week-ends. Students are required to attend over two full days, Saturday and Sunday, approximately every third weekend during the academic year. At the end of the relevant year, both the full-time and second-year modular students take the same assessments. The first modular course commenced in October 2008. Of the 189 students commencing the vocational degree course that year, 75 opted to take it on a modular basis with the remaining 114 taking it on a full-time basis. The number of modular students commencing in 2008 was higher than in subsequent years, probably as the start of a modular course had been flagged and some students were waiting to commence once it became available. In subsequent years, the numbers commencing on the modular course have varied between thirty-eight and fifty-five, and in the same period those on the full-time course between 107 and 160. The first modular students qualified as barristers in July 2010 and in general the results of modular students have been consistent with those of the full-time students.

STUDENT NUMBERS AND PROFILE

In addition to the radical change in the nature of the degree course since 1988, there has been a dramatic increase in the number of persons taking the course each year and a significant change in the gender profile of the classes. This is demonstrated by a comparison of those admitted as barristers in the three years 1986–88 with those qualifying in the three years 2010–12, as recorded by the registrar of King's Inns (see Table 1).

Table 1. Call to the bar 1986–88/2010–12[7]

	Male		Female		Total	
	No.	%	No.	%	No.	%
1986	96	68	46	32	142	100
1987	95	68	44	32	139	100
1988	63	62	39	38	102	100
Total 1986–88	254	66	129	34	383	100
2010	113	55	93	45	206	100
2011	114	60	76	40	190	100
2012	110	56	88	44	198	100
Total 2010–12	337	57	257	43	594	100

Over the three year period 1986–8 the total number called to the bar was 383 of which 129 (34 per cent) were female.

Over the three year period 2010–12 the total number called to the bar was 594 of which 257 (43 per cent) were female.

There was an increase of 55 per cent in the total number called to the bar in the 2010-12 period compared with 1986–8. The total number of males called to the bar increased by 33 per cent and the total number of females increased by 99 per cent in the 2010–12 period compared with 1986–8.

The significant increase each year in the total numbers taking the King's Inns degree course and qualifying as barristers and, in particular, the increase in the number of women has caused a dramatic increase in the practising bar and change in its gender profile over the twenty-five years since 1988 (see Table 2).

7 Source: Registrar of King's Inns.

Table 2. Members of the Law Library

	Total	Male No. %	Female No. %	Senior Counsel	Male Senior Counsel No. %	Female Senior Counsel No. %
October 1988[8]	722	566 78	156 22	104	100 96	4 4
January 2013[9]	2302	1382 60	920 40	321	271 84	50 16
Increase	1580	916	764	217	171	46
% Increase	219%	162%	490%	209%	171%	1150%

In 1988, the members of the Law Library were 78 per cent male and 22 per cent female. In 2013 they are 60 per cent male and 40 per cent female.

In 1988, 96 per cent of the senior counsel were male and 4 per cent female. In 2013 84 per cent are male and 16 per cent are female.

The total membership has increased by 219 per cent since 1988 and the female members by 490 per cent.

The number of female senior counsel has increased by 1150 per cent as compared with 1988!

Commentary on the effect of the above increases and change in profile of the practising bar is beyond the scope of this article.

THE DIPLOMA IN LEGAL STUDIES

In 2006, the council of King's Inns appointed a further working group under the chairmanship of Paul Gallagher SC, to review the Diploma in Legal Studies.[10] The principal conclusion of the Gallagher working group was that the focus or objective of the diploma should continue to be to enable the students to acquire the knowledge and understanding of substantive law appropriate for both practice at the bar and to equip

---

8   Source: Ivana Bacik, Cathryn Costello and Eileen Drew, *Gender in justice: feminising the legal professions* (Dublin, 2003), p. 72.
9   Source: Bar Council.
10 The members of the working group comprised Conor J. Maguire SC, Ms Justice Mary Finlay Geoghegan and Ms Justice Elizabeth Dunne, Brian Murray SC, Maurice Collins SC, Professor Tom O'Malley BL and Dean Sarah Macdonald.

them to participate fully in the vocational course leading to admission to the degree of barrister-at-law. It also recommended that a secondary objective should be to enable those students who do not ultimately wish to pursue a professional legal qualification, to obtain, through the diploma, a knowledge and understanding of substantive law and legal skills which would be of use in employment in the public service, private sector or in the provision of services. It also made detailed recommendations on the delivery of the diploma teaching and, in particular, that there should be an increased emphasis on seminar/tutorials in small groups and self-directed learning.

In implementation of the Gallagher working group recommendations, the council of King's Inns appointed Dr Eimear Brown as the diploma co-ordinator. She has comprehensively implemented the recommendations of the Gallagher group, resulting in an enhancement in the teaching methods and quality of the diploma course in recent years. In the present economic climate and with the increased availability of other post-graduate law courses, King's Inns faces competition and challenge in the delivery of this course. In my view, the quality of the course and its particular focus on the teaching of substantive law in a manner appropriate for those intending to practise at the bar will ensure its continued success.

The developments outlined above have been achieved by the creation of a law school within King's Inns with both full-time and part-time persons employed. The law school team is presently led by its dean, Mary Faulkner, and the registrar, Marcella Higgins, and includes course coordinators, a large panel of teaching staff drawn from practising barristers and administrative support staff. The increase in numbers of students and their full time presence in the Inns have required an enhancement of facilities and library, IT and ancillary services. The society's under treasurer, Camilla McAleese, achieved a remarkable transformation of No. 11 Henrietta Street for educational use. Similarly, the librarian Jonathan Armstrong and his assistants combine with great skill up-to-date student library services with the preservation of the historical library of King's Inns. The IT services available to students, both as part of library services and in the delivery of the courses, are continually updated.

The focus of all working in the law school is the continued development of King's Inns as a centre of excellence for the delivery of professional legal education. In recent years, there have also been developments beyond the core degree and diploma courses. I propose briefly mentioning three of these.

IRISH LANGUAGE EDUCATION

King's Inns has introduced courses relating to the use of the Irish language in the practice of law or related work. Since 2008, the society provides, as part of the vocational degree course, a course of instruction in Irish legal terminology and the understanding of legal texts in the Irish language pursuant to its obligations under the Legal Practitioners (Irish Language) Act 2008.[11] In addition, degree students have the option of the advanced Irish language course. The Legal Practitioners (Irish Language) Act 2008 repealed the Legal Practitioners (Qualification) Act 1929, which had required the chief justice to be satisfied that a person (with certain exemptions) possessed 'a competent knowledge of the Irish language' prior to calling such person to the bar. In practice, this was done by an examination administered by a person nominated by the chief justice and facilitated by the society. That examination has now ceased.

Further, King's Inns, with financial support from the Department of Arts, Heritage and the Gaeltacht, since 2010, delivers three advanced diploma courses through the medium of Irish. These are,

i. Ard-Dioplóma sa Dlítheangeolaíocht agus san Aistriúchán Dlíthiúil (Advanced Diploma in Lawyer-Linguistics and Legal Translation)
ii. Ard-Dioplóma san Aistriúchán Dlíthiúil (Advanced Diploma in Legal Translation)
iii. Ard-Dioplóma sa Dlí-Chleachtadh trí Ghaeilge (Advanced Diploma in Legal Practice through Irish)

The need for such courses was prompted by the fact that on 1 January 2007 Irish became a co-official language of the European Union. This created opportunities within the EU institutions for Irish-language speakers but there has been a shortage of legal translators and lawyer-linguists with Irish as their primary language. The primary purpose of the lawyer-linguist and legal translation courses offered by the society are to provide students with an opportunity of qualifying for potential EU posts. However, the diplomas are also of benefit to people who wish to pursue employment as translators in Ireland. In 2011 and 2012 a total of twenty-two persons have graduated with the advanced diploma in lawyer-linguistics and legal translation or in legal translation.

---

11 See s. 1(3)(a) of the Legal Practitioners (Irish Language) Act 2008.

In 2011/2012, King's Inns delivered the first course leading to the advanced diploma in legal practice through Irish. The course is open to legal practitioners who have completed the lawyer-linguistics course. There were twelve participants on the course, eleven of whom were members of the Law Library. Two of the participants have since taken up Irish language positions in the EU institutions.

SPECIALISED COURSES

King's Inns has commenced the delivery of a series of advanced diploma courses in specialist areas of relevance to practising lawyers and to those working in the public and private sectors. The first of these was an advanced diploma in legislative drafting. The need for such a course in Ireland had long been discussed. This is a unique part-time evening course offering legal practitioners, law graduates and persons with relevant legislative drafting experience the opportunity to train in the skill of drafting legislation and regulations. It is delivered through the medium of seminars, workshops and lectures presented by leading experts in the area. The course was developed and designed with support from successive attorneys general and in conjunction with the Parliamentary Draftsman's Office. Those participating in the course include civil servants from a variety of departments and practicing barristers and solicitors. Places on each course are limited by reason of the workshop format. Three successful programmes have now been completed with a total of forty-two persons graduating.

The most recent diploma course introduced in King's Inns is an advanced diploma in corporate, white collar and regulatory crime. This is a twenty-week evening diploma course delivered by practitioners. The lead lecturer is Shelley Horan BL, with the benefit of an advisory panel of Patrick Gageby SC, Shane Murphy SC and Remy Farrell SC, who also, with other practitioners, have participated as guest lecturers on the course. It was launched by the director of public prosecutions, Claire Loftus, in February 2012. Sixty-four persons graduated from the first course and sixty-one are taking the current course. The primary aim of the programme is to provide participants with a comprehensive practical knowledge of the issues facing the prosecution and defence, investigators, sentencing bodies, public/private sector interests and law reformers. The numbers participating indicate a keen interest in the topics and issues treated.

CONCLUSION

Since my election as a bencher in 1996, I have been involved in education in King's Inns. I participated as a member of each of the Shanley, Gleeson and Gallagher working groups and chaired the implementation committee for the new Vocational Course in 2004. I currently chair the development committee of the Law School in King's Inns. The views expressed in this article are inevitably subjective.

It is my belief, nonetheless, that there has been a radical change for the better to the education delivered by King's Inns over the past twenty-five years. During the period, a professional full-time law school has been established. There is now a clear delineation between the academic study of substantive law which may be pursued in multiple institutions and the subsequent professional course in King's Inns building on that and primarily providing training in the essential skills required of a person commencing practice at the bar in Ireland.

There is, of course, no room for complacency. The maintenance of King's Inns as a centre of excellence for the delivery of professional legal education faces many challenges, particularly in the context of the Legal Services Regulation Bill 2011. King's Inns continues to review and develop the education and training provided, bearing in mind its long tradition and history, but focused on the requirements of legal practice in the twenty-first century.

As a footnote, those who were students in King's Inns may be glad to learn that the tradition of student dining remains but with changes. Twice a term, benchers dine at tables with students. Benchers are sufficiently delusionary to believe that the students enjoy and benefit from this interaction!

The regulation and education of the solicitors' profession in Northern Ireland, 1976–2012

ALAN HEWITT

To understand the significance of 1976 as the starting point of this account, it is necessary first to look briefly at the previous history of the regulation of the solicitors' profession in Northern Ireland.

The Government of Ireland Act 1920[1] – the legislative basis of the partition of Ireland – received the Royal Assent on 23 December 1920 and came into effect on 1 May 1921. The state opening of the first parliament of Northern Ireland by King George V took place on 22 June 1921.

The 1920 Act created separate parliaments and supreme courts of judicature for Northern and Southern Ireland. However, the Treaty gave Ireland the same status within the British Empire as the Dominions of Canada and New Zealand, the Commonwealth of Australia and the Union of South Africa and, in the event of Northern Ireland refusing to join the new Irish Free State in this arrangement (which in retrospect was inevitable), provided for a boundary commission. This commission did not meet until 1924 and its intended findings were never officially published. Apparently these would have been that no changes should be made except the addition of a small part of County Donegal to the six counties of Antrim, Armagh, Down, Fermanagh, Londonderry and Tyrone that constitute Northern Ireland. Instead, a deal was struck whereby, in exchange for the abolition of the boundary commission, the financial obligations of the Irish Free State to Britain under the Treaty were revoked.

The 1920 Act also provided that from the appointed day (1 October 1921), solicitors of the supreme court of judicature in Ireland should automatically become solicitors of the supreme courts of both Northern Ireland and Southern Ireland, but that thereafter (with an exception for apprentices who were in articles at the time) new solicitors were to be

---

1 10 & 11 Geo. V, c.67.

entitled to practise only in that part of Ireland in which they had qualified.

Prior to partition, solicitors in both parts of Ireland had been regulated by the Incorporated Law Society of Ireland. That society had fought a long battle in the nineteenth century to achieve independence from the Society of King's Inns, to which attorneys and solicitors as well as barristers were obliged to subscribe. A landmark in this battle was the Attorneys and Solicitors (Ireland) Act 1866,[2] which,

> consolidated the existing laws on the admission of solicitors and on the regulation of the profession, but changed them in certain respects, most importantly by providing that after its passing no fees other than those authorised therein (payable to the Law Society as examination fees) were to be payable by any person seeking to be bound as an apprentice or to be admitted and enrolled as a solicitor. This meant that membership of, and payment of fees to, the Society of King's Inns would no longer be a condition of admission as a solicitor.
>
> Similarly, responsibility for the education of apprentices was ... conferred upon the Law Society, acting with the consent of the Judges, terminating the Benchers' responsibility. The Law Society [was] appointed as registrar of attorneys and solicitors to work in conjunction with the registrars of each of the separate Courts of Common Law and the Court of Chancery.[3]

The regulatory functions of the Incorporated Law Society of Ireland were substantially increased by the Solicitors (Ireland) Act 1898, which repealed the 1866 Act and transferred control of education and important disciplinary functions from the direct supervision of the judges to that of the Society.

THE NORTHERN LAW CLUB

At the time of partition, the only organisation existing specifically for the benefit of solicitors in the northern counties of Ireland was the Northern Law Society, formed as 'The Northern Law Club' in 1861. It had changed its name to 'The Northern Law Society' in 1876 and was

---

2   29 & 30 Vict., c.84.
3   Daire Hogan, *The legal profession in Ireland, 1789–1922* (Dublin, 1986), p. 122.

incorporated in 1911.[4] This society had no statutory or regulatory powers; membership was optional and in practice was drawn mainly from solicitors practising in Belfast and Counties Antrim and Down. Its stated objectives were,

> to watch proposed changes, either by Parliamentary enactment, or regulations of the Courts of Law or Equity, affecting the practice, privileges and emoluments of the Profession of Attorney and Solicitor; and in conjunction with other Societies, to oppose or promote them as may be advantageous, by its intervention, when necessary to sustain the rights and respectability of the Profession; to prevent or adjust professional differences and by social intercourse, to promote good feeling and harmonious action amongst its Members; and generally to undertake or assist in such objectives as may appear to be conducive to the interests of the Profession or the Society.

There was a strong social element in the Northern Law Society's activities, but undoubtedly its formation also reflected a genuine desire to see the status and standards of the solicitors' profession enhanced. It sought constantly to prevent unqualified and unsuitable people from attempting to act for the public in areas of work that solicitors considered to be their exclusive territory, and it pressed for the appointment of solicitors to judicial and public office. By the early years of the twentieth century it had also established an impressive library. This was good enough to attract the attention of northern barristers, but the Committee of the Society resolved in 1907 that 'it would be inadvisable to extend the privileges of the Library to the Local Bar'.

In common with the other representative bodies in England and Ireland the Northern Law Society protested for many years about the much-resented solicitors' licence duties exacted by the Chancellor of the Exchequer. And, of course, it agitated for better fees.

The scope for the Northern Law Society, as a voluntary regional organisation with no statutory powers, to change the way in which the profession operated was fairly limited, but it applied itself enthusiastically to the task. Its relationship with the Incorporated Law Society of Ireland was usually cordial, and it assisted the governing body on many occasions. For example, it joined in deputations to London in 1863, 1866, 1867 and 1888, the first two sorties ending successfully with the

---

4 For a fuller account of the society, see Alan Hewitt, *The Law Society of Northern Ireland: a history* (Belfast, 2010), pp 11–22.

enactment of the Conveyancers (Ireland) Act 1864[5] and the Attorneys and Solicitors (Ireland) Act 1866[6] respectively, the last two less successfully when a couple of the many attempts to have the certificate duty abolished failed. However, like their counterparts in Cork, the northern apprentices and solicitors regularly complained about the inconvenience of having to travel to Dublin for lectures and court hearings.

BIRTH OF THE LAW SOCIETY OF NORTHERN IRELAND

With the advent of the new constitutional arrangements the Northern Law Society decided to take steps to acquire for a new body the same powers in relation to solicitors in Northern Ireland as the Incorporated Law Society of Ireland had until then exercised for the whole of Ireland.

On 25 February 1922 a Royal Charter was granted establishing 'The Incorporated Law Society of Northern Ireland' (which for convenience is referred to hereafter as 'LSNI'). The word 'incorporated' would be dropped from the title in 1982, when a supplementary charter was granted. The 1922 charter appointed Samuel G. Crymble (who at the time was the president of the Northern Law Society) as the first president, John McKee and Samuel Ross as the first vice-presidents and eighteen other council members, to hold office until the first general meeting of the new society. All of them had been officers or committee members of the Northern Law Society immediately prior to the grant of the Royal Charter.

The charter, although granted in February, was not actually enrolled until 12 September 1922 and the first official meeting of LSNI's Council took place on that day, but it is obvious from the minutes that the council members had been busy making preparations in the intervening months. In particular, they had arranged for the presentation to the new parliament of a Solicitors Bill giving effect in Northern Ireland to the Solicitors (Ireland) Act 1898, with appropriate amendments. It was reported at the council meeting on 24 October 1922 that the Bill had been passed that day without amendment, becoming the Solicitors Act (Northern Ireland) 1922.[7] The Act consisted of a mere six sections and for the most part simply replaced the references in the 1898 Act to the Incorporated Law Society of

---

5 27 Vict., c.8.   6 29 & 30 Vict., c.84.   7 12 & 13 Geo. V, c.19.

Ireland, the judges of the supreme court of Ireland, the benchers of the King's Inns, *et al.* with references to the Incorporated Law Society of Northern Ireland, the supreme court of judicature of Northern Ireland, the judiciary of Northern Ireland, and so on. All regulations and rules in force under the 1898 Act, as amended by the 1922 Act, continued in force for the time being. The society's powers included the power of making regulations for the completion of articles by those apprentices of solicitors practising in Northern Ireland who had already been in articles at the date of commencement of the Act. The rule-making authority became the lord chief justice of Northern Ireland, acting with any one of the president of the Incorporated Law Society of Northern Ireland and a judge of the supreme court of Northern Ireland.

One of the chief concerns of the council in the early days of LSNI's existence was to establish an admission procedure for those now urgently seeking to enter the profession. A deputation visited the formidable Dr R.M. Jones, principal of the Royal Belfast Academical Institution, to discuss the appointment of examiners for the society's preliminary examination in English subjects, Latin, Mathematics and French. The requirement to pass the preliminary examination was waived in 1928 for the holders of any degree (other than an honorary degree) from any university in Great Britain, Northern Ireland or the Irish Free State. In 1932 it was also waived for anyone holding the Senior School Leaving Certificate, provided that credit marks had been obtained in English, Latin and History and that the candidate had also passed in Elementary Mathematics and one other subject.

As well as its preliminary examination, the society organised intermediate and final examinations in law for apprentices. The apprenticeship period was four years, shortened to three for those holding BA, MA, LL.B or LL.D degrees from any university in England, Scotland, Wales or Ireland recognised by LSNI's regulations. A proposal in 1928 that the period be similarly shortened for the holders of *any* degree from those universities was rejected by the Council.

THE SOLICITORS ACT (NORTHERN IRELAND) 1938

The most significant event for LSNI in the years between the two world wars was the enactment of the Solicitors Act (Northern Ireland) 1938,[8] which came into effect on 1 January 1939. Broadly speaking, the 1922 Act had made only sufficient modifications to the 1898 Act to make the

---

8   2 Geo. VI, c.14.

latter operable in Northern Ireland after partition. The 1938 Act finetuned the existing disciplinary procedures and added to LSNI's disciplinary powers. It established a Disciplinary Committee, appointed by the lord chief justice from among members and former members of Council, whose findings would be forwarded to the lord chief justice in cases where it was considered that striking off or suspension was the appropriate sanction; the committee itself could only censure or impose fines of up to £100, plus costs, although even this was an advance.

After the 1938 Act (surprisingly, for the first time), a solicitor who had been adjudicated bankrupt could no longer practise until permitted by the lord chief justice. Section 43, supplementing earlier prohibitions of unqualified conveyancers, provided that (subject to minor exceptions) it would be an offence for any person other than a barrister or solicitor holding a practising certificate to prepare any document for the purposes of registration of title. Section 44 introduced a similar monopoly in probate matters, and Section 45 made it an offence for a solicitor to share profits or fees with a non-solicitor.

Section 33 of the 1938 Act empowered LSNI to make new accounting regulations; this had long been overdue, although the regulations which were adopted pursuant to the Act seem rudimentary to modern eyes. They provided, first, that every solicitor should keep such books and accounts as might be necessary to show all moneys received for or on account of and all moneys paid to or on account of each of his clients, and second, that he should, at least once in each year, prepare such balance sheet and statement as would show in summary form all moneys held for or on account of each of his clients and where, at that date, the moneys were held. While this was a considerable improvement on the previous position, until 1976 it was the practice of LSNI simply to write to each firm once a year asking it to certify (that is, self-certify) that it had complied with the society's accounts regulations. Only if something untoward had come to its attention did LSNI ask for accountants' reports or the production of documents and accounts. Moreover, the regulations did not require solicitors to keep a *separate* client account.

THE SOLICITORS (NORTHERN IRELAND) ORDER 1976

The 1938 Act was a considerable step forward, but fell far short of giving LSNI all the powers it wanted. It was to be another thirty-eight years before the next significant advance – the Solicitors (Northern

Ireland) Order 1976, which remains the most important of all modern statutes relating to the profession in Northern Ireland. This Order had an extraordinarily long gestation period. In November 1955 the then president, Henry Maginness, informed a general meeting of LSNI that the council intended to present a Bill to parliament giving LSNI 'additional powers to deal with accounts regulations, a Compensation Fund, the admission of apprentices, the professional conduct of members of the profession and other matters.' However, the Bill ran into difficulty, particularly with the then lord chief justice, Lord MacDermott, and at a meeting of the council over a decade later, in April 1969, it was pointed out that the draft Bill, which was about to be presented to parliament again, had never been seen by roughly a quarter of the profession who had qualified since 1960, and should therefore be circulated to them together with the new draft accounts regulations which it was intended to bring in as soon as the Bill had been passed. However the Bill was again overtaken by events, LSNI's annual report for 1970/71 recording that 'the redrafting of the new Solicitors Bill was completed in June 1971, when it was discovered that the Law Society [of England and Wales] was preparing to bring a Bill amending the English Solicitors Acts before parliament in the autumn.' As LSNI did not want to miss the opportunity of incorporating in the Northern Ireland Bill any provisions of the English Bill that might prove advantageous, the matter was again postponed. A 'Solicitors Measure' was eventually introduced to the Northern Ireland Assembly in 1974, and had actually passed the first three of its four stages, but the day before it was due to pass the fourth and final stage the Executive resigned in the wake of the Ulster Workers' Strike and the assembly was prorogued. It was announced that a new Order in Council was to be prepared for passage at Westminster, but it must have seemed to everyone involved that the proposed legislation was blighted.

However, despite this sorry sequence of events, the president of LSNI was able to report to the AGM in 1975 that the council had approved government amendments to the draft Order providing for the appointment of a Lay Observer and for compulsory professional indemnity insurance and enabling *all* solicitors to be able to exercise the powers of commissioners for oaths – these changes mirrored provisions in the Solicitors Act 1974 applying to England and Wales, and to that extent some of the extraordinary delay may have been worthwhile. Finally, and no doubt to the astonishment and relief of all, LSNI's Annual Report for 1975-6 was able to record that the Solicitors (Northern Ireland) Order 1976 had come into effect on 1 September

1976, that draft Accounts, Compensation Fund and Practising Certificate regulations had been prepared by LSNI for approval by the lord chief justice and that a compulsory professional indemnity insurance scheme was under consideration. The regulations were soon approved and promulgated, and a vastly better structure for the regulation of the profession, which had taken a mere twenty-one years to achieve, was at last in place.

Despite its late arrival, the 1976 Order effected fundamental changes, and although it was updated in 1989, with a few significant additions, it is still the basis on which the profession is regulated today.[9] The 1976 Order also, at last, repealed in its entirety what was left of the 1898 Act.

LSNI's regulatory powers were greatly enhanced by the 1976 Order. Article 6 provided that 'the Society may, with the concurrence of the lord chief justice, make such regulations as they think proper with respect to the education, training, qualifications, conduct, experience and control of persons seeking admission as solicitors', and Article 26 (1) that 'the Society may make regulations as to the professional practice, conduct or discipline of solicitors'.

The Order also gave LSNI important powers to deal with property in the control of solicitors, their partners and employees. Article 36 (1) provides that where LSNI has reasonable cause to believe that a solicitor or 'his' employee has been guilty of dishonesty in connection with his practice or any trust of which he is a trustee, or that there has been any undue delay or (and perhaps most importantly) that any sum of money due from the solicitor or his firm to, or held by him or his firm on behalf of, his clients or subject to any trust of which he is a sole trustee or co-trustee is in jeopardy while in the control of the solicitor or his firm, and the council passes a resolution to that effect, the provisions of Schedule 1 to the Order apply to that solicitor. In the years since 1976 these provisions have become a vital tool in the hands of the Society. Schedule 1 also applies automatically to any solicitor who is adjudicated bankrupt, or enters into arrangements with his creditors, or has money judgments made against him, or has become mentally or physically incapable of carrying on practice. It can also be applied where the council has resolved that it is satisfied that the solicitor has failed to comply with accounts regulations.

Schedule 1 is extremely wide-ranging. When applied to a solicitor, it gives LSNI the ability to control not only clients' money and property

9 Solicitors (Northern Ireland) Order (S.I. 1976, no. 582); Solicitors (Amendment) (Northern Ireland) Order (1989, no. 1343, N.I. 14).

in the possession of the solicitor, but also the solicitor's own property and money. If necessary, LSNI may apply to a judge of the high court for an order requiring compliance with LSNI's directions, appointing LSNI the attorney of the solicitor and/or preventing payments being made by banks or others out of moneys emanating from the solicitor. If appointed attorney, LSNI may itself operate the solicitor's bank accounts, take possession of or recover property, sell property and assets, and has the power 'generally to act in relation to the solicitor's practice and estate as fully and effectively as the solicitor could do'.[10]

There were also significant advances in accounting requirements, the 1976 Order empowering LSNI to make regulations, which it did immediately, requiring that separate client and office accounts be kept and that clients' money be held on deposit. Each firm was also required, for the first time, to deliver an accountant's report to LSNI annually. It seems astonishing in retrospect that some of these requirements had not existed before. Since 1976 the accounting rules have been strengthened continually, and in addition to the annual accountant's report, LSNI's own accountancy staff now makes inspection of each firm's accounts at least once every two to three years, and more often if it seems necessary – one of the advantages of regulating in a comparatively small jurisdiction.

The 1976 Order completely revamped the conduct of serious disciplinary matters. LSNI itself was given responsibility for the initial handling of all complaints against solicitors, which it did mainly through two of its committees, the Professional Conduct Committee (now the Client Complaints Committee) and the Professional Ethics and Guidance Committee. It was empowered to issue directions to solicitors and – in cases where unsatisfactory service had been provided – to order that costs be reduced or waived. However, the Order still did not enable LSNI to impose the ultimate sanctions of suspension from practice or striking off. Those powers were reserved to a new body, the Disciplinary Committee (now the Solicitors Disciplinary Tribunal). This consisted originally of not less than five nor more than twelve persons appointed by the lord chief justice, after consultation with the council, from among practising solicitors of not less than ten years' standing. The amending Order of 1989 added a requirement to have lay members, and removed the numerical restrictions, although three members must be present, at least one of whom is a lay member; the president of the tribunal must be a solicitor and the number of solicitor members present must exceed the number of lay members present.

10 Solicitors (Northern Ireland) Order 1976, Schedule 2, Part II, Para. 21.

All complaints were still made to LSNI in the first instance, but cases appearing to merit the more serious sanctions were referred by LSNI to the tribunal. Despite all efforts to remove confusion, LSNI still struggles with the inability of the public at large to grasp that the tribunal is a statutory body quite distinct from LSNI, especially when the tribunal's decisions are not to everyone's liking.

The Order of 1976 also opened the way for the establishment of both a Compensation Fund to which practitioners were required to contribute, so providing a fund for clients who suffer as a result of their solicitor's default, and also the 'Master Policy' of professional indemnity insurance, which compulsorily covers the entire profession in Northern Ireland. Before 1976 around one-third of the profession in Northern Ireland had no professional indemnity insurance. These two developments provided a powerful boost to the profession's claim to be relatively risk-free from a client's point of view. The benefits of the Master Policy have also proved extremely advantageous to practitioners, despite escalating premiums: the unfortunate experiences in recent years of solicitors in England and Wales and in the Republic of Ireland, whose regulators left them to find their own insurance cover, has been striking.

Article 42 of the Order provided also for the appointment of one or more lay observers (in practice there has never been more than one at any one time), who were to make annual reports to the lord chief justice, the head of the Department of Finance and the council 'on the nature of complaints being made to the Society about the conduct of solicitors and the manner in which the complaints are being dealt with by the Society'. The amending Order of 1989 added the duty to 'examine any written allegation made by or on behalf of a member of the public concerning the society's treatment of a complaint about a solicitor or an employee of a solicitor'. The Lay Observer's annual reports have provided a plethora of statistics and analyses over the years; for the most part they have been reasonably complimentary about LSNI's treatment of complaints, while consistently suggesting refinements and improvements, and they have undoubtedly helped to keep LSNI on its toes, as have the regular meetings between the Lay Observer and LSNI's officers and staff. Often what has been required has been to let justice be seen to be done rather than to remedy any actual failure of justice; public perception is always vitally important where self-regulation is concerned.

THE INSTITUTE OF PROFESSIONAL LEGAL STUDIES

The year 1976 was a momentous one for the solicitors' profession in Northern Ireland, not only because of the 1976 Order but also because it saw the first significant change in the apprenticeship system in the twentieth century. Although LSNI had taken over the administration of the system from the Incorporated Law Society of Ireland in 1922 (after which apprentices no longer had to travel to Dublin for lectures), and a university degree in law became the norm in 1951, the basics had remained unchanged for decades: a three-year apprenticeship (for graduates), the entirety of which was spent by the apprentice in his master's office, apart from the occasional escape to courts, court offices and registries or to the lectures provided on a few afternoons each week by LSNI's part-time lecturers; and an examination at the end of each summer term. The system had its strengths: if a master was able and conscientious, the method of learning by imitation had much to commend it, and some at least of the lecturers were very good indeed and had a very practical grasp of their subjects – others were not, and practitioners of my own vintage will remember without affection the uninspiring venue for the lectures, in the old consultation rooms at the Royal Courts of Justice in Belfast, with competing traffic noise from May Street.

Nor was entry to the profession restricted to the wealthy: grants were available for university courses, and the practice of firms charging for articles finally died out in the 1960s. Apprentices were rarely well-paid, but it was possible to make ends meet.

However, there were clearly several deficiencies in the system, and in 1972 the then Minister of Education for Northern Ireland appointed a committee under the chairmanship of Professor A.L. Armitage, Vice-Chancellor of Manchester University, to consider and make recommendations upon (a) education and training for professional qualifications in the two branches of the legal profession in Northern Ireland and (b) the additional resources which would be needed to implement those recommendations. The Armitage Report was published in September 1973.[11] It identified the basic problem, rather starkly, as being 'the almost complete lack of any satisfactory form of direct professional training'. The main deterrent to the provision of such training, it considered, was 'the small number of students – which makes the cost of running comprehensive courses prohibitive – the lack

---

11 *Report of the Committee on Legal Education in Northern Ireland* (Cmnd. 579, HMSO, 1973).

of accommodation, the lack of suitable library facilities and textbooks on Northern Ireland law and practice ... and the lack of professionally qualified teachers'.[12]

The report recommended that education for both branches of the profession should be in three stages – academic, professional and continuing. The academic requirement should normally be a recognised law degree. Queen's University Belfast should 'continue to be the home of the only law school in Northern Ireland and should provide also the professional course'.[13] The (one-year) vocational courses for both branches of the profession should be provided by Queen's through an Institute of Professional Legal Studies situated near to the law faculty and the university library. The governing body of the institute, the Council of Legal Education (Northern Ireland), should reflect the interests of all parties concerned, that is, the two branches of the profession and Queen's. There were detailed recommendations about the content of the common vocational course, which should be followed by 'in-training appropriate to each branch of the profession'. Courses of continuing education should be provided at the institute and be self-financing. Crucially, each branch of the profession should retain control over entry, and 'the only means of financing the Institute would be by an ear-marked initial capital grant for its establishment, such grants to be payable by the Government to the University.'[14]

The need for legal reference works and textbooks on Northern Ireland law and procedure should be met and would require assistance from central funds. Not least, the report maintained, 'the success of any system of professional legal education requires an adequate system of grants to students to ensure that the profession is open to all ... the continuance of the support by way of awards for the mandatory professional year will ensure this.'[15]

Given the fairly revolutionary nature of the proposals, the ensuing process from receipt of the report by the government in June 1973 to implementation was handled with what might almost pass for expedition, and with relatively little divergence from the Armitage recommendations. The Council of Legal Education, representative of LSNI, the Northern Ireland Bar and Queen's University and chaired by the lord chief justice or his nominee, was established by a statute of the university. The first director of the Institute of Professional Legal Studies, James Elliott, was appointed in 1976.[16] The institute opened its

12 Ibid., para. 24.   13 Ibid., para. 66.   14 Ibid., para. 105.   15 Ibid., para. 94.
16 His successors as director have been James Russell (1982–86), Mary McAleese (1987–97) who was subsequently elected President of Ireland, and Anne Fenton.

doors to prospective solicitors and barristers in September 1977 in an old building in Upper Crescent in Belfast, close to the university: those who had to work there would probably agree with one writer that 'the accommodation was appalling and the surroundings not conducive to study'[17] and it eventually relocated to much better premises owned by the University in Lennoxvale, an avenue off Belfast's Malone Road, where it remains today after refurbishment and extension in 2001.

The Institute immediately ran into problems. It had initial capacity for seventy trainees (solicitors and barristers), but even in the first year there were over one hundred applications for places. It was decided by LSNI's council that this was unfair to those who had embarked on their university courses in the expectation of entering into an old-style apprenticeship, and accordingly it authorised a transitional apprenticeship scheme available only to those who had commenced their university studies in the years 1973 to 1975 and who had applied for and failed to obtain a place at the institute. This extension in turn proved insufficient, and a series of reprieves were given to the old-fashioned apprenticeship; the old and new systems existed side by side, somewhat uneasily, until the last of the old-style apprentices qualified in 1986.

In 1979, the Royal Commission on Legal Services (of which more later) reported and, *inter alia*, while commenting favourably on the provision of professional legal education in Northern Ireland, recommended a review after three years' operation of the institute. The review took somewhat longer than that to get under way, but in 1983 the government appointed a committee under the chairmanship of Professor Peter Bromley of the law faculty at Manchester University to carry it out. The Bromley Report was published in 1985. It concluded that the institute had 'broadly fulfilled the objectives set out in the Armitage Report', and that with very few exceptions (notably for clerks with seven years' experience) the institute should henceforth be the only route for entering the profession. However, the report noted that there was one marked difference between its recommendations and those of Armitage: 'Experience has shown that training at an institute cannot replace training on the job. ... we believe that it is of the utmost importance that training at an institute and training in practice should be more closely integrated'.[18]

The report recommended that, to this end, each student seeking admission to the Institute should first register with LSNI as an

17 Ray MacManais, *The road from Ardoyne* (Brandon, 2004), p. 253.
18 Report of the Committee on Professional Legal Education in Northern Ireland (The Bromley Report), (HMSO, 1985), p. 3.

apprentice and that intending solicitors should be apprenticed for two years; they should spend the first three months of their apprenticeship in their masters' offices, the whole of the next twelve months at the institute and the final nine months back in the office. They should maintain close links with their offices throughout their time at the institute and should return there during institute holidays. One other significant recommendation was that instead of admission criteria being based only on academic qualifications there should be a written test to assess the candidates' ability to apply their knowledge of the law. This resulted in the controversial 'aptitude test', which remains the subject of much debate and diverse opinions.

After considerable discussion, the Bromley recommendations were accepted and implemented by the society and the institute. In an effort to ensure closer correlation between theory and practice, practising solicitors were appointed as consultants for several of the institute's courses, and some tutors were also recruited from the profession's ranks.

The years since Bromley have seen enormous changes both in the profession and in Northern Ireland generally. The easing of the Troubles and a return to a more normal society had several effects: as confidence rose and (until the recession of 2007 onwards) prosperity increased, not only was there an apparently ever-increasing demand for legal services, but also many of Northern Ireland's best young people were prepared to try practice there rather than in London or elsewhere. The demand for places at the institute grew exponentially: the hundred or so applications in the first year eventually rose to well over five hundred a year. This had a number of effects: first, the number of bursaries offered by the Department of Education (now, sadly, discontinued altogether) failed to keep pace, so that many students had to find their own funding; second, many applicants with excellent qualifications were inevitably disappointed; and thirdly, the University of Ulster entered the professional training field with its Graduate School of Professional Legal Education ('GSPLE'), which opened at the university's Magee campus in Londonderry in 2008. Currently, the institute offers 120 solicitor trainee places and thirty bar trainee places, while GSPLE offers twenty-eight solicitor places (but none for would-be barristers). A joint selection test is operated by the two bodies.

Perhaps even more striking than the increase in students generally has been the change in the ratio of women to men since the early 1980s. In 1977-8, the first year of the institute, only 19 per cent of its students were women; by 1993, this figure had risen to 64 per cent. In 2002 it was 72 per cent and in 2004 (the highest so far) 80 per cent. There have, of course, been fluctuations, but at no time in the last decade has the percentage of women students been less than 60 per cent, with an average in that period of 67 per cent.

In November 2007 the society began a major review of the training and qualification system. After wide-ranging consultation with all interested parties and much debate, final recommendations were approved in June 2012. They have not been implemented at the time of writing, but the main changes proposed are that:

1. All applicants for admission must possess either a degree in law containing stipulated core subjects or alternatively possess another acceptable degree and demonstrate an acceptable level of knowledge of the core subjects at degree level.
2. The alternative route to admission for experienced law clerks will be discontinued and the alternative route for exceptionally well-qualified candidates who do not meet all the normal requirements will continue to be allowed only in truly exceptional cases.
3. The approved providers of vocational training (at present IPLS and GSPLE) should ensure that the existing course content is expanded to include additional teaching on costs, taxation of costs and advocacy skills and to ensure that the core values of the profession 'are reflected and pervasive in all their teaching'.
4. The providers are also to have the option to offer part-time training. In such cases the full qualification period will be three-years rather than two, the training by the providers being spread over two years rather than one.
5. A new Plenary Council of Legal Education, supported by both branches of the profession, will be set up to supervise all vocational training providers.

LEGAL PUBLICATIONS

As already noted, the Armitage Report of 1973 had identified the lack of textbooks on Northern Ireland law and practice as one of the deficiencies in legal education, and for many years this remained a source of major frustration for trainees and solicitors alike. The small market for such publications and the improbability of profit made publishers extremely wary. While LSNI, from its earliest days, had tried to provide a decent library, books on English law always had to be read with great caution, as in many areas of law there were crucial differences between the two jurisdictions. LSNI had produced the *Northern Ireland Legal Quarterly* from 1943 to 1961. This was taken over, in turn, by Queen's University Belfast in 1964, by SLS (see below) in 1982 and by the School of Law of Queen's in 2008, becoming of an increasingly academic bent in the process. LSNI also produced its *Gazette* from 1950 until 1982, and has published *The Writ* since 1986, but neither of these journals, though practical and useful, lessened the need for textbooks. LSNI, to its credit, did manage to sponsor the production of a number of books, starting in 1956 with W.A. Leitch's *Handbook on the Administration of Estates Act (Northern Ireland), 1955*.[19] However, the real breakthrough in publications for Ulster lawyers came in 1980 with the advent of Servicing the Legal System ('SLS'). This company was a joint venture between Queen's University, LSNI, the Northern Ireland Bar and the Northern Ireland Court Service, with funding from the court service, LSNI and the bar. In the first few years there was also funding from the Nuffield Foundation and the Northern Ireland Bankers' Association.[20] After 1980 SLS produced a large number of excellent textbooks as well as the Bulletin of Northern Ireland Law (available online since 2002) and other periodicals.[21] LSNI's library has been developed to the point where it can hold its own with any professional library, and with the explosion in the availability and use of legal materials on the internet the legal publications scene in Northern Ireland has been transformed. As Heather Semple, LSNI's head of library and information services, wrote in 2006:

> So where does that leave us in Northern Ireland? Put simply – ahead of the rest of the U.K. Suddenly small is beautiful. In this jurisdiction there is a superb range of home-grown products for the Northern Ireland lawyer providing practitioners with complete legal portals. There are several reasons for this:
> - The proportionately smaller output of case law and legislation from the Courts and Government in Northern Ireland has

---

19 For a list of LSNI's publications see Hewitt, *Law Society*, p. 102.
20 Ibid., p. 103.
21 Ibid., pp 157–64 for a full list of SLS publications from 1980 to 2009. Sadly, as this book goes to print, news has been received of the demise of SLS. It is understood that one or two of its periodicals are being taken over by LSNI but that other publications, including the Bulletin, have ceased.

made the creation and updating of legal information portals manageable by smaller organisations and publishers. Libero (the database of the Law Society Northern Ireland library) and the Bulletin of Northern Ireland Law (published by SLS) are examples of non-commercial and commercial versions respectively ...

- A lack of bibliographical material in Northern Ireland created a willingness to embrace the internet as an alternative resource of publishing and accessing information. Northern Ireland was the first jurisdiction in the UK to introduce a Statute Law Database. The Statutory Publications Office launched The Updated Statutes of Northern Ireland in November 2002, creating a web-based set of primary Northern Ireland legislation in its revised form. Four years later, the GB version is still in preparation.
- The cost of these products can also be kept low. Some of the legal portals are partially or totally subsidised, and the commercial remainder are currently available at very attractive rates ... The size and makeup of the legal profession in this jurisdiction has made for easier marketing and awareness of economic products.[22]

GOVERNMENT INTERVENTION

In the thirty-seven years which have elapsed since the Solicitors (Northern Ireland) Order 1976, LSNI has taken a great many initiatives to improve its regulation of the profession and the quality of service provided by the profession to the public. For example, it established the Home Charter as a quality assurance scheme in conveyancing matters and promoted LEXCEL as a quality 'kitemark' for firms, it runs an annual advanced advocacy course, has encouraged and supported specialist groupings in environmental and planning law, employment law, corporate and commercial law and other areas, and, not least, has promoted a continuing professional development (CPD) scheme which now requires all solicitors to undertake a stipulated number of hours of study each year. It has actively promoted risk management and client care and has constantly improved and refined its client complaints and disciplinary procedures. However, as I somewhat mischievously said in my history of LSNI, 'despite the plethora of initiatives on the part of

---

22 Heather Semple, 'The online lawyer', *The Writ: Journal of the Law Society of Northern Ireland*, 172 (March 2006, 3–4), 3.

the Society ... the appetite of Government for interfering with the professions on doctrinaire grounds remained unsated.'[23] A Royal Commission on Legal Services, chaired by Sir Henry Benson, was in 1976 appointed to enquire into the law and practice relating to the provision of legal services in England, Wales and Northern Ireland, 'and to consider whether any, and if so what, changes are desirable in the public interest in the structure, organisation, training, regulation of and entry to the legal profession, including the arrangements for determining its remuneration, whether from private sources or public funds, and in the rules which prevent persons who are neither barristers nor solicitors from undertaking conveyancing and other legal business on behalf of other persons'.[24] Its terms of reference could hardly have been wider.

The fifteen members of Benson's commission met in plenary session on seventy-four occasions, with another sixty-seven meetings in sub-committees. They also visited Belfast and several other cities throughout the UK, where they met members of the profession and other interest groups. As the majority of the members were not lawyers, they visited, individually and in small groups, solicitors' offices, barristers' chambers, courts, tribunals, the Inns of Court, law centres and legal advice centres, citizens' advice bureaux, building societies, schools of law, polytechnics, colleges, local authorities, the (English) land registry, other government offices and some prisons, all in an endeavour to remedy their self-confessed 'limited knowledge of legal practice and the way lawyers work'.[25] They took written and oral evidence from innumerable organisations, including LSNI, the General Council of the Bar in Northern Ireland and the Law Faculty of Queen's University. All the consultees spent copious amounts of time and energy on their responses, and the resulting twenty-four volumes of written evidence and five volumes of oral evidence may be found in the Queen's University Law Library.

The commission's report was published in October 1979. Space does not permit here to detail its conclusions regarding such issues as fusion, rights of audience, practice structures, publicly funded services, monopolies, disciplinary procedures, remuneration and education.[26] Suffice it to say that the end result was extremely limited, partly because in many areas the commission actually recommended that there should

23 Hewitt, *Law Society*, p. 119.
24 *Report of the Royal Commission on Legal Services* (Cmnd 7648, HMSO, 1979).
25 Ibid., para. 1.24.
26 For further reading, apart from the report itself, see Hewitt, *Law Society*, ch. 9.

be no change. Few of the changes which it did suggest ever came to fruition. In Northern Ireland, the main results were probably the relaxation of restrictions on advertising (although the Monopolies Commission had already started that process and the Office of Fair Trading was to continue it), greater lay involvement in disciplinary procedures and the suggested further review of professional legal education which, as already mentioned above, was to culminate in the Bromley Report. Whether this justified the collective time and effort which went into the commission must remain an open question.

It was to be another ten years before the government returned to the fray, with the presentation to parliament by the then lord chancellor, Lord Mackay, of three Green Papers: 'The Work and Organisation of the Legal Profession', 'Contingency Fees' and 'Conveyancing by Authorised Practitioners'. These were followed in May 1989 by a 'Northern Ireland Supplement' issued by the Department of Finance and Personnel. Again, the detail of the proposals may be found elsewhere.[27] Some of the proposals were quite alarming to the profession, but concerted opposition on both sides of the Irish Sea resulted in a complete government retreat. The profession was thus able to see out the rest of the twentieth century in relative peace, but by 2001 the appetite of 'New Labour' for interfering was no longer to be restrained, and the first shots in its new campaign were fired in that year by the Office of Fair Trading with its report 'Competition in the Professions', dealing with perceived restrictions on competition in several professions, including solicitors. While the report dealt only with professions in England and Wales, it stated that, 'it is our intention that the lessons learned will inform work on the professions in Scotland and Northern Ireland', so LSNI felt obliged to respond.

The Office of Fair Trading produced a follow-up report in April 2002; by that time the Law Society of England and Wales ('LSEW') had voluntarily made changes to its regulations and had promised others. For example, it had agreed to change its regulations to allow solicitors employed by non-solicitors to provide services to third parties, had agreed to reconsider its ban on sharing fees with non-solicitor professionals, had abolished its prohibition on competitive fee advertising and on 'cold-calling' (although only to business clients). LSEW had also started a bewildering series of changes and reversals of those changes in its rules about referral fees and had indicated that it was willing to withdraw fee guidance in respect of probate and

27 Hewitt, *Law Society*, pp 87–9.

conveyancing work. LSNI and the Law Societies of Scotland and Ireland regarded this as abject capitulation and the resulting tension between them and LSEW came to a head in 2002 when they refused to join with LSEW in signing and releasing a declaration endorsing the core values of the legal profession, because they felt that LSEW had by then seriously compromised those values by its concessions to government. The three dissenting societies later signed and published a joint article 'What Price the Core Values' defending and elaborating their position.[28] Nonetheless, the government juggernaut, so unnecessarily encouraged, was rolling on, and in July 2002 the lord chancellor's department produced a consultation paper entitled 'In the Public Interest?', which set out five matters arising from the Office of Fair Trading report that fell within its remit, relating to conveyancing, probate, multi-disciplinary partnerships, legal professional privilege and the QC system. Although the paper related only to England and Wales, it had already been indicated that the response to it would 'inform' proposals for Scotland and Northern Ireland, so again LSNI felt obliged to respond, making a robust defence of the core values.

The government's next step was to ask Sir David Clementi to carry out an independent review of the regulation of legal services in England and Wales. His final report, published in December 2004, found that,

> There are no clear objectives and principles which underlie this regulatory system; and the system has insufficient regard to the interests of consumers. Reforms have been piecemeal, often adding to the list of inconsistencies. The complexity and lack of consistency has caused some to refer to the current system as a maze.[29]

Clementi put forward proposals for reform which were accepted by the government in a White Paper in October 2005. As expected, Scotland and Northern Ireland were not forgotten. In Scotland there was an exercise similar to the Clementi review and in the first session of the new Scottish parliament its Justice 1 Committee held an enquiry into the regulation of the profession in that jurisdiction. In respect of Northern Ireland a review group was established and a consultation paper, 'Regulation of Legal Services in Northern Ireland', issued in

---

28 See Hewitt, *Law Society*, pp 121–2 and Appendix Five.
29 Review of the Regulatory Framework for Legal Services in England and Wales (Final report, 2004), p. 2.

September 2005.[30] This cast doubt, arguably without any credible analysis, on the principle of self-regulation and stated that 'we find the principles and arguments advanced by the Clementi review compelling, but it will be for Northern Ireland's Review Group to ensure that they are applied in a way that suits circumstances here.' The chairman of the review group, Professor Sir George Bain, already had a close knowledge of Northern Ireland, having been from 1998 to 2004 president and vice-chancellor of Queen's University Belfast. The group's terms of reference were (in light of the findings of the Clementi Review, the subsequent White Paper and the responses to the Northern Ireland consultation document) to bring forward firm proposals for the regulation of legal services in Northern Ireland that were consistent with,

- protecting and promoting consumer interests
- promoting competition through the removal of unjustified restrictions
- promoting public understanding of citizens' legal rights, and
- encouraging a strong, effective and independent legal profession.

LSNI carried out an enormous amount of work in a relatively short period and submitted a response to the consultation paper in February 2006. While welcoming the review process, it cautioned against the importation of solutions from another jurisdiction: 'We do not accept the presupposition that regulation as it has evolved and operated in Northern Ireland by the LSNI within the statutory framework has failed in some fundamental way to serve the interests of consumers. We contrast the position in Northern Ireland with the position in England and Wales, where there has been clear evidence of systemic regulatory failure and dysfunction.'

Having collected written responses, the Bain Review Group held meetings with LSNI, the Bar Council, the benchers and the Office of Fair Trading, and also held a series of meetings around Northern Ireland to which they invited, as well as lawyers, representatives of voluntary and consumer organisations and local business people.

---

30 In the Republic of Ireland, the Competition Authority published in February 2005 a preliminary report on legal services, and in December 2006 a final report entitled Competition in professional services: solicitors and barristers.

THE BAIN REPORT

Admirably, the Legal Services Review Group reported on time in October 2006. In his foreword to the report, Professor Sir George Bain said,

> As the reader of our report will discover, we fully accept Clementi's principles and objectives for the regulation of legal services. But we have not accepted some of the recommendations for England and Wales because we believe that they are inappropriate for Northern Ireland. Northern Ireland is different – different in size, different in the nature and structure of its legal professions and different in its history of regulation. Hence different recommendations are needed ... [our recommendations] will place consumers in Northern Ireland in at least as good a position as those elsewhere in these islands, but without excessive costs and complex structures.[31]

The report covered the three main areas of regulation, complaints and competition. With regard to regulation, it concluded that,

1. The legal profession should continue to discharge regulatory functions, subject to a more effective and transparent oversight by an independent legal services oversight commissioner.
2. Lay persons should have an increased involvement in relation to general regulatory matters.
3. The professional bodies should undertake greater and targeted consultation on rules they intend to make.
4. The legal services oversight commissioner should have an audit function in relation to professional rules.
5. The lord chief justice should have an advisory role in relation to professional rules.
6. The regulatory and representative functions of the professional bodies need not be separated for general aspects of regulation, but should be for complaints handling.[32]

---

[31] Legal Services Review Group, Legal services in Northern Ireland: complaints, regulation, competition (TSO, 2006), pp i–ii.
[32] Ibid., p. ix.

The oversight commissioner would be supported by a small staff, and his office would be funded by the two branches of the profession through a two-part levy: a general levy on all practitioners and a specific levy on those found guilty of poor service or misconduct. The group also recommended that the bar, for the first time, should have similar complaints handling procedures and oversight to those of solicitors, and not surprisingly the question of how funding should be split between the two branches has proved contentious.

With regard to complaints handling, the group found that, 'whatever way the statistical evidence is interpreted, the level of dissatisfaction with lawyers in Northern Ireland seems to be lower than in other jurisdictions'.[33] The most important reform required, it believed, was greater lay participation, and it proposed that LSNI's client complaints committee should be serviced by a dedicated secretary and should be functionally separate from the council; members of the council should not be permitted to hear complaints.[34] Laypeople should be in a majority on the committee, a layperson should chair it[35] and there should be better training for lay members. The Solicitors Disciplinary Tribunal should continue to exercise its functions, with an ability to impose more serious penalties if required, and should be chaired by a professional lawyer, but with a majority lay membership.[36]

There was lengthy consideration of the issue of who should be allowed to complain, and a recommendation that, effectively, *anyone* should, subject to legislative parameters, instead of just 'the client' (which tended to be too restrictive, excluding, for example, a disappointed beneficiary under a will or someone who wished to complain about someone else's solicitor). It was also proposed that the client complaints committee should have wider power to award financial redress, with an initial limit of £3,500; it was thought that this would help to keep minor cases out of the courts.

With regard to competition, Bain also considered, but rejected, alternative business structures for the profession, including multi-disciplinary partnerships, legal disciplinary partnerships (barristers and solicitors practising together), 'Tesco Law' and, in the case of the bar, chambers rather than the existing Bar Library system. It concluded that 'the Northern Ireland model, consisting of solicitors in general practice and an independent Bar Library, is a competitive model with a good range of choice to the consumer'.[37] To LSNI's pleasure, it agreed with

---

33 Bain Report, para. 4.34.   34 Ibid., para. 4.40.   35 Ibid., para. 3.37.
36 Ibid., para. 4.42.   37 Bain Report, para. 6.36.

the extension to solicitors of advocacy rights in the higher courts, something for which LSNI had long campaigned.

LSNI issued a press release welcoming the publication of the report and confirming that it would engage constructively with the government to bring forward an agreed reform agenda, based on the report.

Draft legislation intended to give broad effect to Bain's recommendations is still languishing somewhere in the political wilderness, despite being placed on the parliamentary schedule in 2012; at the time of writing it has still not been produced to the Assembly for debate. While one cannot yet quite draw a comparison with the rate of progress of the 1976 Order, after over six years the members of the Bain review group, who produced their report so expeditiously, may feel more than a little disappointed.

'You just have to get on with it': the advance of women in the legal profession, 1901–2012

COLUM KENNY

A century ago this year, the newspaper of the Women's Social and Political Union of the United Kingdom marked the publication by the Irishwomen's Reform League of a pamphlet entitled *Women's need of women lawyers*. The pamphlet had been written anonymously by 'a woman LL.B. of T.C.D.' The reviewer was pleased that

> This pamphlet puts into a concise and readable form some of the main reasons why women should be admitted to the practice of the legal profession, and refutes some of those arguments most frequently put forward against this much-needed reform. The writer maintains that even if it be true that men are more inclined to be lenient to women than women themselves, yet this is no reason for continuing the present state of affairs – what women are asking for is fair play ... University examinations have proved the capacity of women to deal with the theory of law ...[1]

Ninety-nine years later, an Irish newspaper headline proclaimed, 'Women barristers set to outnumber men in decade.'[2] In the article beneath this headline, Dearbhail McDonald, legal editor of the *Irish Independent*, pointed out that four of the most senior legal positions in the Republic of Ireland were, for the first time, held by women. She had in mind Chief Justice Susan Denham, Attorney General Máire Whelan SC, Director of Public Prosecutions Claire Loftus and Chief State Solicitor Eileen Creedon. She added that, 'Irish lawyer Patricia O'Brien holds the top legal post at the United Nations and two of Ireland's

---

1 *Votes for women*, new series, vi, no. 282 (1 August 1913). There is a copy of the pamphlet at the National Library of Ireland, 3A 4105. Perhaps the author was one Miss Duggan LL.B who delivered an address entitled 'The need of [*sic*] women lawyers' at a meeting of the Irishwomen's Reform League the following year (*Weekly Irish Times*, 28 Feb. 1914).
2 *Irish Independent*, 6 Oct. 2012.

"magic circle" law firms are headed by female solicitors.' She quoted the new Bar Council chairman, David Nolan SC, who told her, 'The figures debunk the concept of the bar being an old, male-dominated, cigar-smoking profession'.

In Northern Ireland too there have been advances, with a significant growth in the number of women practising law in recent decades.

*

At the beginning of the twentieth century, the position of women who aspired to practise as barristers in Ireland was explained succinctly by the benchers of King's Inns. Miss Weir Johnston had written 'asking if a lady could become a member of the Irish Bar'. In October 1901 the society directed its under-treasurer to inform her that 'it was not competent for a lady to enter this Inn as a student, or become a member of the Irish bar.'[3]

In 1906 Francis Sheehy-Skeffington (1878–1916), who two years earlier had resigned as registrar of University College Dublin after publicly criticising its reluctance to admit women on equal terms with men, took issue with J.A. McNerney, who in a newspaper had defended the continuing exclusion of women from the bar. Skeffington wrote to the editor that,

> He [McNerney] is gravely concerned at the 'subtle influence' which a lady barrister might exert on judge or jury, to the detriment of justice. But he has admitted that, logically, the feminine demand must include the right to act as jurors; and a sprinkling of women in the jury box would be the best safeguard against undue female influence from the Bar – which would be further counteracted whenever the judge happened to be a woman, as would frequently occur in a state of social equality.[4]

However, thirteen more years and a great war passed before parliament enacted the Sex Disqualification (Removal) Act, in December 1919. This ensured that any woman living in what was then the United Kingdom of Great Britain and Ireland might become a lawyer, and could not be prevented from doing so on the grounds of her gender

---

3   Minute book of the council, 1901–17 (King's Inns MS, p. 6).
4   *Irish Independent*, 28 April 1906; *Dictionary of Irish biography*, ed. James McGuire and James Quinn, 9 vols (Cambridge, 2009) for Skeffington, by Patrick Maume.

alone. The benchers and law societies of Dublin and London were obliged to take note.

It was, of course, not only women living in the United Kingdom who aspired to practise as lawyers, and women had earlier been admitted to practise in the United States and in the courts of some European countries.[5] Moreover, in Canada on 2 February 1897, Clara Brett Martin, the daughter of Anglican Irish immigrants, had been 'admitted as a barrister and a solicitor, the first woman in the British empire to achieve such status.' In New Zealand, on 10 May 1897, Ethel Rebecca Benjamin was admitted as a barrister and solicitor, on foot of the Female Law Practitioners Act 1896.[6] In 1903 Victoria became the first Australian state to allow women to practise. Its Irish-born chief justice, John Madden, wished women barristers well and described Flos Greig's call in 1905 as 'the graceful incoming of a revolution', but he made no secret of his personal reservations about women's suitability for the bar and bench. No doubt partly because of such sentiments, Greig's 'realism led her, as a pioneer, to practise as a solicitor rather than a barrister.'[7] Cornelia Sorabji, who had studied law at Oxford between 1889 and 1892, afterwards appeared in the courts of certain Indian princely states and acted as a legal adviser to the court of wards in Bengal, Bihar, Orissa and Assam, but was not called to the English bar until 1923 and could not practice in the upper courts of India before they were opened to women in 1924.[8]

Women were first called to the bar in Ireland on 1 November 1921, more than six months before Ivy Williams (1877–1966) became on 10 May 1922 the first woman to be called in England. Relative to Britain at any rate, Ireland had 'led the way in respect to priority of women's call to the Bar', as one Irish writer proudly recalled a decade later.[9]

The first two women admitted as students by King's Inns, and later called to the Irish bar, were Averil Deverell and Frances (known also as

5   Ellen A. Martin, 'Admission of women to the bar', *Chicago Law Times*, 1 (1887), 76–92; J.C. Albisetti, 'Portia ante portas: women and the legal profession in Europe, ca. 1870–1925', *Journal of Social Studies*, 33:4 (Summer 2000), 825–57.
6   *Dictionary of Canadian biography* (online) for Martin, by Constance Backhouse; *Dictionary of New Zealand biography* (online) for Benjamin, by Carol Brown.
7   *Sydney Morning Herald*, 2 Aug. 1905; 'Women as lawyers' in *Press* (Canterbury, NZ), 12 Aug. 1905; *Australian dictionary of biography* (online) for Greig, by Ruth Campbell and J. Barton Hack; ibid., for Madden, by Ruth Campbell. Born in Cloyne, Co. Cork, Madden (1844–1918) was the son of an attorney who went to Australia in 1857.
8   *Dictionary of national biography* for Sorabji, by Suparna Gooptu; Lisa Trivedi, Review of *India calling: the memories of Cornelia Sorabji, India's first woman barrister* (Oxford, 2001), *Journal of Colonialism and Colonial History*, 3:3 (Winter, 2002).
9   *Irish Independent*, 17 March 1930.

'Fay') Kyle. Following 'lengthened' discussion about the admission of 'ladies' to King's Inns, the benchers of the society had on 19 January 1920 facilitated the progress of these two women by not insisting that they attend once more certain lectures that they had already attended at Trinity College Dublin before being admitted as students to King's Inns. On the printed form that was to be completed and signed by any applicant for admission as a student, someone in Deverell's case had changed by pen the relevant pronouns from 'he' to 'she' and 'him' to 'her', but not in Kyle's case.[10]

On 29 January 1920, the *Freeman's Journal* reported Deverell's admission to King's Inns and published 'the most recent photograph' of this 'lady of the law'. For her part Kyle proceeded to distinguish herself by becoming the first woman to win the John Brooke scholarship. The benchers had established this annual award in June 1878 on foot of an endowment of £4,000 from the 'Misses Brooke' in honour of their late brother, John Brooke QC. It was granted to the person who obtained first place in the final examinations at King's Inns, provided that the person was subsequently called to the bar and practised. Other recipients have included Liam Hamilton and Ronan Keane, each later to become chief justice of Ireland, and in 2003 Rosemary Healy-Rae, 'the daughter of the irrepressible South Kerry TD'.[11]

On 25 October 1921, on a show of hands by seventeen votes to eleven, the benchers further excused Kyle and Deverell from keeping the complete number of terms' commons (dinners) prescribed by the rules of King's Inns, 'the first in consideration that she had entered this Hon. Society at the earliest possible date, and obtained the John Brooke Scholarship, the second that she had entered at the same time, in consideration of her war services.' Her services had consisted of driving an ambulance. The fact that King's Inns also relaxed its requirements for a number of men at this time, including war veterans such as John Clarke MacDermott (1896–1979), a future lord chief justice of Northern Ireland, suggests that the two women benefited at least partly

10 Minute book of the council, 1917–28 (King's Inns MS, p. 94, pp 97–8). Ibid., p. 112 (25 Oct. 1920) records a like allowance made for Mary Dillon-Leetch, who would become in 1923 the third woman called in Dublin. Deverell's memorial for admission as a student is dated 8 January 1920, a few days before that of Kyle, but both are shown to have paid the duty for admission as students on the same date, 11 February 1920. Oddly, when it came to completing Deverell's memorial for admission to the degree of barrister-at-law, it was written in the appropriate blank space on the printed form that she had been admitted a student in Michaelmas term 1919 (King's Inns MSS).
11 Minute book of the council, 1870–85 (King's Inns MS, pp 299–307); Minute book of the council, 1917–1928 (King's Inns MS, p. 148); *The Kerryman*, 25 July 2003.

from the benchers being eager to tie up loose ends as they struggled to come to terms with the impact of Ireland being partitioned, rather than from any particular wish on the part of the society to see Irish women called to the bar as soon as possible.[12]

Less than a week later, at what was described as a 'special meeting' in King's Inns, the benchers passed a series of resolutions dealing with the consequences of the political partition of Ireland and aimed in vain at ensuring that both counsel and judges north and south would continue to participate in the governance of King's Inns. They also agreed that 'students who have been admitted to the degree of Barrister-at-Law by the King's Inns shall be admitted to audience in the courts of both Northern and Southern Ireland.' MacDermott, who with Kyle and others was due to be called on the following day, had been so concerned that his admission in Dublin might not be recognised in Belfast that he personally telephoned Sir John Ross (1853–1935), 'who had so recently become President of the High Court of Appeal for Ireland' – in an ex-officio capacity as the recently appointed and last lord chancellor of Ireland – and asked him for an assurance in the matter. Ross informed MacDermott that Sir Denis Henry (1864–1925) had agreed to recognise the forthcoming call of 1 November as valid throughout the island. Henry, unusually, was a Catholic unionist. A former member of parliament, he had served both as the solicitor general and attorney general of Ireland before being appointed lord chief justice of Northern Ireland in August 1921.[13]

Kyle and Deverell were both 'admitted to the Bar on the first call-day in Dublin since the Irish judiciary has been divided'.[14] Among the seventeen men called with them on 1 November 1921 was Paddy McGilligan (1889–1979), a future minister for finance and attorney general of the Republic of Ireland and the professor of constitutional, international and criminal law at University College Dublin from 1934 to 1959. He and MacDermott had tied for first place ahead of Kyle

12 Minute book of the council, 1917–28 (King's Inns MS, pp 148-9, 150–5, 157).
13 Ibid., pp 152–3; J.C. MacDermott, *An enriching life* ([Belfast], 1979), p. 151; *Dictionary of Irish biography* for Henry, by A.D. McDonnell. John Ross, *The years of my pilgrimage* (London, 1924), p. 295 for the high court of appeal for Ireland: 'The new Court, which had power to hear appeals from H.M. Courts of Appeal in Southern and Northern Ireland, was a necessity under the federal system intended to be set up by the [Government of Ireland] Act of 1920. The High Court got through a great deal of important work while it lasted.' (*Freeman's Journal*, 6 Dec. 1922). Both the court and the office of lord chancellor of Ireland were abolished in December 1922.
14 'First Irish Portias', *Daily Sketch*, 3 Nov. 1921 (with photograph of the two women); MacDermott, *An enriching life*, p. 143.

when she came third in the junior class examinations at King's Inns in May 1920, but MacDermott and McGilligan came second and third respectively to her first place in the senior class examinations of May 1921.[15]

The Anglo-Irish Treaty had not yet been signed by then, although King George V had already opened Northern Ireland's new parliament. As Kyle had excelled in the examinations at King's Inns she was the first person to be called on the day. Lord Chief Justice Thomas Molony (1865–1949), presiding now where formerly the lord chancellor had been accustomed to do so, congratulated her: 'A crowded court silently re-echoed the congratulations, and Miss Kyle blushed slightly as she resumed her seat.'[16] Within eight months, the building in which the last chief justice of all Ireland had now admitted her to practise would be entirely gutted by explosions and fire during the civil war.

Kyle's home was in Belfast and, a few days after her call in Dublin, she was also called to the bar of Northern Ireland.[17] John Clarke MacDermott was persuaded to accompany her, as he later explained:

> I returned to Belfast that same week only to find that the question of my status as a barrister there was still, apparently, in some doubt. Miss Kyle telephoned to say that she had seen Lord Justice [William] Moore, a member of the new Northern Ireland Court of Appeal who had previously been a judge of the High Court in Dublin [and treasurer of King's Inns 1918-20], that he said that she must be called again by Sir Denis Henry in Belfast and that this had been arranged with him for the following Monday in the Crumlin Road Courthouse at 11a.m. I, thinking as I still do, that Sir John Ross's assurance was well founded, said the Dublin Call would suffice: but she said that Lord Justice Moore was adamant, that she was going to be called on the Monday and that I should know what was on foot. I thanked her, pondered over the matter and came to the conclusion that the uncertainties of a career at the Bar were sufficiently numerous without being increased by some question of status which could easily be avoided, and arranged accordingly to present myself once again for Call.[18]

15 Minute book of the council, 1917–1928 (King's Inns MS, pp 104, 139, 148, 157); *Irish Times*, 2 Nov. 1921.
16 *Irish Independent*, 2 Nov. 1921.
17 *Irish Independent*, 9 Nov. 1921; McDermott, *An enriching life*, pp 152–3.
18 MacDermott, *An enriching life*, p. 152.

And so he did, and was called along with Frances Kyle who, according to her obituarist, 'practised her profession for a short time before returning to private life at her family home in Belfast.' Polden writes that, 'Frances Kyle from Ulster may claim to be the first UK barrister, having qualified at the Irish bar and held a brief, in Northern Ireland, before any Englishwoman.'[19]

Averil Deverell's father William was clerk of the crown and peace for Co. Wicklow.[20] She won the distinction of being entitled as a barrister to carry her briefs in a red bag, this being an indication that she had appeared before the privy council in London, in her case as a junior with Alfred Dickie KC. Her own first brief was not reported until late 1922, being an old chancery suit before the master of the rolls. Her first purchase from her earnings as a barrister was said to have been a cairn terrier, and she subsequently set up kennels in Greystones, Co. Wicklow, from which she supplemented her earnings from the bar.[21] When she succeeded in persuading Mr Justice William Dodd to affirm the decision of the recorder of Dublin to dismiss an action for £40 against her client, the *Irish Times* thought this sufficiently newsworthy for its short report on the matter on 26 July 1923 to carry the headline, 'Lady barrister wins.' She herself is said to have disliked the term 'lady barrister' and insisted that a sign with those words that was hung on the women's dressing room at the Law Library be replaced with one that read 'Women Barristers'. She came to enjoy in Dublin the title 'Mother of the Bar', just as the senior male barrister in practice was known as the 'Father of the Bar'.[22]

If Deverell bolstered her income from a source outside the bar, she was by no means the only woman barrister in Britain or Ireland to do so. Another was Helena Normanton (1882–1957), a feminist campaigner admitted to practise in London six months after Ivy Williams. Normanton 'felt betrayed by members of the legal profession who fabricated myths that were damaging to her career', and found that her relatively low earnings from the law compelled her to supplement her income.[23]

In 1906 an Irish bencher and the future recorder of Belfast, Charles Matheson KC, had expressed the hope when speaking at King's Inns

19 Obituary, *The Times*, 25 June 1958; Patrick Polden, 'Portia's progress: women at the bar in England, 1919-1939.' *International Journal of the Legal Profession*, 12:3 (2005), 332.
20 *Irish Times*, 12 Nov. 1934.
21 *Irish Independent*, 26 July 1928; *Irish Times*, 14 Dec. 1922, 24 July 1928 ('London letter'), 18 April 1952, 4 Aug. 1961, and 1 March 1968, 3 March 1979 ('An appreciation').
22 *Dictionary of Irish biography* for Deverell, by Maria O'Brien.
23 *Dictionary of national biography* for Normanton, by Joanne Workman.

that, 'please goodness, he would live to see the day when they should have a Portia among them in the Four Courts.' Then and for some years afterwards, one finds references to women barristers as 'Portias'. It is an allusion to the name of the heroine in Shakespeare's *Merchant of Venice* who appears in a court of justice dressed as a doctor of laws and who argues that 'The quality of mercy is not strained.' Unfortunately Matheson died in May 1921, and did not live to see the day less than six months later when his hopes were realised.[24]

For their part, according to Cruickshank, the United Kingdom's male solicitors wondered after 1919 'would women flood the profession, or would they fail because they lacked the requisite qualities?'[25] An Irish commentator in 1921 was pleased that, 'In addition to having the first lady barristers, Ireland also has the honour of having the first lady M.P. (Madame Markievicz) – a fitting record for a nation which has been noted throughout the ages for its chivalry towards women.' However, this commentator also thought that, 'The career of the lady barristers will be followed with interest by those who are anxious to test whether ladies can "make good" at the professions.'[26] It has been suggested that 'making good' in legal practice for women can mean having to act in accordance with male stereotypes: 'Just like Portia, women are accepted within the legal profession only if they "appear" to be men, preferably if their disguise is so successful that we are convinced that they are men'.[27]

When Averil Deverell appeared again before him, in January 1923, Judge Dodd made a comment that in its reported form seems quite cryptic. It may reflect concerns that had been expressed that women advocates would exercise a 'subtle influence' and that judges, finding it difficult to resist or to rebuff the perceived charms or weakness of female advocates, might be more lenient to them than to their male colleagues. He addressed Deverell, telling her that 'she had won on her merits, not on any outside grounds'. What she had won was an order of a grant of administration *de bonis non* of the personal estate of a deceased person.[28] Later in 1923 Deverell was joined at the bar of the

---

24 *Irish Independent*, 24 October 1906; *Irish Times*, 23 May and 'Obituary', 3 Aug. 1921; 'First Irish Portias', *Daily Sketch*, 3 Nov. 1921; Albisetti, 'Portia ante portas'.
25 Elizabeth Cruickshank, 'Building a profession', *The Law Society Gazette*, 26 June 2003. See also E. Cruickshank, *Women in the law: strategic career management* (London, 2003), ch. 1.
26 *Sunday Independent*, 6 Nov. 1921.
27 Margaret Thornton, *Dissonance and distrust: women in the legal profession* (Melbourne, 1996), p. ix; Jean McKenzie Leiper, *Bar codes: women in the legal profession* (Vancouver, 2006), pp 7–40.
28 *Freeman's Journal*, 27 Jan. 1923.

Irish Free State by Mary ('Molly') Dillon-Leetch, who became the third woman to be called in Dublin. The sister of two solicitors in Ballyhaunis, Co. Mayo, Dillon-Leetch practised on the western circuit before her marriage to C.E. Callan, a solicitor in Boyle, Co. Roscommon. In November 1954 their daughter Sylvia Callan was to be called to the bar on the same day as Miriam Hederman, Joan Knipe and fourteen men who included the future chief justice Ronan Keane. Two of their other children became solicitors.[29]

In Ireland from 1921 the new women barristers simply donned the usual barrister's wig, but in England some lawyers thought that women ought to wear something different on their heads and a senior group of judges and benchers met solemnly to consider the matter. One suggestion was that 'they shall wear a biretta, such as is worn by Portia on the stage', a notion that may have been calculated to deter them from practice. In the end the committee opted for the standard barrister's wig, but its requirement that this 'should cover and completely conceal the hair' was surely more demanding of women than of men.[30] Some skittish, if patronising, comments made about the appearance of female barristers also reflected a certain discomfort in their presence. In 1923, for example, one Irish observer noted that 'Miss Deverell is both young and attractive looking, and her manner of wearing her wig is rather more coquettish than that adopted by the male stars of the profession. I should never dare to refer to any part of the equipment of such important personages as Mr [Patrick] Lynch and Mr [William] Jellett and their eminent confreres … , but I am sure it will interest their juniors who do not see them in court to know that they favour a somewhat rakish angle when adjusting their wigs.' Thankfully, Irish female barristers appear not to have scandalised their male colleagues in the manner that women of the Paris bar reportedly did, by appearing in their robes in the corridors of the law courts with a cigarette between their lips. Or if the Irish women did so, nobody seems to have complained about it.[31]

Only ten women were called in Dublin between 1921 and 1930, and by 1968 the accumulated total stood at a mere seventy.[32] Male barristers long addressed and referred to such newcomers as 'Miss —', while customarily using first names for colleagues of their own gender.

29 *Irish Press*, 2 Nov. 1954; *Leitrim Observer*, 14 Feb. 1959.
30 *Irish Times*, 14 May 1922 and 8 April 1992.
31 *Irish Independent*, 21 Dec. 1923 and 30 Apr. 1927.
32 Ferguson (ed.), *King's Inns barristers, 1868–2004*, pp 93–98.

There were also Irish women practising in England. They included Ida Duncan, a graduate of Trinity and a daughter of T.J. Duncan of Dun Laoghaire who entered the Middle Temple and was called in London in 1923. She earned the distinction of being the first woman barrister to argue a case before the court of criminal appeal. She won the appeal against a conviction at Monmouth assizes.[33] Polden writes that, 'Ida Duncan, from Éire, was on the Oxford circuit and held dock briefs before securing a place as a lunacy commissioner'.[34] He also notes that one Irish woman, Ellice Hearn (later Eadie), along with Betty Harris, 'broke into that most select of preserves, the Office of the Parliamentary Counsel'. Hearn, a clergyman's daughter from Cork with Oxford firsts in jurisprudence and the BCL, both taken while she was a student at Gray's Inn (1934, call 1937), was the first to do so 'but soon left to join the WAAF [Women's Auxiliary Air Force]'.[35]

A woman sat as a magistrate for the first time in Ireland in February 1920, at Dundrum, Co. Dublin.[36] The first women jurors sat in January 1921, in the Dublin City sessions. Anna Haslam, president of the Irish Women Citizens' and Local Government Association thought that, 'The generous welcome extended to women jurors in a recent speech by the Lord Chief Justice should be an encouragement to all who have the privilege of rendering such service.' Citizens who enjoyed that privilege were householders or tenants of flats rated on their own valuation. However, women were not obliged to sit on juries and those who volunteered to do so could be and often were challenged. For years to come most juries would consist entirely of men.[37]

In January 1923, Mary Dorothea Heron became the first woman to be admitted a solicitor in Ireland, although she did not take out a practising certificate with the Law Society. A graduate in classics of Queen's University Belfast, she worked at her uncle's firm of solicitors in Belfast until the 1940s. In June 1923 Helena Early became 'the first lady practising as a solicitor' in the Irish Free State, and was later president of the Irish Soviet Friendship Society.[38] The first woman

---

33 *Irish Independent*, 3 Dec. 1924; 'Modern Portias', *Northern Advocate*, 18 April 1925, p. 10.
34 Polden, 'Portia's progress', pp 297, 314.
35 Ibid., p. 317.   36 *ILT & SJ*, 21 Feb. 1920.
37 *Irish Times*, 19, 22 and 26 Jan. 1921; *Irish Independent*, 21 Feb. 1928 and 18 Aug. 1948.
38 *ILT & SJ*, 28 July 1923; Daire Hogan, *The legal profession in Ireland, 1789-1922* (Dublin, 1986), pp 146-8; Mary Redmond, 'The emergence of women in the solicitors' profession in Ireland' in E.G. Hall and Daire Hogan (eds); *The Law Society of Ireland, 1852-2002: portrait of a profession* (Dublin, 2002), pp 110-11; *Irish Independent*, 21 Feb. 1928 and 18 Aug. 1948.

admitted to the Law Society of Northern Ireland was Kathleen Donnelly, in 1926. 'Even then', writes Dermot Feenan, 'women took time to regard entry to the legal profession as a suitable vocation, and those that did typically came from middle or upper-middle class backgrounds. Women began to enter both branches of the legal profession in equal numbers in Northern Ireland only in the late 1980s.'[39]

Not until 1941 was a woman, Frances Moran, called to the inner bar in Dublin. She had in 1924 become the fourth woman admitted to practise in Dublin and was in charge of the law school at Trinity College Dublin for several years, even before being appointed in 1944 its first female Regius Professor of Law. Known as 'Fran', she was said to have been a 'splendid lecturer' and to have had 'an exquisite sense of humour'.[40] Other women who since then have risen to prominence in academia include Norma Dawson, who is currently professor of law at Queen's University Belfast and who was president of the Irish Legal History Society 2009–12, and Mary McAleese, formerly the director of the Institute of Professional Legal Studies in Belfast and formerly Reid Professor of Criminal Law, Criminology and Penology at Trinity College Dublin. McAleese went on to be elected head of state in the Republic of Ireland in 1997.

In 1946, the fact that Alice Elizabeth Blayney was the only woman called that year in Dublin merited special notice and a photograph of her in the *Irish Times*.[41] Her younger brother John would be called two years later and would subsequently become a judge of the supreme court. She married the future chief justice, Thomas A. Finlay.

In 1964 Eileen Kennedy was appointed the first woman judge in Ireland, as a justice of the district court in Dublin. It was not until 1980 that Mella Carroll became the first woman judge of the high court in the Republic of Ireland, and in December 1992 Susan Denham became the first woman appointed to the supreme court in Dublin. In 1994 Catherine McGuinness became the first female circuit court judge, being later elevated to the high court and supreme court in turn.

The appointment of Mella Carroll to the high court in 1980 was of particular importance, because she was one of an emerging generation of women whose professional standing was fully acknowledged as being significant by their senior male colleagues. Hugh Geoghegan has

---

39 D. Feenan, 'Applications by women for silk and judicial office in Northern Ireland.' A report commissioned by the commissioner for judicial appointments for Northern Ireland (University of Ulster, 2005), p. 21.
40 *Irish Times*, 1 July 1944; *Dictionary of Irish biography* for Moran, by Matthew Russell.
41 *Irish Times*, 25 June 1946.

written that, 'At the junior bar, Carroll's primary practice as a conveyancer meant that her appearances in court as an advocate were rare. This dramatically changed after she became a senior counsel in 1976. Not only did she develop a reputation for competence in court advocacy but she even accepted briefs in civil cases involving juries.'[42] Carroll (1934–2006) was the first female to be elected chairman of the Bar Council, and also later became the first woman chancellor of Dublin City University and president of the International Association of Women Judges. Other practitioners who followed her onto the high court bench included Mary Laffoy in 1995 and Fidelma Macken in 1998. In 1999, the Irish government nominated Macken to the European court of justice. A total of almost eighty men had sat in that court from its establishment in 1952, but she became the first woman to do so.

If progress for women lawyers had been gradual south of the border, it was slower in some respects in Northern Ireland. Elsewhere in this volume, Lord Carswell recalls that,

> When I first walked through the door of the Bar Library in 1957 with the other newly called members of the bar of Northern Ireland, it was entering a different world from that which our successors encounter today. For a start, there were only four of us, but that was regarded as a 'big call', whereas the annual September call in Belfast now numbers some twenty-five or so new barristers. We were all men, while calls today are more or less evenly divided between men and women. There was one woman member of the Bar Library, but she was engaged in law reporting and did not take part in advocacy. There was a sprinkling of women solicitors, but no women at any judicial level.

In Northern Ireland, as Feenan observes, 'Historically, the pool of female candidates available for judicial office and silk has been smaller than that for male candidates.'[43] In 2005 he found that there were still only five women holders of silk in Northern Ireland, representing 8 per cent of the total who held silk, and noted that the commissioner for judicial appointments for Northern Ireland had reported in 2003 that the ratio of female to male members of the bar, with ten years or more

---

42 *Dictionary of Irish biography* online addition for Carroll, by Hugh Geoghegan (2012).
43 Feenan, 'Applications by women for silk and judicial office in Northern Ireland', pp 20–1. He refers to a speech by Noelle McGrenera QC to the 'Women in Law' Conference, Belfast, 2003, entitled 'To infinity and beyond: making the dream come true.'

experience was forty-eight females to 214 males. Of the sixty-eight queen's counsel only five were females. Therefore, only 10 per cent of the eligible females at the bar had been awarded silk compared to 29 per cent of eligible males. Three years later he wrote that, 'There are still no female High Court, or Court of Appeal, judges. The number of women holding high legal office in Northern Ireland is low compared to other countries.'[44] In September 2012, Lord Chief Justice Sir Declan Morgan expressed his concern at continuing female under-representation among senior judges. He thought that 'hopes that historical imbalances would diminish naturally over time through recruitment on merit do not seem to be bearing fruit.'[45]

In 1978 Thomasena ('Tommy') McKinney became the first woman president of the Law Society of Northern Ireland. Her career is said to have 'started somewhat unpromisingly in 1938 when she joined the firm of John McKee & Son as a typist', and she was not admitted as a solicitor until 1953.[46] Since then Margaret Elliott (1990), Antoinette Curran (1998), Catherine Dixon (1999), Attracta Wilson (2005) and Imelda McMillan (2012) have also served as president.[47] Meanwhile, south of the border, in 1980 Moya Quinlan became the first woman president of the Law Society of Ireland, in which office she has been followed by two other women, Elma Lynch (2001) and Geraldine Clarke (2002).

The benchers of King's Inns, who in the late eighteenth century had adopted the conservative motto *Nolumus mutari* ('We do not wish to change/be changed'), departed from custom in 1996 when they appointed Camilla McAleese the society's first female under-treasurer since its foundation in 1541.

Ms Justice Mary Finlay Geoghegan and some of the other contributors to this present volume remark on recent increases in the ratio of women to men studying and practising law. However, researchers such as Bacik and Drew who have traced the development of women in legal practice in Ireland believe that such evident advances still mask certain difficulties.[48] Hegarty wrote in 2003 that 'subtle barriers affect

---

44 D. Feenan, 'Women judges: gendering judges, justifying diversity', *Journal of Law and Society* 35:4 (2008), 500.
45 *Belfast Telegraph*, 6 September 2012.
46 Editorial, *N. Ir. Legal Q.*, 38, no. 4 (1987), 297–8.
47 Alan Hewitt, *The Law Society of Northern Ireland: a history* (Belfast, 2010), pp 95–7.
48 Ivana Bacik and Eileen Drew, 'Struggling with juggling: gender and work/life balance in the legal professions', *Women's Studies International Forum*, 29 (2006), 136–46; Ivana Bacik, Cathryn Costello and Eileen Drew, *Gender injustice: feminizing the legal profession?* (Dublin, 2003).

female barristers' progression at the Bar'. She had found from interviews conducted in the course of her research that, 'The main barriers were as follows; networks, family responsibilities, contacts and political affiliation.'[49]

In 1996 Margaret Magennis and others formed the Association of Women Solicitors in Northern Ireland. South of the border, the Irish Women Lawyers Association 'strives to encourage and support women in the legal profession in Ireland by facilitating professional, social and educational networking between women lawyers and advocating for and advancing the interests of such women.'[50] During 2012 this association held a gala dinner to celebrate its tenth anniversary, where references were made to 'trailblazers' who were identified as, 'the first women to become a law graduate, Lelita Walkington (1888), a lawyer to hold public office, Georgie Frost[51] (1919), barristers, Frances Kyle and Averil Deverell (1921), a solicitor, Mary Heron (1923), a law professor, Frances Moran ([Reid professorship, TCD]1925[–30]), a judge, Eileen Kennedy (196[4]) and a high court judge in Ireland, Mella Carroll (1980).'[52] One might mention here also Mary Robinson SC, the first woman barrister to become President of Ireland. She later served as the United Nations High Commissioner for Human Rights.

The progress in the legal profession that women have made since 1921 is underlined by reference to some early newspaper reports of their appearance at the bar in particular. It may be seen from the following news extracts that, although some practical obstacles to equality remain, a phenomenon that was once remarkable took only a few decades to become commonplace.

*

Women and law
Irish Times, 26 October 1921

We congratulate Miss Frances Kyle who, after a distinguished career at Dublin University, has won the John Brooke Scholarship at the King's Inns. She is the first woman who has achieved this honour, and she has

49 Martina Hegarty, 'A study of the career histories of female barristers in Ireland from 1983 to 2003' (Undergraduate thesis, National College of Ireland, Dublin, 2003), p. 98.
50 IWLA mission statement. At http://www.iwla.ie/about (4 April 2013).
51 *Dictionary of Irish biography* for Frost, by Maria O'Brien; *Frost v. The King* [1919] 1 IR 81.
52 *Law Society Gazette*, Aug./Sept. 2012, p. 16; 'University news', *Irish Times*, 5 July 1930.

achieved it at a very critical and confusing time in the history of the Irish Bar. Yesterday the ancient homogeneity of our country's legal institutions was broken. Separate High Courts of Justice for 'Northern' and 'Southern' Ireland were opened in Dublin and Belfast. The future of the King's Inns is uncertain; for Belfast is credited with the intention of starting a Law School of its own. Curiously enough, Miss Kyle, who may be not only the first woman Brooke Scholar, but the last Brooke Scholar of an undivided Law School, is a native of Belfast. We print today the second part of 'Solicitor's' article on the prospects of the legal profession in Ireland. His criticisms and proposals seem to us to be both sound and important; but, although he has touched on many subjects, he is silent on the possibility which Miss Kyle's victory suggests – namely, a women's invasion of the law. We are a liberal-minded people, as our universities have shown, and a large accession of women to the law would be quite consistent with the adventurous spirit of the age. 'Solicitor' believes that, sooner or later, the two branches of the profession will be amalgamated. The arrival of women as barristers and attorneys is likely to hasten the change.

First woman barristers: double record
Irish Times, 2 Nov. 1921 (with a photo of the men and women called that day, of which the negative does not survive)

There was a crowded audience in the Court of Appeal yesterday when the Lord Chief Justice of Ireland (Right Hon. T.F. Molony), with whom sat Lord Justices Ronan and O'Connor, called twenty law students to the Bar.

Hitherto the function was performed by the Lord Chancellor, but the Government of Ireland Act 1920 has changed all that, and more. Barristers of long standing who have witnessed scores of calls, mingled with the throng of ladies and gentlemen, friends of the candidates in the galleries. The occasion was unique, inasmuch as two ladies were amongst the 'calls'.

The ladies wore the usual wig and gown, and well the garb became them. The Lord Chief Justice congratulated Miss Kyle on being the first lady to have the distinction of being admitted to the Bar, and also upon having won the John Brooke Scholarship of £50 per annum for three years, the highest honour that a law student could win. The other lady barrister (Miss Deverell) was called in company with her [twin] brother (Captain W[illiam].B.S. Deverell).

Ladies and the law. First Irishwomen to be called to the bar
Freeman's Journal, 2 Nov. 1921

For the first time in the history of the Four Courts two ladies were called to the Bar yesterday, and the circumstance invested 'call-day' with unusual interest.

The Benchers met first, and while they were in conference a number of those qualified for the profession filed into the Court of Appeal and took the places customarily allotted to those who await the call.

Among them were two ladies, one of whom Miss Frances Christian Kyle, Sen. Mod., B.A., LL.B. (Dublin University) led the file, having won that distinction in competition with many candidates of the harder sex and at least one of her own. And she comes all the way from Belfast. She is the daughter of Mr. Robert Alexander Kyle, of 17 Wellington Park, Belfast.

After Miss Kyle came Mr. John Clarke MacDermott, LL.B. (Queen's University Belfast). He was a lieutenant in the Machine Gun Corps, and won the M.C.

Miss Kyle and Mr. MacDermott had taken first and second places, because while the former carried off the John Brooke Scholarship of £50 per annum for three years, the latter was awarded the Society's prize of £21.

Called a second time. Unique experience of recently admitted barristers-at-law
Freeman's Journal, 9 Nov. 1921

In the King's Bench Division of Northern Ireland yesterday, Lord Chief Justice Henry 'called' to the Bar at Belfast Miss Frances Christian Kyle, LL.B., and Mr. J.C. McDermott, LL.B., who were 'called' last week in the Four Courts.

His Lordship, having congratulated the new barristers, wished them successful careers at the Bar.

First lady called to northern bar
Irish Independent, 9 Nov. 1921

Miss Frances Christian Kyle, LL.B., who was called to the Bar by Lord Chief Justice Molony in the Four Courts a few days ago, was also called to the Bar in the King's Bench of 'Northern Ireland', the same formalities being observed as in the Court of 'Southern Ireland.' Lord

Chief Justice Henry congratulated Miss Kyle as Lord Chief Justice Molony had done, on being the first lady barrister in Ireland and the first lady to win the Brooke scholarship. Mr J.C. MacDermott, LL.B., was called in a similar manner in both Courts.

Woman's place in the professions
Irish Times, 25 March 1925

On the subject of 'Careers for women', Miss G. Fitzgerald B.A., lecturing before the Irish Women Citizens and Local Government Association at its annual meeting ... said that ... In the branch of law they had four women barristers, two of whom had won the Brooke Scholarship [Frances Kyle and Frances Moran], one of them taking the Victoria Prize two years in succession. She believed that the profession was overcrowded at present, but at the same time thought that more women should become solicitors, as there were better prospects in that direction, and the prejudice did not seem to be strong against women solicitors and women barristers.

Meath lady barrister
Meath Chronicle, 7 Nov. 1925

The call to the Irish Bar last Monday of Miss Antonia E. MacDonnell is but the culmination of a career of varied scholastic success and achievement. She is Meath's first lady Barrister [and the sixth to be called] ... Miss MacDonnell entered the National University obtaining a Scholarship in Irish and modern languages. From the National University she went to the Edinburgh School of Cookery and Domestic Economy where she won the College Bursary and obtained first place and first-class certificate with silver badge at her final examination in June 1922, at which examination over four thousand students competed. She ... is a sister of Mr. R. MacDonnell, LL.B., Solicitor.[53]

English women turn from law
Associated Press, London, July 1927

LONDON. —There is a noticeable falling off in the number of women candidates at the bar examination since the pioneer barristers, Miss Fay Kyle and Miss Helena Normanton, were 'called to the bar.'

---

53 Also see Margaret Ó hÓgartaigh, 'Antonia MacDonnell, Meath's first female barrister and the legal profession in Ireland in the early twentieth century', *Ríocht na Midhe, Records of the Meath Archaeological and Historical Society*, 19 (2009), 273–6.

University women of today declare the examinations are not nearly so difficult as at first thought. They prefer to put their energies into something which pays better than waiting about the law courts for work which comes in only slowly.[54]

Letter to the editor
Irish Times, 4 Feb. 1930

I suggest that provision be made in the [Illegitimate Children] Bill for the appointment of women magistrates to sit with men District Justices to hear affiliation order cases. We have in Dublin several women barristers and solicitors who are admirably fitted for the task. Yours etc., Mary Mulvey, Peace Commissioner, U.D.C., Dundrum, Co. Dublin.

Women and the law
An Irishman's Diary, *Irish Times*, 26 March 1930

Irish feminists appear to be making little capital out of the distinction conferred on one of their number by the inclusion of Miss Kathleen Phelan, barrister-at-law, on the delegation representing the Irish Free State at the International Conference on the Codification of International Law, now sitting at The Hague ... A number of countries – including Great Britain – compromised by bringing a woman to The Hague in the position of 'technical adviser', but the Free State Government showed itself to be made of more advanced stuff and appointed a woman delegate.

Miss Phelan ... practises in Dublin and on Judge [James] Sealy's [southern] circuit, being one of the few women to venture into the provinces in search of briefs. Before she turned to law, her studies were in the chemical field, and she is an M.Sc (Honours) of the National University.

Welcome to woman barrister
Irish Times, 14 Jan. 1931

When a licensing appeal was called at Lurgan Quarter Sessions, before County Court Judge Greene, K.C., Dr Brian Maginess, Barrister-at-law [future attorney general and government minister in Northern

---

54 This AP report was picked up by editors across the United States (e.g., *Niagara Falls Gazette*, 22 July 1922; *Spokane Daily Chronicle*, 1 Aug. 1927).

The advance of women in the legal profession, 1901–2012 145

Ireland],[55] introduced Miss M.K. Sheil, Barrister-at-law (who appeared in the case), and said that she was a sister of Mr C[harles] L[eo] Sheil, Barrister-at-law, a well-known practitioner in that court [and future judge of the king's bench division in Northern Ireland].

Judge Greene said that he was very happy to welcome Miss Sheil, and he hoped that she would be very successful in her career at the Bar. It was the first time he had had the pleasure of a lady barrister in his court.

Women barristers
Irish Independent, 13 Nov. 1931
(includes a photograph by Lafayette of Deverell in wig and gown)

Seeing the name of Miss A.K. Deverell BL (who, by the way, has a reputation among her colleagues for witty repartee), figuring in the Metropolitan Garda case, reminds me that the men barristers in the Bar Library are distinctly piqued about the dimensions of the room which has been allotted to the women members of the bar.

When the courts moved back to their old abode the women barristers scorned the room assigned to them on the grounds that it was too small. The harassed legal gentlemen who had the allocation of the rooms caved in at once and permitted the fair ladies to have an apartment in which, remarked one of the piqued males, they could give a ball.

Legal profession
Irish Times, 21 Jan 1932

There are now a fair number of women barristers in the Free State. One of them, Miss Kathleen Phelan, was sent to the Codification of the International League as the Free State representative. Among the young women who have qualified as solicitors recently is Miss Keller, LL.D., T.C.D. She won a gold medal for oratory and is present secretary of the International Federation of University Women.

Women lawyers
Quidnunc, *Irish Times*, 6 Feb. 1935

Visitors to our Courts of Justice now, when they see a young lady legally begowned, regard it as a matter of course as a convention with which we

---

55 *Dictionary of Irish biography* for Maginess, by Bridget Hourican.

have long been familiar. Though it is only a few years since the fair sex were admitted to practise in Ireland, it is a little over fifty years ago since a brilliant and determined lady, Mrs Carrie Burnham Kilgore, broke down an old tradition, and overcoming almost insuperable difficulties, became a member of the United States Bar [in Pennsylvania in 1886].[56]

Echoes of the town
Weekly Irish Times, 29 March 1937

And so, in response to many requests and comments to write something on the position of women in Ireland, the only letters I received are from those who do not think I have been quite fair, as some women are not fully qualified for such posts as, for example, District Justice. Now there is not an intelligent woman who would wish any position for which she was not fully qualified. I am told by one correspondent that no woman barrister is yet in the rank for such a post. So that settles that. [Kitty Clive writing]

Women in strange employment
Weekly Irish Times, 21 October 1939

Based on the returns of the 1936 census … [t]here are 12 women carpenters, 6 cabinet-makers, 5 motor mechanics … 10 women barristers and 36 solicitors … and 14 pawnbrokers.

Muriel Bowen's scrapbook
Sunday Independent, 13 November 1949

During the week there was a 66 per cent increase in the number of women barristers practising in Ireland. The two ladies called to the Bar a fortnight ago —Miss Mary Neylon, of Clare [and a future librarian of King's Inns], and Miss Britta Donnellan, Maynooth — have both taken their places in the Law Library.

They join three distinguished colleagues there: Miss Frances Moran, S.C., Miss Averell [sic] Deverell and Miss Agnes Cassidy … About 40

---

56 *Notable American women, 1607–1950: a biographical dictionary*, ed. E.T. James (Boston, MA, 1971 ed.), pp 329–30 for Kilgore. Martin, 'Admission of women to the bar', pp 76–92, indicates that Kilgore was preceded by others elsewhere in the US, the earliest being Arabella A. Mansfield in Iowa in June 1869.

women have been called to the Bar in the past 25 years, but the vast majority prefer work outside the Courts.

Cherchez la femme
An Irishman's Diary, *Irish Times*, 13 Oct. 1951

In the early days of the century strange things began to happen in and around Trinity. Feminism began to rear its ugly – or, in the case which I am about to recount, its pretty face! The Board of T.C.D. [which] always had a fairly keen eye for the main chance ... decided, for a small financial consideration ... to give a degree to any woman student who had satisfied her English examiners that she was worthy of it ... Now comes the case of Miss [Isabel] Marion Weir-Johnston. This young lady – and she was exceedingly young at the time – not more than about sixteen years of age – was a native of Derry, or Londonderry, whichever way you like it. She startled everybody suddenly when she wrote to the British legal authorities requesting their permission at a later stage to read for the Bar, and become the first female barrister in the United Kingdom. There was apparently quite a to-do about it at the time. Being completely ignorant of Miss Weir-Johnston's age, both Mrs Pankhurst and Mrs Drummond [suffragettes] got all hot and bothered, believing that they had secured the recruit of a lifetime. What they said when they found out the girl's age has not been recorded. [As noted above, she also wrote to King's Inns in 1901, enquiring if a woman might be admitted to that society and called in Ireland.]

However, to make a long story as short as I can, Miss Weir-Johnston, who had gone to school in England, arrived one day [in January 1904] in Trinity to become the first woman student in the College. Needless to say, there was a great deal of heavy weather about it all; But the Board had decided at last to take the fateful step ... She never graduated. 'Cos' why? Because Stephen Barnabas Kelleher fell in love with her, and she married him ... [57]

Court welcome for woman barrister
Leitrim Observer, 4 Dec. 1954

That it was the first time he had had the pleasure of welcoming a woman barrister in the Court and that it gave him much pleasure to do

---

57 For Weir-Johnston see Judith Hartford and Claire Rush (eds), *Have women made a difference? Women in Irish universities, 1850–2010* (Bern, 2010), pp 61–2.

so, was stated by Judge Lynch, at Sligo Circuit Court, when Mr. H. O'Neill, Barrister-at-Law, introduced Miss Sylvia Callan Barrister-at-Law, on her first appearance. [She had been admitted to practise that term and was the daughter of the fourth woman called to the bar in Dublin, Mary Dillon-Leetch]

Eight women among 36 called to bar
Irish Times, 30 July 1976

This is believed to be the largest number of barristers called at one time.

Women prove their equality case at the bar: Ireland's women barristers believe that they are on the verge of an exciting era
by Noirin Hegarty, Irish Times, 17 Oct. 1986

Senator [Mary] Robinson admits that she sometimes finds the whole format and language of the Bar absurd. 'Everything about the Bar is in the masculine gender. One says "My Lord;" and when I fill in forms for my junior colleagues I refer to the women as "he;" also we talk about a "Master/Devil" relationship', she says.

Senator Robinson also criticised the lack of crèche facilities for both men and women at the Law Library. 'It is a very young Bar and yet there is no facility for working mothers or fathers.'

Mrs Robinson remembers a time when she was pregnant as a senior counsel. 'This sounds absurd', she says, but 'I had to abandon the waistcoat we wear, because nobody ever thought when designing the clothes, that a woman silk would ever be appointed, much less get pregnant.'

Not all roses for sisters in law
by Carol Coulter, Irish Times, 7 Nov. 2000

Maureen Clark SC came to the bar 25 years ago ... 'Every single barrister I met then warned me I wouldn't make a living, I wouldn't be up to it, clients wouldn't like me. A lot of us believed it', she says. But she adds: 'It's a very different climate now.' [She continues,] 'The solicitors on circuit were great. You just have to get on with it.' [In 2003 Ms Clark was appointed a judge of the International Criminal Court, and subsequently of the High Court in Ireland]

Catherine McGuinness, recently appointed [in January 2000] a Supreme Court judge ... felt comfortable doing crime and other work as a barrister. 'I never felt the bar was highly discriminatory. You didn't feel as out of place as in political life. A hewer of sandwiches and a drawer of tea was what you were meant to be in politics. There might have been a certain adjustment involved, but there was certainly no discrimination from judges. We survived, most of us.'

May the Irish Legal History Society flourish!

– R.F.V. Heuston, 30 September 1988

The society's foundation

W.N. OSBOROUGH

The inaugural general meeting of the Irish Legal History Society was held in Trinity College Dublin in September 1988. This was when the constitution of the society was adopted and the first council elected. The occasion concluded with an address delivered by Professor Robert Heuston (1923–95), 'Legal history and the author: some problems of authorship'.

The society itself had been established a few months earlier, in February 1988 and at another event in Trinity. At this reception, held in the provost's house courtesy of the late Professor W.A. Watts, the then provost, the birth of the society took place in the presence of the chief justice of Ireland of the day, the Hon. Mr Justice Finlay, and of the then lord chief justice of Northern Ireland, the Rt Hon. Lord Lowry.

As it happens the shade of a third Irish chief justice might have been invoked for his presence on the occasion as well. This was since there was placed on display at the reception on this auspicious occasion the 'Gold Collar SS' that once belonged to Sir Thomas Molony (1865–1949), the last lord chief justice of Ireland. Molony who had strong links with Trinity College – he became its vice-chancellor in 1931 – bequeathed his 'Gold Collar SS' to the college for so long as the office of lord chief justice of Ireland should not be re-instituted. Trinity's tutelage of this unusual and priceless artefact, I reckon, looks assured for some considerable time to come.

There was much to be done in the interval between the reception of February 1988 and the inaugural general meeting the following September, and indeed for some considerable time after that. To make sure that the society became a going concern it was essential to attract a sufficient membership. Publicity too was of the essence. A number of flyers containing membership forms were printed off thanks to the late Michael Adams, our publisher, and became ready for publication. I had received delivery of a batch of these flyers and it was arranged that I would liaise with the late John McLean, under-treasurer at the inn of court of Northern Ireland, one Saturday morning at the ferry terminal at Dun Laoghaire, to transfer a portion of this batch into John's keeping for distribution in Belfast and in Northern Ireland generally. We met. I opened the boot of my car. John opened the boot of his, and the transfer of flyers took place without any mishap. I could not help reflecting after this rendezvous that two less suspicious individuals handling contraband goods close to a place of shipment could hardly have been visualised.

One question raised in the early days concerned the possible name to be bestowed on the new society. Precedent elsewhere suggested that the proper course to follow might have been to name the society after some distinguished luminary of the past. Two European continental societies offered possible models. The Société Internationale Fernand de Visscher pour l'Histoire des Droits de l'Antiquité for one: this society as it happens had visited Dublin in 1972. Again, rather better known, there was the Société Jean Bodin, named after the distinguished French writer of the sixteenth century. Bodin (1530–96) was celebrated above all for his classic work *Les six livres de la République*.

Nearer to home, the Scottish and English legal history societies are again named after actual historical figures. Scotland's Stair Society is called after the great institutional writer, James Dalrymple (1619–95), first Viscount Stair, whose *Institutions of the Law of Scotland* appeared first in 1681. The Stair Society was established in 1934. England's Selden Society was a much earlier creation – in 1887. John Selden (1584–1654), the prominent legal antiquarian, was not perhaps the most obvious choice of individual for the English society to be named after. Earl Clarendon, it is true, viewed Selden as a man 'of stupendous learning in all kinds and in all languages', but in his *Table-talk* (1689) Selden uttered one memorable sentiment which could just have been held against him in any open competition: 'There was never a merry world since the fairies left dancing and the parson left conjuring.'

A possible black mark could have been entered against Jean Bodin too for his belief in witchcraft. The difficulty in securing for the Irish Legal History Society a completely non-contentious eponymous figure was a difficulty that might perhaps have been anticipated – John Davies and Christopher Palles, both suggested, were shot down for very different reasons. And, in the end, pragmatically, the decision was arrived at to opt for the anodyne title – the Irish Legal History Society. Significantly, this approach – not to name the society after any individual at all – was to be followed when the fourth legal history society for these islands was inaugurated in 1999. This is the Welsh Legal History Society: Cymdeithas Hanes Cyfraith Cymru.

February 2013

Celebrating the society

The Irish Legal History Society, supported by academics from a number of Irish universities and by judges, counsel and solicitors from both Northern Ireland and the Republic of Ireland held an inaugural meeting on 12 February 1988 in the provost's house, Trinity College Dublin. The prime mover in the foundation and development of the society has been Professor W.N. Osborough. In February 2013 the society returned to Trinity College Dublin for its spring discourse and in order to celebrate its twenty-fifth anniversary. There Dr Patrick Prendergast, the college's provost, welcomed members. His address included the following references to the Irish Legal History Society.

The society's stated objective is to encourage the study of the history of Irish law, and to advance its study through annual lectures and publications. It has succeeded admirably in both objectives over the past quarter of a century.

One of the society's defining characteristics is that it brings together scholars and practitioners from both parts of the island of Ireland. This cross-border dimension has been one of its most significant contributions.

A driving force in the establishment of the society was Professor Nial Osborough. On the society's tenth anniversary in 1998, he delivered the autumn discourse and admitted then that the programme of work he had devised ten years earlier would have kept the society busy until the year 2088. The impressive list of publications and of discourses over the past twenty-five years would, I think, be the envy of any society.

Fifteen years ago, in 1998, the late great R.B. McDowell, then a mere 85 years old, gave the spring discourse on 'Edmund Burke and the law'. R.B. quoted, with approval, Burke's view of the law as

> a subject whose study carries no difficulty to those who already understand it – and no difficulty to those who will never understand it! But all those poor unfortunates caught between those two extremes will 'have a hard task of it'.

It seems probable that Burke cast himself as one of those 'poor unfortunates' since, as we know, he didn't get too far with his study of the law. However he did at least enrol in the Middle Temple in London, unlike his Trinity contemporary, Oliver Goldsmith, who was given £50 by his uncle to go to London to study law, but promptly lost the money, gambling in Dublin ...

Goldsmith and Burke now have pride of place in the college, gazing out on College Green from the front of Regent House. This should not be taken as the college's endorsement of their laxity towards legal studies!

The medieval historian Dr Peter Crooks delivered the spring discourse four years ago, in the Science Gallery, on 'Reconstructing the past: later medieval Ireland and the Irish chancery project.' I had the great pleasure of launching last year the website of the chancery project, which is a tremendous online public resource, hosted on Trinity's server. In this, and in other projects to encourage the study of the history of Irish law, the Legal History Society's and Trinity's aims often dovetail. I know we will continue our mutual support and partnership.

One of the great strengths of the Irish Legal History Society over the past twenty-five years is that it has acted as a bridge between north and south, creating a forum for the exchange of ideas and for co-operation on intellectual and scholarly pursuits.

Speaking in 1998, Professor Osborough recognised the four qualities needed for success in the world of legal history: 'skill, dedication, imagination, and perseverance'. They could serve as a suitable motto for this society, and they are indeed qualities I like to encourage in our students.

I congratulate the society on reaching this important anniversary – and in doing so in such style. I wish you all the best over the next twenty-five years.

The Irish Legal History Society

(www.ilhs.eu)

SUCCESSION LISTS 1988–2013

Established in 1988 to encourage the study and advance the knowledge of the history of Irish law, especially by the publication of original documents and of works relating to the history of Irish law, including its institutions, doctrine and personalities, and the reprinting or editing of works of sufficient rarity or importance, the society over twenty-five years has been served by a succession of officers and council members identified on the volumes published. Below is a succession list of officers during those years together with an alphabetical list of members who have served on the council. The titles of honour prefixing names are those applicable at the conclusion of the period of office. Those in office at the date of going to print are identified by the year of election and the word 'Date'.

Patrons

The Hon. Mr Justice Thomas A. Finlay	1988–94
The Rt Hon. Sir Brian Hutton	1988–97
The Rt Hon. Sir Robert Carswell	1997–2004
The Hon. Mr Justice Liam Hamilton	1994–2000
The Hon. Mr Justice Ronan Keane	2000–4
The Rt Hon. Sir Brian Kerr	2004–9
The Hon. Mr Justice John Murray	2004–11
The Rt Hon. Sir Declan Morgan	2009–Date
The Hon. Mrs Justice Susan Denham	2011–Date

Lord Lowry was closely involved as lord chief justice of Northern Ireland in the initial steps to form the society. He ceased to be the chief justice upon his appointment as a lord of appeal in ordinary in August 1988 and was elected a life member of the society. He was not formally a patron.

Presidents

The Hon. Mr Justice Declan Costello	1988–91
His Honour Judge Anthony Hart QC	1991–4
Daire Hogan	1994–7
Professor D.S. Greer QC (hon)	1997–2000
Professor W.N. Osborough	2000–3
His Honour Judge John Martin QC	2003–6
James I. McGuire	2006–9
Professor Norma Dawson	2009–12
Robert D. Marshall	2012–Date

Vice-presidents

Professor G.J. Hand	1988–95
His Honour Judge Anthony Hart QC	1988–91
Professor D.S. Greer	1991–7
James I. McGuire	1995–2006
J.F. Larkin BL	1998–2000
His Honour Judge John Martin QC	2000–3
Professor Norma Dawson	2003–9
Robert D. Marshall	2006–12
The Hon. Sir Donnell Deeny	2009–Date
Dr Patrick Geoghegan	2012–Date

Honorary secretaries

Professor W.N. Osborough	1988–2000
Dr Alan Dowling	1993–6
Professor Norma Dawson	1996–2000
Dr Kevin Costello	2000–5
Sheena Grattan	2001–5
Dr Patrick Geoghegan	2005–9
Dr Jack Anderson	2005–6
Dr David Capper	2006–8
Dr Niamh Howlin	2008–12
Dr Thomas Mohr	2009–Date
Dr David Capper	2012–Date

Honorary treasurers

Daire Hogan	1988–94
J.L. Leckey	1993–2000
Robert D. Marshall	1994–2006
John G. Gordon	2001–Date
Robert Heron	2007
Felix M. Larkin	2007–12
Yvonne Mullen BL	2012–Date

The offices of secretary and treasurer respectively have been held jointly since October 1993 by an officer resident in Dublin and another in Belfast.

Council members

Dr Jack Anderson	2004–5
Rosemary Carson	2003–7
His Honour Judge James Carroll	1988–91
Dr Art Cosgrove	1988–93
The Hon. Mr Justice Declan Costello	1991–7
Dr Kevin Costello	2004–Date
Dr D.V. Craig	1988–91
Professor Norma Dawson	2000–3; 2012–Date
Dr Seán Donlon	2004–Date
Dr Kenneth Ferguson BL	2009–Date
The Hon. Hugh Geoghegan	1999–Date
Dr Patrick Geoghegan	2009–12
Professor D.S. Greer QC (hon.)	1988–91; 2000–Date
Professor G.J. Hand	1995–2002
Sir Anthony Hart	1994–Date
Dr Robin Hickey	2008–Date
Robert Heron	2006–7
Daire Hogan	1997–Date
Professor Colum Kenny	2003–Date
Felix M. Larkin	2006–7; 2012–Date
John F. Larkin QC	1988–97; 2009–Date
James I. McGuire	1993–5; 2009–Date
J.A.L. McLean QC	1992–7
His Honour John Martin QC	2006–Date
Eanna Mulloy SC	2002–9

Dr Thomas Mohr	2008–9
Yvonne Mullen BL	2010–12
Roderick O'Hanlon BL	1994–2002
Professor Jane Ohlmeyer	2003–Date
Professor W.N. Osborough	2003–10

Index

Act of Union (1800), 71, 72
Adams, Michael, 153
administrative law, 64
advancement, presumption of, 33, 34
AG v. Healy, 88
AG v. McGann, 88
AG v. Murray, 87
AG (SPUC) v. Open Door Counselling Ltd, 28
Ahern v. Molyneaux, 58–9
Anderson, Jack, 158, 159
Anecdotes of the Connaught circuit (Burke), 81
Anglo-Irish Treaty 1921, 132
Anglo-Irish Truce 1921, 69–70
Anne, queen, 52
Annesley, earl of, 82
Antrim, 103, 105
Archbold, John F., 86
Argus, 49
Armagh, 6, 7, 10, 103
Armitage, A.L., 113
Armitage case, 87
Armitage Report (1973), 113–14, 115, 117
Arms Trial (1970), 48
Armstrong, Jonathan, 99
Assam, 129
assizes, 5–8, 17, 37, 38, 69, 78, 79, 81, 82, 83, 85
Assocation of Women Solicitors in Northern Ireland, 140
Associated Press, 143
Athlone, Co. Westmeath, 39, 44
attorney general, 28, 48, 75, 87, 127, 131
attorney general for England and Wales, 15, 16, 81

attorney general for Northern Ireland, 15–16
Attorneys and Solicitors (Ireland) Act 1866, 104, 106
Aughinish Alumina, 61
Austen, Jane, 82
Australia, 35–6, 93, 103, 129

Babington, Tony, 5, 71
Bacik, Ivana, 139
Bain, Sir George, 123, 124
Bain Report, 124–6
Ballibay, [Ballybay], Co. Monaghan, 84
Ballyburley, Co. Offaly, 41–2
Ballyhaunis, Co. Mayo, 135
Bar, 79, 80, 86, 128, 129, 131, 132; *see also* Law Library; Northern Ireland Bar
  barrister-at-law, degree of, 90
  calls to the bar, 90, 97
  circuit life, 37–40
  court dress, 135
  criminal bar, 69–88
  fees, 13, 15
  Northern Ireland, 3–22
  regulation and education; see King's Inns
  specialisation, 40
  women barristers, 3, 97, 127, 128–36, 139–49
Bar Council of England and Wales, 93
Bar Council of Ireland, 38–9, 123, 128, 138
Bar Library, Belfast; *see* Northern Ireland Bar
The bar life of O'Connell (O'Flanagan), 85

Barna, Co. Galway, 48
Barr, Robert, 32
Barry, Patrick/Philip, 78
Belfast, 3, 105, 120, 131, 132, 133, 136, 138, 141, 142, 154
  courthouses, 8–9
Belfast city commission, 7, 8, 17
Belmont Castle, 75
Belvedere, earl of, 82
benchers; *see* King's Inns
Bengal, 129
Benjamin, Ethel Rebecca, 129
Benson, Sir Henry, 120
Bewley, Charles, 87
Bihar, 129
Binchy, Daniel, 46
Binchy, James, 46
Binchy, Michael, 46, 47
Binchy, William, 46, 58
Birr, Co. Offaly, 39, 43, 45, 47
Black and Tans, 50–1
Blackburne, Lord, 25
Blackhall Place, Dublin, 66
Blake, re, 28
Blake v. Wilkins, 76
Blascáod mor Teo v. Commissioners for Public Works, 62
Blasket Islands, 62
Blayney, Alice Elizabeth, 137
Blayney, John, 29, 137
Bodin, Jean, 154
Bond, Oliver, 73
boundary commission (1924), 103
Bowen, Muriel, 146
Boyle, Co. Roscommon, 39, 135
Brady, Joseph, 71
Breheny (sergeant), 4
Brehon Law, 46
Brett, Sir Charles, 8, 9, 10
British Army, 24, 142
British empire, 103
Bromley, Peter, 115
Bromley Report, 115–16, 121
Brooke, John, 130
Brooke Scholarship, 130, 140–1, 142, 143

Brougham, Lord, 77–8
Brown, Eimear, 99
Budd, Declan, 62
Bulletin of Northern Ireland Law, 118, 119
Burke, Edmund, 155–6
Burke, James, 23
Burke, Major John, 23–6
Burke, Oliver J., 75, 77, 80, 81
Burke's estate, re, Burke v. Burke, 28
Burnham Kilgore, Carrie, 146
Burrowes, Peter, 74, 78
Burton, Charles, 84
Byrne, Matthew J., 50, 51
Byrne, William, 73

Callan, C.E., 135
Callan, Sylvia, 135, 148
Callery, Peter, 62
Campbell, Burrowes, 78, 79n
Campbell, Sir James, Lord Glenavy, xv, xvi, xviii–xxi
Canada, 35, 59, 103, 129
Canson Enterprises Ltd v. Boughton, 27
Capper, David, 158
Caravat trials, 74, 79
Carleton, Viscount, 72, 73
Caroline, queen, 77
Carrigan, William, 87
Carroll, James, 159
Carroll, Mella, xxi, 137–8, 140
Carson, Edward, 86
Carson, Rosemary, 159
Carswell, Sir Robert, 3, 138, 157
Cassidy, Agnes, 146
Catholic Association, 74n, 76
Cavan, 47
Censorship of Films Appeal Board, 47
Censorship of Publications Board, 46
central criminal court (Dublin), 44
Chancellor of the Exchequer, 105
charitable trusts, 28–9
Charleville, Co. Cork, 46
Cherry on land law, 52
Cherry, Richard, 41, 52
Chief State Solicitor, 127

China, 60
Chitty on contract, 52
circuit court, 37–8, 49
circuit court judges, 40, 137
  midland circuit, 41–9
circuit life, 37–40, 42
'father of the circuit,' 39, 81
circuits, 37–8
civil bill cases, 37–8
civil bill courts, 38
civil legal aid, 66
Civil Liability Act 1961, 54, 59
civil litigation, 18–19, 37–8, 58, 66, 94
Civil Partnership and Certain Rights and Obligations of Cohabitants Act 2010, 34
civil partnerships, 34
civil procedure, 20
civil war, xviii, 42, 50, 132
Clancy's *Irish Digest* (1994–9), 64
Clare, 146
Clarendon, earl of, 154
Clark, Maureen, 148
Clarke, Frank, 92n
Clarke, Geraldine, 139
Clementi, Sir David, 122
Clementi review, 122, 123
Clerk and Lindsell on tort, 52
clients, 60, 125
Clive, Kitty, 146
Clogher, Co. Tyrone, 6
Clonmel, Co. Tipperary, 79
Codification of the International League, 145
cohabitants, 34, 35
Colet, John, 56, 57
Collins Barracks Museum, Dublin, xviii
Collins, Desmond, 46
Collins, Michael, 55
commissioners for oaths, 109
commissions, 69, 79
Committee on Professional Legal Education in Northern Ireland, report; *see* Bromley Report
common intention constructive trusts, 34–5

common law bar, 82
common law courts, 25, 26, 38, 104
Commonwealth of Australia, 103
Compensation Fund, 112
competition, 121, 123, 125–6
Competition Authority, 123n
Connaught Bar Society, 76
Connaught circuit, 69, 75
Constitution of Ireland 1937, 27–8, 34, 54, 55
Constitution of the Irish Free State 1922, 26, 27, 55
constitutional jurisprudence, 27
constitutional law, 64
constructive trusts, 31–2, 34–6
consultative council of European judges, 48
contract, 27
contributory negligence, 59
Conveyancers (Ireland) Act 1864, 106
conveyancing, 52–3, 59, 60, 65–6, 119
Cork, 46, 56, 61, 65, 106, 136
Cosgrove, Art, 159
Costello, Declan, 30, 158, 159
Costello, John A., 58, 87
Costello, Kevin, 158, 159
Coulter, Carol, 148
Council of Legal Education (Nothern Ireland), 114
county courts, 13, 17, 20, 37, 38, 41, 87, 144
court for crown cases reserved, 70
court of appeal, 141, 142
court of appeal (Northern Ireland), 7, 19, 131n, 132
court of chancery, 104
court of criminal appeal, 87, 88, 136
court of first instance of the European Communities, 48
court of king's bench, 78, 79
courthouses (Northern Ireland), 8–10
Courts of Justice Act 1924, xix, 37, 38
Cox Reports, 70–1, 77
Craig, D.V., 159
Crampton, Philip, 84
Cranworth, Lord, 26

Craughwell, Co. Galway, 23
Creedon, Eileen, 127
Crimean War, 24
criminal bar, 69–88; *see also* criminal trials
criminal courts of justice, 69, 95
Criminal Justice (Legal Aid) Act 1962, 88
Criminal Justice Evidence Act 1898, 86
criminal law, 55–6, 66, 70, 94–5; *see also* criminal bar
Criminal Law and Procedure Act 1887, 86
criminal legal aid, 63, 70, 88
criminal libel, 75
criminal trials, 8–9, 17–18, 69, 70–86
  murder cases, 10, 13, 17, 48, 70–1, 75, 78, 79, 80, 85, 86, 87, 88
Cromwell, Oliver, 63
Crooks, Peter, 156
Crossmaglen, Co. Armagh, 10
Crotty, James, 56
Crown, 70, 73, 74, 81
crown counsel, 80, 85–6, 87
crown judges, 6–7
Cruickshank, Elizabeth, 134
Crumlin Road Courthouse (Belfast), 8–9, 132
Crymble, Samuel G., 106
Curran, Antoinette, 139
Curran, John Adye, 80–1, 85
Curran, John, junior, 81n, 85
Curran, John Philpot, 69, 71, 72, 73, 74–5, 77, 79, 82
Curran, Patricia, 13
Curran, Sarah, 74
Curran, William Henry, 76
Cymdeithas Hanes Cyfraith Cymru, 154

Dáil Éireann, 47
Dalrymple, James, Viscount Stair, 154
damages, 63
David Copperfield, 53
Davies, John, 154

Davitt, Cahir, 44
Davitt, Michael, 25
Dawson, Norma, 137, 158, 159
Day, Robert, 73, 75, 79
De Tocqueville, Alexis, 80
Deeny, Sir Donnell, 158
Deery, John, 49
Deery, Matthew, 49
Delany, T.W., 44
Denham, Susan, 49, 127, 137, 157
Denman, Thomas, 77, 83, 84
Denning, Lord, 31, 32, 63
Department of Arts, Heritage and the Gaeltacht, 100
Department of Education (Northern Ireland), 116
Department of Finance (Northern Ireland), 112
Department of Finance and Personnel (Northern Ireland), 121
Department of Justice (Northern Ireland), 16
Department of Public Prosecutions (Northern Ireland), 12, 16
Derry, 147
Deverell, Averil, xvi, 129–31, 133–5, 140, 141, 145, 146
  portrait, xv, xx, *back cover*
Deverell, William, 133, 141
Dicey, A.V., 55
Dickens, Charles, 52, 53, 62, 77, 78
Dickie, Alfred, 133
Dillon, John, 86
Dillon-Leetch, Mary (Molly), 130n, 135, 148
'Diplock' courts, 17, 18
Diplock, Lord, 26–7
director of public prosecutions, 48, 127
director of public prosecutions (Northern Ireland), 12, 15–16
Directorate-General for Competition (European Communities), 47
district justices/judges, 56, 64, 144
Dixon, Catherine, 139
Dixon, Kevin, 28
Dodd, William, xv, 133, 134

Donegal, 47, 103
Doneraile conspiracy trial, 72
Donlon, Seán, 159
Donnellan, Britta, 146
Donnelly, Kathleen, 137
Doran, Joseph, 73
Dowling, Alan, 158
Down, 6, 70–1, 103, 105
Doyle, Tommy, 46
Drew, Eileen, 139
Drogheda, 43
Drummond, Flora, 147
Dublin, 37, 39, 40, 44, 53, 58, 69, 70, 73, 74, 75, 76, 78, 83, 86, 106, 113, 129, 131, 132, 133, 137, 141, 144, 148, 154, 156; *see also* Four Courts; Green Street courthouse; King's Inns
Dublin Castle, 83
Dublin circuit, 46, 48
Dublin circuit court, 46
Dublin city sessions, 136
Dublin City University, xxi, 138
Dublin University, 140, 142
Ducluzeau (grand jury member), 72
Dugdale, Rose, 48
Duggan, Frank, 58, 61
Dun Laoghaire, Co. Dublin, 136, 153
Duncan, Ida, 136
Duncan, T.J., 136
Dundalk, Co. Louth, 11, 49
Dundrum, Co. Dublin, 136, 144
Dunmanway, Co. Cork, 56
Dunne, Elizabeth, 98n
Dunton, John, xvii

Eadie, Ellice, 136
Early, Helena, 136
eastern circuit, 45
Edinburgh Review, 77
Edinburgh School of Cookery and Domestic Economy, 143
Elliott, James, 114
Elliott, Margaret, 139
Elmhurst (Limerick), 48
Emmet, Robert, 74–5, 78

employment litigation, 20–1
English Bar, 77, 129
English bill, 38
English decisions, 28, 31
English White Book, 20
Enniskillen, Co. Fermanagh, 6
equitable estoppel, 29, 31; *see also* proprietary estoppel
equitable remedies, 27, 28
equity, 23–36
Europa Institute, University of Amsterdam, 47
European arrest warrant, 39
European Central Bank, 57
European court of human rights, 89
European court of justice, 138
European Economic Community, 47, 60
European general court, 48
European law, 63, 67
European Union, 60, 89, 100
evidence, 18, 32, 33, 73, 81, 82, 86

faction parties, 79
Faculty of Advocates (Scotland), 93
family law, 19, 32–4, 39, 40, 62, 66
farm families, 60
Farrell, Remy, 101
Fatal Injuries Act 1956, 54
Faulkner, Mary, 99
Feale, river, 57
Feenan, Dermot, 137
fees, 13, 53, 58, 80, 88, 105, 108, 121–2
Female Law Practitioners Act 1896, 129
female lawyers; *see* women lawyers
feminism, 147
Fenton (solicitor), 75
Fenton, Anne, 114n
Ferguson, Kenneth, 159
Fermanagh, 103
Fianna Fáil, 47–8
The Field (J.B. Keane), 58
Fine Gael, 47
Finlay Geoghegan, Mary, 89, 92n, 98n, 139

Finlay, Thomas A., 31, 49, 137, 153, 157
Finnegan, Joseph, 92n
Fishery Board, 57
Fitzgerald, Miss G., 143
Fitzgerald, James, 72
Fitzgibbon, John, xvii
Fitzgibbon, Katie, 46
Fitzgibbon, Paddy, 60, 61
Fitzpatrick, Hugh, 78
Fitzpatrick, Michael, 61
Fogarty, Andrew, 70–1
Four Courts, Dublin, xix, xvi–xvii, xviii, 43, 69, 75, 83, 95, 134, 142
Fox, Billy, 48
France, 154
Fraser, Sir Alasdair, 16
Freeman's Journal, xv, 47, 130, 142
French, George, 81
Frost, Georgie, 140
Fundamental Rights in the Irish Law and Constitution (Kelly), 55, 64

Gabbett, Joseph, 72n, 86
Gaelic Athletic Association (GAA), 58–9
Gaelic League, 43, 44
Gageby, Patrick, 69, 101
Gallagher, Paul, 98
Gallagher working group, 98–9, 102
Galvin, Barry, 65
Galway, 23, 48, 61, 76, 80
Gaming and Lotteries Act 1956, 54
Gandon, James, 23, 69
Gannon, Sean, 49
Garda Síochána complaints appeals board, 49
Garrow, William, 77, 78
Gavan Duffy, George, 28
Gazette, 54, 62
Gazette (Northern Ireland), 118
General Council of the Bar in Northern Ireland, 120
Geoghegan, Hugh, 30, 48, 49, 137–8, 159
Geoghegan, Patrick, 158, 159

Geoghegan-Quinn, Máire, 48
George, Rev Richard, 41
George V, king, 103, 132
George, William, 41
Gibson, John George, xvi
Gleeson, Dermot, 92
Gleeson, Joseph, 44
Gleeson, William J., 44–5, 87
Gleeson working group, 92–3, 102
Gogarty, Oliver D. ('Noll'), 45
Goldsmith, Oliver, 156
Gordon, John G., xvi, 159
Gort, Co. Galway, 61
Government of Ireland Act 1920, 103, 141
Graduate School of Professional Legal Education (University of Ulster), 116, 117
grand juries, 6, 81
Grattan, Sheena, 158
Gray, Samuel, 74n, 84
Gray's Inn, 136
Great Britain, 144
Greene, George C., 144
Green Street courthouse, Dublin, 69, 72, 85, 86
Greer, D.S., 158, 159
Greig, Flos, 129
Greystones, Co. Wicklow, 133
Griffith, Arthur, 45
Griffith College, Cork, 65
Griffith, Nevin, 45
Groarke, Raymond, 49
Guthrie, John, 76
Guthrie v. Sterne, 76, 77

Hale, Matthew, 84
Hale, Brenda, 35
Hamilton, Liam, 130, 157
Hand, G.J., 158, 159
Handbook on the Administration of Estates Act (Northern Ireland), 1955 (Leitch), 118
Harris, Betty, 136
Harrison's *Irish Digest 1949–1958*, 54, 64

Hart, Anthony, 158, 159
Haslam, Anna, 136
Haughan v. Ruttledge, 29
Haughey, Charles, 62
Hawkins Pleas of the Crown, 72
Hay Gordon, Ian, 13
Hayes, Edmund, 86
Healy, Maurice, 9–10, 43
Healy-Rae, Rosemary, 130
Healy, T.M., 11, 86
Hearn, Ellice, 136
Hederman, Miriam, 135
Hegarty, Martina, 139–40
Hegarty, Noirin, 148
Henry, Sir Denis, xx, 131, 132, 142, 143
Heron, Mary Dorothea, xx, 136–7, 140
Heron, Robert, 159
Heuston, Robert, 153
Hewitt, Alan, 103
Hickey, Robin, 159
Higgins, Marcella, 99
high court, 49, 61, 62, 132, 137–8, 141, 148
high court of appeal for Ireland, 131
high court of justice (Northern Ireland), 13–14, 17, 141
high court on circuit, 38
Hillas, Robert, 75
Hogan, Daire, 158, 159
Home Charter, 119
Hong Kong, 59, 93
Honorable Society of King's Inns: *see* King's Inns
Horace, 22
Horan, Shelley, 101
House of Lords, 20–2, 77
Howlin, Niamh, 158
Huband, William G., 86
Huston, John, 23
Hutton, Sir Brian, 157
Hynes v. Independent Newspapers Ltd, 27

Illegitimate Children Bill, 144
illustrations, xv–xxi
Incorporated Law Society of Ireland; *see* Law Society of Ireland
Incorporated Law Society of Northern Ireland; *see* Law Society of Northern Ireland
India, 129
'inequality of contract,' doctrine of, 32
inns of court (London) *see* London inns
Institute of Professional Legal Studies (Queen's University Belfast), 92, 113–17, 137
Institutions of the Law of Scotland (Stair), 154
International Association of Women Judges, 138
International Conference on the Codification of International Law, 144
International Criminal Court, 148
International Federation of University Women, 145
International Monetary Fund (IMF), 57
Invincibles, The, 86
The Irish bar (O'Flanagan), 85
Irish Digests, 54, 64, 70
Irish Free State, xxi, 26, 37, 50, 87, 103, 107, 135, 136, 144, 145
Irish house of commons, 71
Irish Independent, 47, 127, 142, 145
Irish language, 43–4, 100–1
Irish Law Times and Solicitors Journal, 54
Irish Legal History Society, 89, 137, 153–4, 155, 156–7
  succession lists 1988–2013, 157–60
Irish Society, the, 6
Irish Soviet Friendship Society, 136
Irish Times, xvi, 44, 133, 137, 140–1, 143, 144, 145–6, 147, 148
Irish Volunteers, 47
Irish Women Citizens' and Local Government Association, 136, 143
Irish Women Lawyers Association, 140
Irishwomen's Reform League, 127

Japan, 60
Jebb, Richard, 75
Jellett, William, 135
Jennings, Ivor, 55
Johnson, Richard, 57, 61
Johnston, Francis, 10
Jones, Doctor R.M., 107
Jones v. Kernott, 35
Joy, Bruce, xvii
Joy, Henry, xvii
Joyce, Hugh, 61
JR, a ward of court, re, 30
judges, xv, 6–7, 14, 15, 64, 67
    Northern Ireland, 13–15, 16, 19, 138–9
    women, 137–9, 140, 148, 149
Judicature (Ireland) Act 1877, 26, 27
Judicature Acts (Wylie), 20
judicial appointments commission (JAC) (Northern Ireland), 14, 138–9
judicial independence, 64, 67
judicial review, 19, 39, 86
juries, 85–6, 136
Justice (Northern Ireland) Act 2002, 14, 16
Justice of the Peace (O'Connor), 86
The justice of the peace for Ireland (MacNally), 78, 82, 86
justices of the peace, 86

Keane, John B., 57, 58
Keane, Ronan, 23, 88, 130, 135, 157
Kelleher, Stephen Barnabas, 147
Keller, Miss, 145
Kells, Co. Meath, 47
Kells Urban Council, 47
Kelly, John M., 55, 64
Kelly v. Cahill, 31–2
Kempton, Violet, 44
Kennedy, Eileen, 137, 140
Kennedy, Hugh, xxi, xx, 55, 87, 131n
Kenny, Colum, 127, 159
Kenny, John, 46
Kenny, William, xvi
Kenny's outlines of criminal law, 55

Kentstown, Co. Meath, 41
Keogh, William Nicholas, 80, 81
Kerr, Sir Brian, 157
Kerry, 49, 82, 130
    legal practice in, 50–68
Kerry Babies tribunal, 48
Kerryman, 49, 57
Kilbeggan, 42
Kilgore, Carrie Burnham, 146
Kilkenny, 78, 79, 80
Killyhevlin Hotel, Enniskillen, 6
Kilwarden, Lord, 74
king's bench division of Northern Ireland, 142, 145
King's Inns, Dublin, xix, xviii, 41, 43, 46, 49, 89, 104, 107, 128, 129, 132, 140, 141, 146
    benchers, 89, 128, 130–1, 139, 142
    Brooke Scholarship, 130, 140–1, 142
    council, 89–90
    development committee, 96
    diploma in corporate, white collar and regulatory crime, 101
    diploma in legal studies, 90–1, 98
    entrance requirements, 90, 91–2
    Irish language education, 100–2
    law school, 89, 90–102
    library, 99
    modular degree course, 96
    specialised courses, 101
    student dining, 102
    student numbers and profile, 96–8
    vocational degree course, 92–6, 102
    women, admission of, 128, 130–1, 142, 147
Kingsdown, Lord, 26, 29
Kinlen, Dermot, 49, 59
Knights of St Columbanus, 44
Knipe, Joan, 135
Kyle, Frances (Fay), xv, xvi, xx, 129–33, 140–1, 142, 143
Kyle, Robert Alexander, 142

Labour party (UK), 121
Lafayette (photography), xv, 145

Index

Laffoy, Mary, 138
Laganside courthouse (Belfast), 9
Lambert, Elizabeth, 42
land agitation, 85
Land law (Wylie), 53
land purchase Acts, 25, 41, 53
land registration, 52, 53
Lanyon, Charles, 8
Laois, 39, 42
Larkin, Felix M., 159
Larkin, John F., 158
Larkin, Martina, 65
'The Lass of Richmond Hill' (MacNally), 75, 83
law books *see* legal publications
law digests, 54, 64
Law Library, 98, 101, 125, 133, 138, 145, 146, 148
law reform, 59, 70
law reports, 21
law schools *see* legal education
Law Society of England and Wales, 109, 121–2
Law Society of Ireland, 41, 46, 66–7, 104, 105, 106, 113, 122, 136, 139
    professional course, 92n, 93
    regulatory functions, 66, 104
    women presidents, 139
Law Society of Northern Ireland, 8, 12, 106–26
    admission procedure, 107, 117
    Council, 106, 107, 108
    disciplinary functions, 108, 111–12
    establishment, 106–7
    government intervention, 119–23
    lay observers, 112
    legal publications, 118
    regulatory functions, 108, 110–12, 119, 122
    women, admission of, 136–7
    women presidents, 139
Law Society of Scotland, 122
Leah, Frank, xix
Leckey, J.L., 159
Lee, Gerard A., 46
Lefroy, Thomas, 80, 82
legal aid, 63, 66, 70, 88
legal costs, 20
legal education, 67
    barristers, 89, 90–102; *see also* King's Inns
    solicitors (Northern Ireland), 113–17
Legal Practitioners (Qualification) Act 1929, 90, 100
Legal Practitioners (Irish Language) Act 2008, 100
legal publications, 52, 55, 56, 59, 61, 63–4, 67, 72, 82, 86
    Northern Ireland, 114, 117–19
legal representation *see* criminal bar
Legal Services Regulation Bill 2011, 66–7, 102
Legal Services Review Group (Northern Ireland), 124–6
legislation, 54, 59, 63, 67, 70
Leinster circuit, 73n, 75, 79
Leinster College of Irish, 43
Leitch, W.A., 118
Leitrim, 47
Leitrim Observer, 147–8
Les six livres de la République (Bodin), 154
Levinge and Molloy, 86
LEXCEL, 119
Libero, 119
Limerick, 48, 61, 83
Listowel, Co. Kerry, 49, 50–66, 65–6
Listowel, Lord, 50–1, 52
Listowel UDC v. McDonagh, 59
Listowel Urban Council, 59
Loftus, Claire, 101, 127
London, 43, 56, 116, 129, 133, 136, 143
London inns, 93, 120, 155–6
Londonderry, 6, 103, 116, 147
Longfellow, Henry Wadsworth, 68
Longford, 39, 42, 44
lord chancellor's mace, xvi, xvii–xix
lords justices (Northern Ireland), 7
Louth, 43, 49
Lowry, Lord, 153, 157
Lurgan, Co. Armagh, 144

Lynch, Elma, 139
Lynch, Fionán, 148
Lynch, Kevin, 49
Lynch, Patrick, 135
Lynn, Alexander, 87

Maamtrasna murder case, 86
McAleese, Camilla, 99, 139
McAleese, Mary, 114n, 137
MacBridge, Seán, 88
MacCann, John, 73
McClachlin, Beverley, 27
McComb, William, 8
MacDermott, Lord (John Clarke MacDermott), xx, 7, 109, 130, 131–2, 142, 143
MacDonagh, Michael, 83
McDonald, Dearbhail, 127
Macdonald, Sarah, 93, 98n
MacDonnell, Antonia E., 143
MacDonnell, R.J., 143
McDowell, Patrick, xvi–xvii
McDowell, R.B., 155
McElligott, Edward, 44
McGilligan, Paddy, 55, 131–2
McGuinness, Catherine, 137, 148
McGuire, James I., 158, 159
Mackay, Lord, 121
McKee (John) & Son, 139
McKee, John, 106
Macken, Fidelma, 138
MacKenzie, R. Shelton, 76
MacKenzie, Patrick, 45
McKinney, Thomasena ('Tommy'), 139
McKnight, Michael, 87
McLean, John, 153, 154, 159
McMahon and another v. Kerry County Council, 30–1
MacMahon, Bernard, 74n
MacManaway, Dean, 6
MacMechan, William, 71
McMillan, Imelda, 139
Macnaghten, Lord, 28
MacNally, Leonard, 71, 72, 73, 74, 75, 78, 79, 82–3, 86

McNerney, J.A., 128
Madden, John, 129
Magee case, 75–6, 83
Magennis, Margaret, 140
Maginess, Brian, 144–5
Maginness, Henry, 109
magistrates, 38, 136, 144
magistrates' courts, 10, 13, 82
Maguire, Conor A., 47
Maguire, Conor J., 98n
Maguire, Conor P., 47–8
Maguire v. AG, 28
Manchester University, 113, 115
Mansfield, Arabella A., 146n
Markievicz, Constance, 134
Married Women's Property Acts, 33–4
Marshall, Robert D., 158, 159
Martin, Clara Brett, 129
Martin, John, 158, 159
Marx, Karl, 71
Matheson, Charles, 133–4
matrimonial home, 32–4
Mayne, Edward, 72
Maynooth, Co. Kildare, 146
Mayo, 135
Meath, 41, 47, 80–1, 143
Meath Chronicle, 47, 143
Meath County Council, 47
Merchant of Venice (Shakespeare), 134
Methuen, John, xvii
Metropolitan Garda case, 145
Middle Temple, London, 136, 155
Middlesex circuit, 77
midland circuit, 39, 42, 45, 47, 48, 49
  judges of, 41–9
Mining Board, 46
Mohr, Thomas, 158, 160
Molloy, Constantine, 85, 86
Molony, Sir Thomas, 132, 141, 142, 143, 153
  portrait, xv, xx, *frontispiece*
Monaghan, 47
Monaghan County Council, 49
Monmouth assizes, 136
Monopolies Commission (UK), 121

Moonan, George A., 43–4
Moonan, Richard, 43
Moore, Thomas, 74
Moore, William, xv, xvi, xx, 132
Moran, Frances, 137, 140, 143, 146
More, Thomas, 56–7
Morgan, Sir Declan, 139
Moyvane, Co. Kerry, 56
Mullan, Fred, 11
Mullen, Yvonne, 159, 160
Mullingar, Co. Westmeath, 39, 48, 85
Mulloy, Eanna, 159
Mulvey, Mary, 144
Munster circuit, 43, 46, 82, 83
The Munster circuit (O'Flanagan), 85
murder trials *see* criminal trials
Murnaghan, George, 46
Murphy, Ned, 5
Murphy, Shane, 101
Murray, Brian, 92n, 98n
Murray, John, 157

Napier, Joseph, 70
National Army, 47
National Museum of Ireland, xviii
National University of Ireland, 44, 46, 143, 144
negligence, 7, 27, 59
Nenagh, Co. Tipperary, 87
'New Labour', 121
New Zealand, 27, 103, 129
Newcastle, Co. Down, 6
Newry, Co. Down, 11
Newtownards, Co. Down, 10
Newtownsandes, Co. Kerry, 56
Newtownstewart, Co. Tyrone, 10
Neylon, Mary, 146
Nolan, David, 128
Nolan, Frances, 44
Nolan, Julia, 47
Norbury, Lord, 72–3, 74, 76, 78, 79
Normanton, Helena, 133, 143
north-western circuit, 47, 75
northern circuit, 47, 49
Northern Ireland, 103, 131
appeals to House of Lords, 20–2
assizes, 5–8
barristers' profession; *see* Northern Ireland Bar
courthouses, 8–10
courts, 3–22
judges, xx, 13–15, 16, 19, 138–9
legal publications, 117–19
legal services review group, 122–3, 124–6
solicitors' profession, 10–12, 103–26; *see also* Law Society of Northern Ireland; solicitors (Northern Ireland)
Statute Law Database, 119
'supergrass' trials, 18
women lawyers, 3, 128, 132, 133, 136–7, 138–9, 140, 142–3
Northern Ireland Assembly, 16, 109
Northern Ireland Bankers' Association, 118
Northern Ireland Bar, 3–22, 114, 118, 125
Bar Library, 3–5, 4, 5, 8, 11, 12
civil trials, 18–19
criminal trials, 17–18
women members, 3, 132, 133, 138–9, 142–3
Northern Ireland Court Service, 16, 118
Northern Ireland Legal Quarterly, 118
Northern Ireland parliament, 16, 103, 132
Northern Law Club, 104–6
Northern Law Society, 104, 105, 106
Nuffield Foundation, 118
Nunn & Walsh, 86
Nuremburg war crimes trials, 47

O'Briain, Barra, 56
O'Brien, Patricia, 127
O'Brien, Peter ('Peter the Packer'), 85–6
O'Connell, Daniel, 70, 72, 75, 76, 78, 79, 82, 83–4, 85
O'Connell, John, 83

O'Connor, Charles Andrew, xvi
O'Connor, James, xv, 86, 141
Ó Dálaigh, Cearbhall, 56, 88
O'Fay v Burke, 23–6, 31, 36
Offaly, 39, 41, 42, 45
Office of Fair Trading (UK), 121, 122, 123
Office of the Parliamentary Counsel, 136
O'Flanagan, Roderick, 71, 83, 85
Óglaigh na hÉireann (National Army), 47
O'Grady, Standish, 72, 79
O'Hanlon, Roderick, 160
O'Higgins, Kevin (judge), 48
O'Higgins, Kevin, TD, 48, 88
O'Higgins, Niall B., 48
O'Higgins, Tom, 45, 49
Ohlmeyer, Jane, 160
Oireachtas, 28, 37
O'Keeffe, Tony, 58
Old Bailey, 74, 77
O'Leary, Cornelius and Hannah, 87
O'Loghlen, Michael, xvi
Omagh crown court, 10
O'Malley, Michael George, 48
O'Malley, Peter, 48
O'Neill, Hugh, 148
O'Nolan, Brian (Myles na gCopaleen), 37
Orangemen, 74n, 84
O'Reilly, P.H., xviii
Orissa, 129
Orpen, William, xv, xx
Orr, Matthew, xviii
Osborough, W.N., 153, 155, 156, 158, 160
O'Shaughnessy, Thomas, 86
O'Shea, Joan, 48
O'Sullivan, Aisling, 65
Oxford, 77, 129, 136

Pale, the, 54, 58
Palles, Christopher, xvi, 7, 85, 154
Pankhurst, Christobel, 147
Paris bar, 135

Parliamentary Draftsman's Office, 101
Parnell, Charles Stewart, 25
partition of Ireland, 103, 131, 141
Penal Laws, 52
Pennefather, Edward, 79, 84
Pennsylvania, US, 146
personal injuries actions, 7, 19
Personal Injuries Assessment Board (PIAB), 63
petty sessions, 13
Phelan, Kathleen, 144, 145
Philippines, 60
Phillips, Charles, 71, 75, 76–8
Phoenix Park, Dublin, 69
Phoenix Park murders, 71
The Pickwick papers, 77, 78
Pierse and Fitzgibbon (Listowel), 60, 61–2, 64, 65
Pierse McCarthy Lucey (Tralee), 65
Pierse, Paul, 65
Pierse, Robert, 50–68
Pierse, Riobard, 61–2, 64, 65
Pierse, Risteard, 61, 65
Pigot, Chief Baron, 71
Pim, J.E., xvi
Plenary Council of Legal Education, 117
Plunkett, William, 72, 73
Polden, Patrick, 133, 136
Ponsonby, George, 72, 73
'Portias,' 134, 135
Portlaoise, 39, 43
Powell, John Blake, xv
Prendergast, Dr Patrick, 155
President of Ireland, 140
Priory, Rathfarnham (Dublin), 75
Prisoners' Counsel Defence Act 1836, 70, 74n, 77
probate, 53, 60, 66
Professional Books, 59
professional indemnity insurance, 112
promissory estoppel, 29
proprietary estoppel, 25–6, 29–31
Protestants, 51, 82, 84
Punch, 78

quarter sessions, 37, 69, 144
Queen's University Belfast, 92, 114, 115, 118, 120, 123, 136, 137, 142; see also Institute of Professional Legal Studies
Quigley, Brigid, 49
Quinlan, Moya, 139

R. v. Corcoran & Ors, 79
R. v. Courvoisier, 75, 78
R. v. Moore, 85
R. v. Parnell, 85
Radcliffe, Thomas, 75
Ramsden v. Dyson, 25, 26, 29, 31
Raymond, James Fitzjames, 50, 51–2
Recollections of John Philpot Curran (Phillips), 77
Redmond, John, 86
registrars, 6
Registry of Deeds, 52
remedial constructive trusts, 35–6
remuneration *see* fees
restitution, 35
resulting trusts, 33, 34
Ridgeway, William, 72
Road Traffic Act 1933, 46
Road Traffic Act 1961, 59
Road Traffic Acts 2011, 63
Road Traffic Law (Pierse), 59, 63
Robinson, Mary, 140, 148
Roche, Bernard, 44
Roe, Frank, 49
Roman Catholics, 76
Ronan, Stephen, xv, 141
Roscommon, 39, 41, 42, 45, 135
Ross, Sir John, xviii, xix, 131, 132
Ross, Samuel, 106
Royal Belfast Academical Institution, 107
Royal Commission on Legal Services, 115, 120–1
Royal Courts of Justice (Belfast), 3, 7, 8, 9, 12, 113
Royal Ulster Constabulary (RUC), 6, 7
RTÉ Radio, 48
rural law practice, 50–68

Russell, James, 114n
Russell, Lord William, 78
Ryan, Christina Mary, 48

St Malachy's College, Belfast, 47
St Paul's Cathedral, 56
Samuels, Arthur, xv
Sandes (Listowel), 51
Sandes, Robert Lindsay, 56
Saurin, William, 72, 75
Scarman, Lord, 32n
Science Gallery, Dublin, 156
Scotland, 93, 107, 121, 122
Sealy, James, 144
Selden, John, 154
Selden Society, 154
Semple, Heather, 118–19
serjeants, 69–70, 82
Servicing the Legal System (SLS), 118
Sex Disqualification (Removal) Act 1919, 128–9
Shakespeare, William, 134
Shanavest trials, 74, 79
Shanley, Peter, 91
Shanley working group, 91, 102
Shaw, Sir Barry, 16
Sheares, Henry and John, 71–3, 79
Sheehy-Skeffington, Francis, 128
Sheil, Charles Leo, 145
Sheil, M.K., 145
Sheil, Richard Lalor, 75, 76, 77, 83
Sherry, Coleman, 61
Sinn Féin, 47, 50
Sinn Féin courts, 50
Sirr, Major Henry Charles, 73
Sketches of the Irish bar, 76
Slieve Donard hotel, Newcastle, 6
Sligo, 41, 47, 75, 148
Smith, Christopher, 88
Smith, Sir Thomas (Master of the Rolls), 24–5
Smyth v. Halpin, 30
Société Internationale Fernand de Visscher pour l'Histoire des Droits de l'Antiquité, 154

Société Jean Bodin, 154
Society for the Protection of the Unborn Child, 28
solicitors; *see also* solicitors (Northern Ireland)
   apprenticeship, 51–2, 113
   regulation; *see* Law Society of Ireland
   rural law practice, 50–68
   women, 59–60, 65, 128, 136–7, 139, 140
solicitors (Northern Ireland), 10–12
   apprenticeship system, 113
   competition, 123, 125–6
   legal education, 113–17, 119, 121
   regulation, 103–13, 119–26; *see also* Law Society of Northern Ireland
   women, 136–7, 139, 140
Solicitors (Ireland) Act 1898, 104, 106, 107
Solicitors Act (Northern Ireland) 1922, 106–7
Solicitors Act (Northern Ireland) 1938, 107–8
Solicitors' Disciplinary Tribunal, 111–12, 125
Solicitors (Amendment) (Northern Ireland) Order 1989, 110n, 112
Solicitors (Northern Ireland) Order 1976, 108–13, 119, 126
Sorabji, Cornelia, 129
Sorahan, Séamus, 72n
South Africa, 103
south-western circuit, 48, 49
southern circuit, 144
Stack v. Dowden, 34–5
Stair Society, 154
Stair, Viscount, 154
Staples, Sir Thomas, 71
State (Healy) v. Donoghue, 70
State (O'Connor) v. O'Caoimhanaigh, 88n
Statute of Frauds (Ir) Act 1695, 57–8
Statutory Publications Office (Northern Ireland), 119

Steele, Mrs, 4
Stuart, Gilbert, xvii
Succession Act 1965, 59
suffragettes, 147
Sullivan, A.M., 69–70, 87
Sullivan, D.B., 86
Sullivan, T.D., 85–6
Sunday Independent, 146–7
'supermarket' law, 66
supreme court, 49, 103, 137, 148, 149
supreme court of judicature of Northern Ireland, 7, 8, 13, 20, 103, 107
Sutton, Ralph, 61
Sweeney, James, 47
Sweeney, Michael J., 47

Table-talk (Selden), 154
Teevan, Thomas, 46
Tennyson, Alfred, 50
Tiernan, Mary Anne, 43
Tipperary, 82
Toler, John *see* Norbury, Lord
Tone, Theobald Wolfe, 71n, 74, 75, 76, 78
Torrens, Robert, 72
Tralee, Co. Kerry, 61, 64, 65
Travellers, 59
treason trials, 71–5
Treaty of Rome, 63
Trim, Co. Meath, 81
Trinity College Dublin, 41, 127, 130, 136, 137, 140, 145, 147, 153, 155, 156
Troubles, the, 50, 63, 116
trusts, 27, 28; *see also* constructive trusts
Tullamore, Co. Offaly, 39, 42
Tyrone, 6, 103

Ulster Workers' Strike, 109
undue influence, 32
United Irishmen, 71–3, 83
United Nations, 127
United Nations High Commissioner for Human Rights, 140

United Scientific Holdings Ltd v. Burnley Borough Council, 26–7
United States bar, 146
United States of America, 93, 129
University College Dublin, 46, 47, 53, 55–6, 128, 131
University of Amsterdam, 47
University of Ulster, 116
unjust enrichment, 35

Vaughan, W.E., 80, 85
Victoria (Australia), 129
Victoria Prize, 143
von Prondzynski, Ferdinand, xxi

Wakely, Francis, 42
Wakely, James, 42
Wakely, John, 41–3, 44
Wakely, John, MP, 41–2
Wakely, Thomas, 42
Wakely, William George, 41
Walkington, Lelita, 140
Walsh, Eamonn, 45, 49
Waterford, 41, 79, 80
Watts, W.A., 153
Webb, Thomas, 71
Webber, Daniel, 72
Weekly Irish Times, 146
Weir-Johnston, Isabel, 128, 147
Welsh Legal History Society, 154
western circuit, 47, 81

Westmeath, 39, 42, 82
Westminster, 109
Whelan, Máire, 127
Whelan, Nora, 47
Whiteboy Acts, 73n
Whiteboyism, 81, 85, 88
Wicklow, 46, 133
Williams, Glanville, 59
Williams, Ivy, 129, 133
Wilson, Attracta, 139
Wilson, Ian, 79
Wolfe, Arthur, 74
women barristers, 129, 135, 143
women jurors, 136
women lawyers, 127–49
    barristers, 97, 127, 128–36, 137–8, 139–49
    judges, 137–9, 140, 148, 149
    magistrates, 136
    solicitors, 59–60, 65, 128, 136–7, 139, 140
Women's Auxiliary Air Force, 136
Women's need of women lawyers, 127
Women's Social and Political Union of the United Kingdom, 127
World War I, 128
World War II, 20
The Writ, 118
Wylie, James Owens, xvi
Wylie, William Evelyn, xvi, 20, 53